S0-BPI-558

Pitt Series in Policy and Institutional Studies

The Impact of Policy Analysis

James M. Rogers

✳

University of Pittsburgh Press

H
97
.R64
1988
West

Published by the University of Pittsburgh Press,
Pittsburgh, Pa., 15260
Copyright © 1988, University of Pittsburgh Press
All rights reserved
Feffer and Simons, Inc., London
Manufactured in the United States of America

Library of Congress Cataloging-in-Publication Data

Rogers, James M., 1949–
    The impact of policy analysis/James M. Rogers.
      p.   cm.—(Pitt series in policy and institutional studies)
    Bibliography: p. 185.
    Includes index.
    ISBN 0-8229-3571-6
    1. Policy sciences. 2. United States—Economic policy—Decision making. 3.
United States—Social policy—Decision making. 4. Social sciences—Research—
United States. I. Title. II. Series.
H97.R64 1988
361.6'1—dc19   87-17181
                                                                                CIP

Contents

✳

Acknowledgments

✳

Many friends and colleagues have contributed to the research and writing of this book. I am grateful to individuals too numerous to acknowledge here who helped me develop my ideas. I thank those named below in particular for their assistance and support.

When I first started this project, Eugene J. Meehan took time to consider my ideas and asked penetrating questions. As usual he challenged my answers vigorously and pressed me further. In so doing he helped me analyze my thinking when clarification was most needed.

When the research was still at a preliminary stage, Frank Sim assessed my reasoning and commented constructively while taking a disciplinary perspective different from my own. Some months later, Frank Sim met an untimely death. His colleagues will surely miss his wit and humor as I do.

As my work progressed I was ably assisted by Robert Pecorella, Mark Kessler, and Andrew Battista, who listened to my ideas and presumptions and provided helpful comments. James Eisenstein, Larry D. Spence, and Nancy Wentzler read drafts and responded to my work with a skillful mix of questions, criticism, and support. More than anyone else, Robert S. Friedman stood by me as I saw this project through to its completion. Without his comments, suggestions, and tireless support, there is no telling what might have happened. I owe a special debt to the forty-three busy professionals in the government agencies and research organizations who gave me their time, usually without hesitation, and rarely failed to answer my questions. Finally, I could have asked for no more diligent and meticulous research assistant than Shawna Mulkay.

All of the individuals named above and others whom I have not mentioned have undoubtedly improved this book. I accept responsibility for any defects that remain.

The Impact of Policy Analysis

1 Introduction

✳

The governance of modern industrial society is a complex task fraught with uncertainty heightened by ignorance. In some situations decision makers have almost no knowledge of the outcomes of their actions. At other times they expect a range of possible consequences but lack a basis for assessing the probability that any one in particular will happen. Only rarely is there enough knowledge to predict with confidence that a given eventuality will occur, but a broad range of issues nevertheless appears on the public agenda and requires action. Demands for a national response to social problems such as poverty, illness, illiteracy, crime, segregation, and discrimination are commonplace. Government is increasingly expected to exert efforts to control the economy, to combat inflation and unemployment. In addition, the heightened interdependence of world actors and events forces modern states to consider affairs beyond their borders. In the domestic and international arenas, it is difficult for heads of state to act with much assurance that they will achieve desired ends. The uncertainty, which stems from elaborate social structures and processes, threatens to incapacitate decision makers. Knowledge is frequently lacking and is costly, if not impossible, to obtain. Nevertheless, nations are compelled to act.

Policy research and analysis represent an attempt to reduce the ignorance and uncertainty confronting key public officials.[1] Analysis employs scientific methods to determine the consequences, for specific groups and for society as a whole, of government policies and actions. Recent developments in communication, information

3

processing, and research technology have expanded the capabilities of analysts. Decision makers often use the new resource; they increasingly call upon internal staffs and external consultants and research organizations to help them govern.

The effectiveness of the new governmental strategy remains an open question, however. Here also the uncertainty attending action is great. In a few limited cases, analysis has succeeded and has helped achieve goals, but notable failures—instances in which analysis has not improved the quality of policy making—are commonplace. We lack the information required to determine the effectiveness and consequences of policy analysis or even to address the relevant questions in anything more than a cursory fashion. In short, government faces a familiar dilemma when it decides whether or not to fund and use the new tool. Public officials are forced to pursue some policy or action to reduce the problem of uncertainty but must do so, as in other areas, without knowing the result of their actions.

The purpose of my research has been to develop a tentative explanation of the impact of policy analysis, tentative because at this stage of the research rigorous tests have not been conducted. My explanation addresses several major questions. What is the impact of policy analysis? How does impact vary across policy contexts, and why? As the research focuses on determining the consequences of government policy with regard to the funding of policy analysis, it exemplifies the subject of study: the research too is policy analysis. Policies may be defined as rules that guide actions,[2] in this case the rules fund analysis to aid policy making. The discussion draws on past research and on my investigation of the negative income tax experiments. If my explanation withstands a series of tests, it can be used to assess the effectiveness of policy analysis empirically. A complete assessment is beyond the scope of this book, but I will examine relevant implications of my explanation in the final chapter.

I will first consider significant developments in the U.S. government's use of policy analysis during the twentieth century. The brief history provides a context for a more detailed description of the current situation that I present later in the book as well as for an appreciation of the research questions.

Science and Government in the Twentieth Century

As close ties have developed between the scientific community and national governmental agencies during this century, interest in the use of analysis for public policy making has grown. The ties between science and government have not developed uniformly but have strengthened and occasionally weakened in response to current events, developments within the scientific community, and changes in government's role in modern society. The use of scientific methods to provide input for public policy is not a new phenomenon; current issues and problems have historical roots. After considering efforts to legitimate science several centuries ago and to establish social science professions in the nineteenth century, we examine three recent historical periods: the progressive era, the depression and World War II, and post–World War II.

Francis Bacon's contributions to research methods included a successful effort to legitimate seventeenth-century science and to promulgate the idea that science can contribute to society. Bacon argued that knowledge is a potent source of power: it can be used to alter the human condition, but it must first be shown to pose no threat to established interests. Despite the inherent difficulties in promoting knowledge on this basis, Bacon was able to give the young science of his time a chance to grow.[3]

Condorcet and other philosophers of the Enlightenment championed the belief that human progress depends on reason. Condorcet was less reticent than Bacon to spell out the political implications of science and forthrightly tied human progress to the rise of democracy. Reason and science thus became the tools of liberal democracy against religion and the old order.[4]

The belief in science and its contribution to human progress extended from the sixteenth, seventeenth, and eighteenth centuries to the latter part of the nineteenth, when social science professions were forming in the United States. An impulse toward reform soon posed problems for the emerging professions.

Social science began to take shape in the United States following the Civil War. At first a large group of nonacademic social investigators shared interests with a smaller number of academics who were just establishing university departments and positions. Members of each group were often first attracted to social inquiry by the belief that social knowledge could be applied to the worst problems of the emerging industrial society. University departments and professional associations were established, and the academics soon emerged as the dominant force in social investigation. As the professional societies began to grow, internal battles, among reformers and those less disposed to support social change actively, threatened the social standing of the nascent disciplines. Bitter disputes were aired publicly. Open disagreement within segments of the scholarly community imperiled the young sciences' claim to authority. After all, what confidence could be placed in a "dispassionate," "objective" method that yielded diametrically opposed sets of results? In addition, pressures from industrialists, often significant benefactors from a university's standpoint, made themselves felt as industrial interests were threatened by reformers. Claims to scientific objectivity and to the authority of the professions were endangered as social science reformers sparked controversy.[5]

Before long, the interest in establishing social science professions took precedence over some scholars' pursuit of social reform. A series of cases concerned with academic freedom dealt the final blow. As school authorities attacked the positions of reform-oriented social scientists in major universities, moderates within the disciplines closed their ranks. The most extreme reformists were purged, and norms regarding permissible advocacy and free speech were established. The disciplines in time came to be viewed more as professional associations of researchers and less as bands of radical reformers. The opportunity to apply a relatively nonthreatening social science expertise to governmental affairs increased.[6]

The tension between reform and professional interests within the social science disciplines has been suppressed but not eliminated.[7] This tension has, however, prompted some reformers to abandon the ivory tower and to address primarily nonacademic audiences.[8] When the conflict resurfaces, as it periodically does, the discussion occurs chiefly within the professions. Any renewed debate, however, takes place in the context of established professional norms which limit its threat to the disciplines and also assure that most scholarly work addresses questions appropriate for the discipline or science and not normative issues concerning change in industrial society.

When the twentieth century began, social science had established a fairly secure place for itself in American society. Science was accepted as legitimate and was not considered to threaten dominant interests. A base for operation in the universities had been created. Government officials in the early 1900s were thus able to seek the assistance of social scientists without great trepidation.

Initial Inroads

Firm ties between social science and the U.S. national government were promoted by several key events early in the twentieth century. The development of statistical and research units within the executive branch (primarily the Bureau of the Census), the enlistment of social scientists in the progressive movement, the emergence of the scientific management movement, the participation of social scientists in World War I, and the creation of various research organizations and commissions all set the stage for later developments.

Social scientists secured a foothold in the government with the establishment of the Bureau of the Census in 1902. The Departments of Labor and Agriculture soon followed with their own research units. Modest undertakings at first, these units and agencies slowly but steadily developed their research capacities. The Bureau of Agricultural Economics, within the Department of Agriculture, made the most extensive use of social research. Early work focused on the economic dislocation of farmers. Establishment of research units in most other departments later in the century followed the pattern set by the early units.[9]

The progressive movement was assisted by social scientists. They supported national social insurance, conservation, child labor legislation, housing reform, efforts to address the problems of blacks, and other issues. Their contributions took the form of surveys and statistical analyses of social conditions. The American Association for Labor Legislation supported research by economists and political scientists, including John R. Commons, Richard Ely (both from the University of Wisconsin), Henry Farnan (Yale University), J. W. Jinks (Cornell University), and Henry Seager and Samuel McCune

Lindsay (both from Columbia University), to serve as a basis for labor legislation and a national insurance system. In presenting the case for reform, the New York Child Labor Committee drew heavily on the work of sociologist Robert Hunter, economist Jacob Riis (Columbia) and Columbia professor of social and political ethics Felix Adler.[10]

The national mobilization for World War I also provided opportunities for social scientists. Various economic planning and research activities were undertaken for war production and coordination. Most of these efforts came to an end with the war, but emerged again with the next major international confrontation.[11]

Additional important research agencies and institutes were established in the years between the world wars. The link between these units and national governmental policy makers was not as close as the tie with the Departments of Labor and Agriculture, but the organizations did help provide a base of information accessible to those responsible for policy. In 1916 the National Research Council was created as the research arm of the National Academy of Sciences. Psychologists and anthropologists within this agency established a base for social scientists. In addition there formed in the 1920s a series of privately financed social science institutes which made themselves available to government. The National Bureau of Economic Research and the Institute for Government Research were among the first. In 1928 they joined with the Institute of Economics to establish the Brookings Institution. Initial research efforts focused on the national budget. The Social Science Research Council, founded in 1923, was somewhat different in character. Its mission was to promote interdisciplinary research and an understanding of the social sciences rather than to undertake major research. Each of these organizations grew in subsequent decades and became sources of analysis for policy applications.[12]

During this period social scientists who wanted to contribute to public policy found themselves with a good friend in the White House. President Hoover's major contribution to social science was the Research Committee on Social Trends, a group financed by the Rockefeller Foundation. The committee's report, *Recent Social Trends in the United States,* issued in 1932, came too late to help President Hoover politically but did signal a new role for social research in government. In it a group of leading scholars thoroughly analyzed American society. Their substantive contribution was overshadowed, however, by prescriptions for the governmental use of social science. The committee not only called for a more active government but also urged that social research become a part of all aspects of governmental decision making. While this objective has yet to be achieved, numerous similar proposals have been made since that time, and the United States is now closer to this goal than it was in 1932.[13]

When the depression struck, social scientists had already demonstrated their usefulness to government. Their studies of social problems, their assistance with the war effort, and their ongoing service in various government and private research organizations all contributed to government. The personalities involved helped develop the governmental connection as much as the research itself. The next several decades would further strengthen the ties.

Response to Crises

The depression and World War II created more opportunities for social scientists than for the immediate application of social research. The crises at hand left little time. Some significant research for policy was undertaken, but more important, social scientists from around the nation came to government. They joined in the national efforts, made recommendations, fortified the capability of the executive branch, exerted some influence on policy, and apparently learned a great deal.

During the New Deal years, interest in the use of social research grew within the executive agencies. The Social Security Administration undertook both long-term study of policy needs and short-term examination of the effectiveness of ongoing programs and administration. The Bureau of Indian Affairs and the Bureau of Agricultural Economics attempted to align their research efforts with policy needs. Already established statistical agencies expanded their capabilities.[14]

A series of boards and commissions, composed of scientists, recommended ways of linking science with government and ways of administering governmental affairs. Some of the recommendations were even implemented. The National Resources Planning Board investigated social and economic coordination and issued in 1934 a report entitled *A Plan for Planning*. President Roosevelt established the Science Advisory Board in 1933 (it was later named the Committee on Government Relations and Science). The board attempted to state the relationship of government to science, but its members found themselves unable to agree as to just what the role of science should be. The president's Committee on Administrative Management, headed by prominent political scientists and public administration specialists, also suffered from internal disagreements, but some of its recommendations for executive branch reorganization were nonetheless implemented.[15]

With the increased governmental role for social scientists, the old dispute between reformers and academics resurfaced. The issue troubled the Committee on Administrative Management and was addressed several years later by Robert S. Lynd's *Knowledge for What?*[16] Lynd attacked empiricism for its own sake and urged social scientists to do applied research. He also suggested that, if science itself cannot make moral judgments, it certainly does not prevent social scientists from doing so.[17] The calls for applied research and an activist social science demonstrated the resurgence of reform-minded individuals. Such demands were also an attempt to legitimate and continue on a larger scale activities that had been carried on throughout most of the previous decade.

World War II engaged the efforts of the physical and social sciences alike. Both emerged from the war stronger than before, although the physical scientists perhaps benefited more, as fewer of their governmental programs were dismantled after the war. The Office of Strategic Research and Development provided a focus for the physical sciences that social science organizations lacked. The physicists also saw the atomic energy program through to its successful completion.[18]

Social experiments and surveys likewise contributed to the war effort. The army undertook social psychological research on adjustment to army life, on combat effectiveness, and on soldiers' expectations regarding their resumption of civilian roles. In addition, psychological methods were applied to personnel work. The Office of Price Administration conducted social surveys to bolster the sale of government bonds. These activities contributed to social psychological knowledge and survey methods and contributed modestly to policy.[19]

Economists joined the war effort by assisting with wartime economic planning and control. New statistical techniques developed as economists received practical experience. As the war ended, there was considerable concern that the economy would again become sluggish. Political demands stemming from this concern led to the Employment Act of 1946 and to the creation of the Council of Economic Advisors.[20]

The depression and World War II drew social scientists to government in larger numbers than ever before. The experience generated increased interest, among both scientists and government officials, in the relationship of research to government. Scientists saw the advantages of government sponsorship for themselves and for their disciplines. Policy makers, confronting new responsibilities, began to realize that science could be useful in government. There could be no return to an earlier era. Instead the immediate objective became the incorporation into standard procedures of mechanisms designed to deal with crisis situations.

Science Becomes Prominent in Government

In the decades that followed World War II, research in the physical and social sciences increased tremendously. A support network emerged that dwarfed any of its predecessors. These developments were accompanied by increased concern with the use of knowledge for policy making. In the wake of the substantial jolts to the support structure for research that came from Sputnik and from the Project Camelot fiasco, many observers reexamined the relation of science to government and exerted pressure for change. The debate over advocacy and objectivity turned to a much closer examination of issues involved in government research support. Some individuals felt that science had suffered an immeasurable loss in autonomy as a result of government sponsorship. People increasingly wondered whether research could be used effectively for public policy. The past few decades have vastly changed the relationship of science to government and have made the public far more aware of the tension and conflict between the institutions.[21]

Postwar social and physical research has depended upon a vast new sponsorship network, with the national government at its apex. Although the foundation was laid during the war, the new structure took shape as a result of a series of debates in the late 1940s and early 1950s. Certain later events also exerted considerable impact. A period of rapid growth and elaboration of the support structure in the 1950s and early 1960s concluded in the mid to late 1960s, but significant activity has continued.

The war demonstrated to scientists the advantages of substantial government sponsorship and highlighted several significant moral questions. Before long, however, the concern with continued growth and support supplanted moral issues. Debate among scientists and politicians over appropriate support mechanisms culminated in the establishment of the National Science Foundation in 1950.[22] Physical scientists led the fight for the new agency as social scientists expressed greater reservations regarding government support. Social scientists were subsequently excluded from the new institution until 1958.[23] Major issues that were raised when the legislation was written pertained to the autonomy of science, accountability for public expenditures, and, consequently, the structure of authority within the new agency and its link to political institutions. The National Science Foundation provided an attractive mechanism for university-based research. Still, scientists in favor of the new agency had felt obliged to promise social dividends from basic research in order to secure the new support structure. The need for the young agency to justify its expenditures for "basic" research in this way would present a problem in the future. Nonetheless, funding grew during the next three decades.

As the National Science Foundation began operations, other agencies sought to bolster their research resources independently. The Office of Naval Research expanded after the war and established its own multisector program. The Atomic Energy Commission also expanded and rearranged its research mechanisms. In the social area, the Public Health Service and its offspring, the National Institutes of Health, became major research actors.[24]

Research and development expenditures grew at a much faster rate than other sectors of the economy. From 1954 to 1958, "basic" research expenditures (expenditures for government and private organizations combined) grew at the rate of 17.9 percent per year, while "applied" research increased 18.7 percent per anum. In comparison, growth in total gross national product was between 5.1 percent and 5.9 percent per year during this period. The total expenditure in 1958 was $10.9 billion.[25] At the same time scientific, technological, and managerial personnel increased in proportion to other sectors of the labor force.[26] At the end of the 1950s, rising research expenditures received an added boost with the launching of Sputnik and continued Cold War tensions.

The launch of Sputnik was widely viewed as signaling a crisis in technological advance. There followed substantial institutional adjustments, primarily in support of technology and the physical sciences but also affecting the social sciences. President Eisenhower created the President's Science Advisory Committee, the special assistant for science and technology, and the Federal Council for Science and Technology. Congress passed the Defense Reorganization Act and the National Defense Education Act, strengthened the National Science Foundation, created the National Aeronautics and Space Administration, and established two new standing committees. In short, science and technology became a gauge of Soviet-American competition.[27] The Defense Reorganization Act of 1958 strengthened the position of the secretary and promoted Department of Defense sponsorship of social research. The newly formed Directorate of Defense Research and Engineering contained a social science unit and soon issued a plan that included long-range goals for social research. These developments stimulated further defense-related social research which later became a salient issue.[28] As the 1960s progressed, social research support advanced on other fronts.

Social research activity increased in the national executive branch during the 1960s. Much of the War on Poverty legislation that created new social programs during the period contained provisions for research and evaluation. President Johnson's extension to all executive agencies of the planning-programing-budgeting-system (PPBS), which had been introduced in the Defense Department, resulted in new planning and research units within major departments.

In addition, external relationships with universities and other research contractors began to proliferate. The National Institute of Mental Health, the Social Security Administration, and the Office of Education were active sponsors of outside research. The Department of Commerce extended its research activity with the Economic Development Act, as did the Department of Labor following the Manpower Act of 1962. The Office of Economic Opportunity (OEO) had a strong research unit and also funded contract research. It established the Institute for Research on Poverty at the University of Wisconsin, an organization which soon became a dominant actor in poverty research.[29] The Departments of Health, Education, and Welfare (HEW), Housing and Urban Development (HUD), and Labor (DOL) each created research units which both conducted policy analysis and served as brokers between outside researchers and policy makers. By the end of the decade a sizable research support structure had been established within the executive branch.

In addition, social research became a focus of debate during several major social policy decisions. Research on the adverse psychological effect of segregation on black youth was aired during adjudication of *Brown v. the Board of Education* in the early 1950s.[30] As the War on Poverty was waged during the 1960s, policy discussion again focused on social research, this time into the causes of juvenile delinquency and poverty.[31] It is difficult to specify in each of these instances the precise role of analysis or its impact on policy decisions.[32] There can be little doubt, however, that, with the postwar period, policy research and analysis assumed new prominence in policy discussion.

With the new institutional arrangements after World War II, the flow of research funds increased. A 1963 survey shows that some $210 million was spent by the national government in support of social science research. Two-thirds of this money came from the Department of Health, Education, and Welfare.[33] From that year through 1975, the rate of growth in support of social science doubled every three years, and from 1966 to 1970, the number of social scientists who received financial support for their research grew by one-third.[34] The National Science Foundation began its social science program in 1958, a year in which the social sciences received $750,000. By 1960 the amount had swelled to $2 million and by 1965 to $10 million.[35] These increases coincided with a massive expansion of the agency's budget in all areas. The support system that emerged for social science was highly decentralized and fragmented. It spanned a broad range of agencies and programs.

A 1978 study of the national investment in social research describes the pluralistic character of the new support system. It found that (1) the pattern by type of activity was far more varied than conventional notions of social research and development might suggest; (2) 60 percent of all support was related to human resources, with 28 percent related to community resources and the remaining 12 percent related to natural resources and the science and technology base; (3) funding programs were strongly decentralized, with 180 separate agencies supporting knowledge production and application activities.[36] Both the physical and the social sciences have experienced unparalleled growth in government support since World War II. Institutional arrangements have altered substantially. The growth in support and research has been accompanied by an increased awareness of the problems surrounding the use and impact of knowledge.

The use and impact of policy analysis were increasingly discussed after a meeting of the Social Science Research Council in 1948. The sociologist Robert K. Merton proposed to the council a large-scale study of the use of research that would focus on the relation of research workers to sponsors and on scientific problems that hampered effective research for policy. The study was not undertaken, but the questions were posed and were to be raised again.[37]

In the late 1960s and 1970s, there came a series of calls for study of the utilization of knowledge and of the relationship of science to government. Carol H. Weiss's proposal for the comparative study of the utilization of evaluation inspired further work in the area.[38]

In addition, a series of major reports completed in the late 1960s proclaimed the need for research on the use of research. A report issued by the National Academy of Sciences, *The Behavioral Sciences in the Federal Government*, focused on improving social agencies' use of research and on bringing more social scientists into the national government. A study prepared jointly by the National Academy of Sciences and the Social Science Research Council, *The*

Behavioral and Social Sciences: Outlook and Needs, concentrated on the implications of use for the structure of social science. A National Science Foundation project, *Knowledge into Action: Improving the Nation's Use of the Social Sciences,* also suggested that more social scientists be brought into government and recommended various improvements in social research. These studies not only highlighted the issue of utilization but also contributed to the understanding of problems associated with research utilization.[39]

The increased interest in use forms a part of a shift that some observers have discerned in the general intellectual climate from the 1950s to the 1960s. According to these observers, the 1950s witnessed emphasis on specialization, adherence to discipline norms, technique, and general, abstract theory. The 1960s, on the other hand, saw a shift to concentration on the concrete analysis of historical periods, cultural change, and relevance. Research became problem and application oriented rather than technique and discipline oriented.[40]

Apart from the increased support for research and the shift in intellectual climate, the controversy surrounding the Department of Defense's Project Camelot helped bring utilization and sponsorship into the spotlight. The reports mentioned above in part responded to this ill-fated research undertaking. Not only was the issue of use raised, but a range of moral and political issues concerning science and government attracted the attention of officials and social scientists.

Project Camelot has been described as the social scientist's atom bomb.[41] The project, which was killed in its infancy by public controversy, enlisted social scientists in an effort to study social processes that led to violent rebellion and the overthrow of foreign governments. The Department of Defense wanted to learn how such movements could be avoided—that is, how to influence social processes in foreign countries. A period of soul-searching, urged upon the social science community by Congress and other political actors, followed the débacle.

Much of the debate centered on threats to academic freedom and the ethical considerations involved in undertaking government research when the researcher has little control over the use of the research product. Social scientists did not like the way they were portrayed in the press, and they sometimes attacked their colleagues engaged in sponsored research. The issue of whether one nation could legitimately study the political processes of another with an interest in intervention grew into a general discussion of the impact of research on research subjects. In addition, questions were raised about the feasibility of government-sponsored research. The challenge to the autonomy of the scientific community that government sponsorship posed came to the attention of many researchers.[42]

The reaction was not restricted to the social science community, however; Congress was also concerned. Senator Harris's bill to introduce a National Social Science Foundation reflected an attempt to incorporate social research into a tried and proven institutional arrangement. It forced social scientists to reconsider their relation to government.[43] Senators Mansfield and Fulbright mounted attacks on Department of Defense social research. Budgets were cut, and a legislative mandate to connect sponsored research clearly to agency missions became law.[44] The Project Camelot episode turned the spotlight on social science and its relation to government. In the years since that time, the light has dimmed only slightly. While there have been some cutbacks in support, government-sponsored social research has gone forward albeit with greater suspicion and heightened tensions.

As a result of such developments, policy research reports have on numerous occasions become front-page news.[45] Policy analysis inevitably becomes embroiled in political controversy as the number of studies increase and particularly as they touch on sensitive issues. The political processes often include "legislators distrustful of 'social engineers' who promote radical ideas or pursue irrelevant academic interests, and social scientists worried that dependence on government might compromise their objectivity."[46] The ties between government and science have strengthened. The research supported sometimes has a direct impact on policy. More often the impact on policy is nil or is indirect and accompanied by other significant consequences. Although government and scientific personnel may be leery of one another, the government continues to fund research, and scientists accept the support. Yet a series of theoretical and political issues persist. We do not understand the impact of policy analysis on society and the political process. Until we do, we will stumble blindly along, buttressed by faith and illusion.

The Impact of Policy Analysis

Several questions have guided the present inquiry. What are the impacts of policy analysis? What factors cause or mediate these impacts? How should these effects be evaluated? The first two questions are empirical and will engage most of our attention. The last question reflects a normative concern and involves value judgments. Specifically, are the impacts of social policy analysis in particular situations to be preferred to the results of inaction (no social policy analysis)? I will try to clarify the normative issues by highlighting the trade-offs involved rather than presenting a detailed answer to the question. It is to be hoped that an analysis of value questions raised by the impact of policy analysis will prove useful for future discussions involving the funding of such analysis.

Our primary interest is the impact of policy analysis on the social condition. What are the consequences for society and for various subgroups? Analysis has direct and indirect effects on identifiable classes of individuals. The former come from the production of policy analysis, from participation in the policy-making process, and from exposure to these processes. Producers of policy analysis reap substantial material and symbolic gains from their activity. Research subjects also gain or lose materially and symbolically. Policy analysis also influences the values, beliefs, and knowledge of participants in the production and policy-making processes and of people exposed to these processes. Changes in individual cognitive structures occur, and in addition, values, beliefs, and knowledge are confirmed. Furthermore, analysis directly bears on the behavior of individuals during the policy process and becomes a political tool that advocates on various sides of a controversy are likely to employ if necessary. Analysis is used to strengthen policy arguments and to attack the position of opponents. In such situations, analysis as a forensic tool alters the terms of debate.[47] Individuals and groups, then, are directly affected by analysis in several ways. Material gains and losses and symbolic impacts are likely to be accompanied by changes and confirmation of individual belief systems.

Indirect consequences stem from the impact of analysis on public policy decisions or outcomes. All policies have some determinable result, even if it is maintenance of the current situation; if analysis contributes to policy, it also contributes to policy impact. Identifiable groups are influenced in a variety of ways. Impact on policy may occur as analysis shapes proposals that are later adopted. Analysis also influences the consequences of decisions by influencing the vote of individual participants. Analysis may be old, produced years prior to present deliberations, or be current and produced with the intent of persuasion. I mean to imply not that analysis is always, or often, a dominant force in policy outputs but that it is often one of several forces at work. The impact of analysis on decisions ranges from none at all to a great deal.

In this book I will endeavor to describe the impact of policy analysis and to explain variations in impact that occur. Do analytic products and the production and decision contexts have attributes that condition the impact of the analysis? If so, what major forces are involved, and how do these components interrelate? These questions have previously received many contradictory answers. I argue in the following chapters that factors relating to production and decision context shape the impact of analysis on decision processes, on individual belief systems, on policy outputs, and on group or class interests. I consider a set of significant cultural, institutional, and social structural conditions and their influence on the impact of policy analysis. In addition I examine the important mediating effects of value conflict and prior individual beliefs. I explain variation in the impact of analysis by referring to specific characteristics of the production and decision contexts.

I also consider normative questions that arise in connection with the explanation of the impact of analysis in particular situations. In terms of impact, is the analysis worth the money? Is the result of producing and using the analysis preferable to the result of doing nothing at all or of expending the funds in some other way? Any position taken on these questions involves a value judgment, a process of reasoned choice, tied to a specific situation.

Chapter 2 critically reviews the literature on the impact and use of policy analysis. In chapter 3 I present my analytic structure and methods, along with an introduction to the field research. Chapter 4 presents an explanation of the impact of policy analysis. Chapters 5 and 6 illustrate the impact of the Seattle and Denver income maintenance experiments on the Carter administration's welfare reform attempts of 1977. Chapter 7 considers the policy implications of this research, normative issues raised by the findings, and directions for future investigations in this area. Chapter 8 examines Congress's reaction to President Carter's program for better jobs and income.

2 Toward an Explanation of the Impact of Policy Analysis

✳

The present book falls within a broad area of inquiry commonly described as the utilization of knowledge and less frequently as the sociology of knowledge application. A wide range of social science disciplines have been represented in the studies so far conducted. Economics, political science, public administration, social psychology, sociology, and history have all contributed.[1] A review of previous research, however, suggests that a unifying paradigm is lacking; a common theoretical base and consistent findings are absent. Writers have addressed diverse questions and hypotheses, pursuing varying methodological approaches. In addition, there is little agreement regarding basic concepts. Only the first few steps along the path to knowledge have been taken.

This chapter critically examines the emerging field of study. It identifies obstacles to theoretical advance and positive steps toward the articulation of theory. It also raises significant questions yet to be addressed adequately and explores the distance still to be traveled in pursuit of adequate answers. The aim is not to review exhaustively or catalog all the previous research but to highlight major problems and research findings so that the quest for further knowledge may be advanced. The critique focuses on three broad areas: conceptualization of events to be explained (dependent variables); explanation of these events; and normative assumptions or judgments that underlie much of the previous research.

Conceptualization of Impact

Although prior research has often attempted to explain the utilization of policy analysis or to describe the interests that benefit from the production and dissemination of analysis, single studies have seldom addressed both questions together. The omission is unfortunate, as each approach considers a significant dimension of the impact of analysis, and the two taken together might be linked to a common set of causal factors. To concentrate inquiry on the use of analysis alone is a gross mistake and impedes further advances. Such a focus narrows the scope of inquiry in a pernicious fashion by failing to consider the major question of the second approach (who benefits) and overlooks other significant impacts (for example, impact on decision processes or on individual belief systems). Apart from this discontinuity in the study of the impact of analysis, each approach has serious problems. Studies that do address the question of interests served by analysis generally tend to consider only one interest that benefits or only a few of them. "Utilization" has also become a very ambiguous term with a variety of meanings.

"Utilization" implies activity undertaken with the aid of analysis. Of prime interest is the use of research to inform policy decisions. Caplan, Morrison, and Stambaugh offered a typical definition: utilization was said to occur when a decision maker "was familiar with relevant research and gave serious consideration to and attempted to apply that knowledge to some policy-relevant issue." In this instance the criterion is attempted application rather than actual impact on policy outputs. The latter criterion has greater political implications than the former but is excluded from study, according to the definition just presented. The definition also fails to differentiate between the use of research to inform decisions and the use of research to justify or legitimate decisions already taken. Russell and Shore mention the incorporation of a range of products, including proposals, into policy decisions in their definition:

> By the uses of social science we mean the incorporation, by the various branches of the federal government—more specifically by the Congress, the office of the President and the civil service—into judgments as to which actions should be taken to

achieve certain desired conditions, of descriptions, causal interpretations and proposals offered by social scientists.[2]

As this definition indicates, much of the literature concentrates on
the utilization of analysis for major policy decisions at the top
levels of the national government, but minor policy decisions are
made every day by officials at all levels of government. Policy
decisions may be made at the national level, may affect millions
of individuals, and may be reached under the public spotlight, or
they may pertain to small questions of program operation at the
local level that are visible to only one or a few individuals. Of
course, there are numerous intermediate steps on this scale. Although some social scientists complain that their research is not
used in decision making, they generally mean that it is not used to
make significant decisions at the national level. Other social scientists present evidence of utilization for a wide range of decision
types.

The application of analysis to immediate policy decisions describes what might be called the ideal of direct impact on decisions.
This model follows a rational conception of policy making, which
holds that decisions should be based on thorough analysis of the
consequences of a range of policy alternatives. Analysis is viewed as
authoritative, as overriding other decision inputs. Acceptance of this
ideal in various forms, with occasional qualifications, is widespread.
It motivates the entire field of policy analysis and the study of utilization and impact. Yet direct impact on decisions as described is so
rare that the National Science Foundation refers to examples of
direct impact on decisions as "nuggets."[3] I will examine the ideal of
direct impact on decisions and other normative issues further in the
final section of this chapter.

Lesser-grade utilization occurs at various policy levels. Caplan,
Morrison, and Stambaugh report "creative and strategically important applications of policy-related social science information" across
the top levels of the national executive branch. Gusfield finds evidence of direct impact on decisions at the operative level in drug
abuse treatment agencies. Scott and Shore argue that decision use
most frequently occurs at the national level with technical matters
concerning daily "governmental business." Scott and Shore also pro-

vide a long list of more salient decisions in which analysis has played a role.[4]

Reports of direct impact on significant decisions span the past fifty years. While direct impact is quite difficult to document so that many reports can be faulted, the extent of the claims and the supporting evidence lend some weight to the conclusion that policy analysis occasionally exerts direct impact on decisions. Lyons finds that research by the Bureau of Agricultural Economics "was continually and systematically related to the formulation of overall policies," as was social research in the Bureau of Indian Affairs.[5] Many other studies reach the same conclusion.

Horowitz and Katz argue that social research played a substantial role in two court decisions involving race, *Brown* v. *Board of Education* in 1954 and *Loving* v. *Commonwealth of Virginia* in 1967. Smith documents the direct effect of the Rand strategic forces study on national security policy. The period of social policy formulation in the 1960s has provided many examples of direct impact on decisions. Moynihan reports utilization of the Ohlin and Cloward research on opportunity structure during the War on Poverty and claims that the Coleman report affected educational policy. Datta describes the effect of the Ohio State/Westinghouse evaluation of Head Start on that program. Williams and Russell and Shore are less specific but argue that analysis contributed greatly to social policy in the 1960s.[6]

If "utilization" meant solely direct impact on policy decisions, it might serve a useful role in inquiry, as one of several significant impacts of analysis, but the concept is often used with reference to quite different phenomena and is thus ambiguous and subject to misunderstanding. Analysis may also be used for political purposes, or, as some observers would have it, analysis may be misused.[7]

Political utilization includes among its various activities attempts to persuade or neutralize critics, to bolster supporters, to shift responsibility, and to legitimate decisions. These uses are generally recognized but are often difficult to distinguish from direct impact on decisions. Social scientists, however, typically frown upon political uses of analysis, and such uses hence receive less research attention than their prevalence and importance might dictate. Political uses do not fit the ideal of direct impact on decisions, the normative model of utilization that dominates the field. They describe not collective ends but rather utilization to serve the ends of specific political actors, individuals, and organizations. In this sense analysis is employed in some manner considered inappropriate during policy formulation or is employed after policy has been made to legitimate the decisions already taken.

Research suggests that analysis is frequently distorted, suppressed, or selectively represented in policy discussions. Primack and von Hippel state that "administration officials have felt free to ignore or distort technical advice when it hasn't been compatible with their bureaucratic or political convenience." Similarly, Hoos argues that analyses are "cited when they bolster a particular ideological position, sealed when they are likely to embarrass persons in power." The prevalence of political use of analysis leads Aaron to conclude that analysis is "a political instrument to be trotted out when it supported one's objectives or undercut one's opponents', and to be suppressed, if possible, when it opposed one's objectives or strengthened one's opponents." Mechanic suggests that the quality of analysis used in this political manner does not much matter, as "in a context where decision makers have difficulty differentiating the counterfeit from the real, the incentive is to trade in bad currency."[8] Analysis may thus be employed in several different ways to influence decisions, yet political uses are often ignored when they are not part of the researchers' ideal conception of utilization.

Political applications exemplify Bacon's and Condorcet's assertions that knowledge is a potent source of power. Recent statements to this effect jibe with the reports of manipulation of analysis in the policy process. Patton argues that knowledge equals power, and its potential lies "in its capacity to empower users of evaluation information." Nelkin echoes this theme: "Scientific knowledge, like land, labor, and capital, is a resource—indeed a commodity—and the ability to manipulate and control this resource has profound implications for the distribution of political power in democratic societies." If knowledge is widely treated as a political resource, as a source of power, then the conception of utilization that ignores this fact is seriously deficient.[9]

Similarly at odds with the ideal of direct impact on decisions is legitimation, the use of analysis to support or justify a decision already made. Legitimation reverses the sequence of events in the ideal scenario, as analysis follows rather than precedes decisions. The frequency with which legitimation occurs adds to the problems surrounding inquiry based on an ideal that envisions direct impact on decisions. Lindblom and Cohen, Scott and Shore, Meld, and King and Melanson all argue that analysis is frequently invoked to legitimate decisions already taken. In addition, 15 percent of Weiss and Bucuvalas's sample of national mental health administrators reported legitimation uses, or instances in which decision makers were "seeking research for its credibility in documenting their arguments." Examples are abundant. Horowitz and Katz discuss the army's use of social science research to legitimate the decision, already taken, to desegregate the troops. Russell and Shore indicate that U.S. senators are particularly adept at legitimation, and these authors cite selective use of social scientists in support of the Child Development Act of 1971 and the supersonic transport proposal.[10]

Utilization, then, is used with reference to direct impact on policy decisions or outputs, to strategic moves to advance particular interests or policy proposals, and also to a wholly different set of phenomena.

Some writers argue that analysis is being utilized when it influences one's thinking about a policy issue or social problem in some way. Exposure to analysis may lead an individual to conceptualize social problems in a new manner. It may alter beliefs about current practices and proposed policies and shape value judgments. Weiss has popularized this view and has named it "the enlightenment function of research." She describes utilization for enlightenment as follows:

> It [analysis] can provide concepts, sensitivities, models, paradigms, theories. Such conceptual derivatives from research can influence which issues are placed on the policy agenda and which kinds of policy options are considered. They can enter into decision makers' orientation toward priorities, the manner in which they formulate problems, the range of solutions they canvass, the criteria of choice they apply.

The process of enlightenment is cumulative and incremental. Multiple experiences, including exposure to a series of research reports, are gradually assimilated, perhaps over long periods of time, into the individual's way of thinking about public problems and policies. As Weiss and Bucuvalas observe, enlightenment does not greatly differ from learning as it is usually defined. Their discussion does, however, emphasize conceptual inputs of analysis over theoretical or relational inputs: "It is the generalizations and concepts from the social sciences that they [decision makers] often find most useful in helping them construct their images."[11] Enlightenment may, nonetheless, influence policy as decision makers bring altered beliefs to the consideration of current policy issues.

Numerous additional studies support utilization as a mechanism of long-range impact on policy. Scott and Shore; Lindblom and Cohen; Caplan, Morrison, and Stambaugh; Smith; Wildavsky; Patton; Alkin, Daillak, and White; and others argue that impact on individual belief systems is a major form of research utilization. Datta provides an interesting description of the enlightenment effect of Head Start evaluations, although she does not use the term. The Head Start evaluation served "to dampen public hope in family or child educational interventions as an effective way to reduce poverty." In addition, "It is widely cited, and its conclusions form part of the belief system of many in positions of national influence." Likewise, the Coleman Report on education, despite the surrounding controversy, influenced thinking about education policy. Aaron likewise discusses the effect of poverty research conducted during the 1960s:

> Scholars analyzed the data and discovered that the problems of poverty and discrimination were a good deal more complicated than most had suspected a decade or so earlier. The faith that complex problems had been understood collapsed. Vigorous action to deal with them lost intellectual respectability. A new and complex understanding of the dynamics of poverty arose that was analytically more satisfying but politically crippling.[12]

The enlightenment hypothesis highlights a significant impact of analysis, but impact on individual belief systems is poorly defined and needs to be conceptualized in a more fruitful manner.

Much of the discussion of enlightenment fails to consider that analysis may confirm prior beliefs, irrespective of their accuracy.

There are several interesting exceptions. Edelman discusses the impact of analysis within the broader context of political language and symbols. He argues that "dogmatic beliefs about problematic issues are the crucial cognitive outcome of political symbols." Spence, after assessing the research on socialization processes, contends that research is more often used to support myth than to challenge beliefs.[13] Obfuscation, or "endarkenment," thus seems to be a cognitive impact that should be kept in mind.

As the preceding discussion illustrates, analysis may be used in different ways with a wide variety of meanings. The sheer range of events described as "utilization" suggests the need for clarification. While various studies have touched on the interests served by analysis, they are not as explicit or direct in examining these political impacts as research in other areas. The finding that particular interests have substantially benefited indicates that analysis influences more than utilization behavior. By the same token, the studies that explore political impact ignore many of the utilization phenomena and are often unduly narrow or overly general.

Researchers may substantially advance their careers by producing policy analysis. Academic social scientists benefit especially from the financial support of their research. Funding confers indirect benefits in the form of recognition, prestige, and professional advancement gained from the command of research money. Blumer develops this argument and suggests that "there is great pressure among social scientists not merely to do research but to have funds for research; the social scientist today who does not have research funds is likely to be regarded as a lowly figure."[14] Promotion and tenure, as well as other professional rewards and advances, stem in part from the successful performance of research. The allocation of money to research does not guarantee professional success, but it does facilitate attainment of the objective.

By producing policy analysis social scientists are also able to enjoy the opportunity to advance their psychological and ideological interests. Research enables the social scientist to confirm firmly held belief systems. As Lindblom suggests, "professional analysts, by definition, are committed to evidence and disciplined analysis. They become partisans, sometimes passionately so, on behalf of reason, even if they slide into partisanship on behalf of other causes as well." Apart from belief in reason, social scientists have an interest in maintaining theoretical, conceptual, and methodological structures acquired through years of disciplinary training and research. To advance or confirm belief in this belief system secures the status of the practitioner and protects past investment in education. But the opposite result is a possibility as well. Roberts suggests that, "when the conceptual system of a science changes, the professional position of a scientist and his past investment in training and experience, can be significantly endangered. Such changes can transform the skills and wisdom of older practitioners from valuable assets into constraining habits of mind that inhibit their use of new concepts and techniques."[15] Research gives social scientists an opportunity to secure their professional skills and habits of thought.

Benefits accrue to the social scientist's organizations as well as to individuals. Disciplines and academic departments gain professional status from participation in sponsored research. Individuals and organizations alike are measured by research performance. In addition, the advancement of belief in disciplinary paradigms benefits organizations as it does members. Furthermore, a new set of material benefits is associated with the rise of profit-making research organizations. Organizations with a record of successful performance of contract research can reap substantial profits. The proliferation of such research organizations is some indication of the benefits at stake.[16]

Social scientists, the organizations for which they work, and the disciplines to which they belong are affected by the production of policy analysis. Rainwater and Yancey argue that it is dangerous to apply social science research to policy issues because of "threats posed to the autonomy of social science by direct or indirect pressures on social scientists to conceal findings." Beals suggests that the danger may already have taken an emotional toll on social scientists: "As the use and support of the social sciences by government agencies have increased, so has the social scientist's fear of losing freedom and honesty and suffering the imposition of secrecy." The concern voiced by Beals is not shared by all social scientists, if we may judge from their avid pursuit of research funds. Social science, however, may already have lost a measure of autonomy, particularly with the increase in government sponsorship. Some observers argue that the integrity of social science has been called into question and that the disciplines have declined in status accordingly.[17] Loss of academic freedom is difficult to document, but some price has apparently been paid for the benefits to social science that stem from the production of policy analysis.

Scientists and their organizations are not the only interests to be affected by policy analysis. It is frequently claimed that policy analysis is generally conservative inasmuch as it constrains innovation and social change. Evaluation research has often found that social programs fall short of achieving their objectives, but it provides few insights into possible remedies. In addition, research may be used to postpone change; the response is frequently: "Yes, there may be a problem with the program, and we'll study the situation." If this statement is true, it undercuts a major argument of those who advocate increased funding of policy research—that policy research promotes effective public programs and policy change.

Conservative impact on policy output may take several forms. Weiss, for example, notes that the tendency to evaluate young, venturesome programs and to find no discernible program impact hurts new and different policy efforts. Aaron suggests that a conservative impact results when multiple interpretations of a common set of findings show that experts are in disagreement. Under these circumstances policy makers are more apt to wait for further resolution of policy questions before taking new action. Aaron concludes that social research conducted during the War on Poverty is presently having such an inhibiting effect on policy makers. The conservative impact on policy output is sometimes far more immediate. Brewer concludes that a project to develop a complex simulation of urban social and economic processes in San Francisco "functioned as an unintended retardant to the development of the Community Renewal Program." Edelman shares Aaron's views on the conservative impact of research through its tendency to provoke opposing interpretations. He contends that "such evocation of multiple realities has profound, if nonobvious, consequences for politics. It encourages both the powerful and the powerless to accept their situations while permitting both to express their abhorrence of poverty and their dedication to reform." Becker and Horowitz also charge that social research is conservative and advances the interests of dominant social groups. They argue that much policy research by sociologists provides "the facts which make oppression more efficient and the theory which makes it legitimate to a larger constituency."[18] A growing body of evidence raises the possibility that policy research is conservative in inhibiting policy initiatives and thereby favoring interests that presently reap the most substantial gains from social, political, and economic institutions.

Studies that focus on utilization also fail to consider impact on decision processes and generally focus on policy output or individual behavior and belief systems. Some research suggests, however, that decision processes are significantly affected. It is frequently claimed that the introduction of analysis increases conflict by bringing into view consequences of policy that seldom meet with all parties' approval. Without analysis the grounds for social division and conflict might not be considered by as many individuals. Policy research reports that became mired in controversy are frequently mentioned in the newspapers. Cases that have become widely known include the 1960s Moynihan report on the Negro family and the New Jersey–Pennsylvania income maintenance experiment. Rainwater and Yancey state that the Moynihan report precipitated "one of the angriest and most bitter controversies yet among government and private individuals all presumably dedicated to realizing Negro rights." Rossi and Lyall describe how the preliminary results of the New Jersey experiment influenced policy discussions as they became engulfed in politics.[19] It is difficult to say, however, whether conflict actually increased or whether existing differences were just being expressed. It is equally hard to trace the impact of debate over research reports on policy outputs. Yet evidence that policy processes have altered raises interesting questions about the impact of these changes on policy outputs.

Some observers think it is good for analysis to be immersed in political controversy. Wildavsky, for example, argues that analysis "could enhance social trust by widening areas of agreement about the consequences of policies and the likely effects of change." Lindblom believes that research-report controversies provide a forum for competing ideas that aid problem solving. In addition, he argues that analysis must realistically be expected to become involved in conflict and in political interaction. He does not, however, address the effect of variation in power among participants on the competition of ideas. Similarly, Morrill claims that the subjection of research and researchers to political attack is a necessary, albeit slow, part of the process of building consensus. These arguments are not supported in a rigorous fashion, and serious questions remain about the effect of analysis on political processes in which actors commanding different amounts of political resources participate.[20] Much study is needed on these interesting and important questions as well as on utilization as it is commonly viewed.

Explanation of the Impact of Analysis

The diversity in the foci of research on the impact of policy analysis is matched by the range of explanations and hypotheses regarding these events. Even when direct impact on decisions is emphasized, many hypotheses presume to explain utilization or nonutilization. When studies that examine other dimensions of impact are considered, the list of hyptheses grows even longer. The theories can be divided into four broad categories: the knowledge specific, the two communities, those concerned with decision-production context, and those concerned with process.

The literature on the impact of policy analysis suffers from significant theoretical shortcomings. First, many fragmented and often conflicting hypotheses presume to explain the impact of analysis. Second, research overemphasizes obstacles to the utilization of analysis. Third, few attempts have been made to integrate hypotheses across the four general categories into a comprehensive explanation of impact. Finally, the several major dimensions of impact have not been placed within a common framework. Research generally focuses on direct impact on decisions, interests served, or enlightenment, but these impacts are seldom viewed together.

Social scientists and decision makers alike often complain that policy analysis is wholly inadequate for policy application. The reasons given are many. The analysis is frequently said to lack an action orientation or program-development focus.[21] Analysis is often considered to stem from and to reflect a disciplinary perspective, so that it is more relevant to the social sciences than to decision makers.[22] When analysis does focus on specific programs, as with evaluation research, the usual finding is minimal program effects or none at all.[23] The implications of negative findings—a significant change in program or policy—are such that direct impact on decisions is frequently thwarted.[24] It is also often complained that analysis is frequently inconclusive or not objective.[25] Multivariate research techniques are commonly regarded as tools inadequate to provide answers to policy questions or are considered to bias research in ways that are sometimes not obvious.[26] Perhaps the most general observation is that analysis is often of such poor quality that it cannot or should not be utilized.[27] It is sometimes very difficult to find research that addresses current or the most pressing policy questions. If these complaints are well founded, the failure to utilize policy analysis may be not only justifiable but also at times beneficial.

Yet studies that criticize policy analysis fail to indicate clearly which faults are the most significant for utilization. Little evidence ranks action orientation, negative results, research technique, or poor quality in importance as explanatory factors.[28] The claims are sometimes also conflicting. Mahoney and Mahoney argue, for example, that comprehensive analysis is more likely to be used, while Harris contends that incremental research, which focuses on relatively small and well-defined policy matters, is the better candidate. Still others contend that there is no relationship between quality and utilization; poor research and good research can both be very useful.[29] A similar disagreement concerns analysis that challenges the status quo or suggests major departures from past policy. Weiss and Bucuvalas argue that research of a challenging nature is particularly useful for enlightenment. Scott and Shore claim that such research is unlikely to exert a direct impact on decisions.[30] The sheer number and variety of hypotheses, and the conflicts among them, leave us with a confused and confusing picture indeed.

Several studies draw upon C. P. Snow's analysis of the gulf between scientific and humanistic cultures to explain why policy analysis is not used. A similar gulf is said to exist between scientists and policy makers. The two are thought to perceive social reality differently, to have different analytic styles, and to use different communication patterns or languages and reward structures, which condition their behaviors. The gap produces hostility and mistrust, as well as the failure of policy makers to find the research products of the scientists useful.[31]

Particular attributes of social scientists or policy makers are also said to hinder utilization without reference to the full two-communities framework. Patton, for example, argues that social scientists fail to understand the politics of analysis (or of policy making) and therefore make it more likely that their work will not be used. Similarly, Myrdal contends that deliberate attempts by social scientists to avoid advocacy produce situations where they "are increasingly addressing only one another" and also make analysis ineffective in bringing about policy change. With regard to policy makers, Morrill maintains that unrealistic expectations for analysis inhibit utilization. Suchman notes policy makers' unfavorable attitudes toward analysis, and Merton describes how distrust affects the approach taken to particular beliefs and assumptions.[32]

Further criticism of the two-communities approach suggests that its value may be limited. Dunn, for example, believes that the approach insightfully addresses the importance of "the subjective interpretation of meaning attached to 'knowlege'" but suffers from lack of clearly defined terms and lack of testable hypotheses. Archibald, on the other hand, claims that the academic role orientations of analysts lead them to identify the communities gap as the source of nonutilization.[33] In other words, the two-communities metaphor is a social artifact rather than an accurate theory.

Moreover, some evidence contradicts the two-communities hypothesis, and additional information suggests that any existing gap is narrowing. The high status or prestige of science in American society, it is often claimed, increases the likelihood that scientific research will be used.[34] If so, prestige would counter the negative effect of the communities gap on utilization. In addition Horowitz suggests, "The fact that an ever increasing number of individuals can with some legitimacy claim both scientific and policy-making statuses tends to blur lines between these issues."[35] An increase in social scientists' willingness to adopt a reform or advocacy stance is perhaps reducing any gap between social scientists and policy makers.[36] Indeed, recent research suggests that national executive administrators display considerable receptivity to social science, although they do not do so uniformly.[37] The mixed research findings on the two-communities theory and the failure to identify adequately the most important explanatory components illustrate the need for further clarification.

There has been much discussion of the effect that various characteristics of the decision-production context exert on the utilization of analysis. In fact, the list of social, cultural, organizational, and political factors affecting utilization is so long that construction of a relatively simple picture of these forces as they influence utilization seems prohibitive. There is, however, greater agreement on several key points than with other sets of hypotheses. The organizational and political context of the production and utilization of research is generally considered critical. Yet as discussion departs from this core belief, the agreement lessens and the range of considerations grows. The many organizational and political hypotheses have yet to be subsumed under a more general framework.

Recent trends have altered the context of policy analysis and are the subject of frequent speculation. Lyons notes the growth of the federal government, the development of the social sciences, and the introduction of new administrative techniques. Aaron considers civil rights victories, the new tools of economic analysis, and the collapse of a general consensus on social problems. Similarly, Moynihan mentions an econometric revolution, the growth of knowledge and research-sponsoring foundations, and the professionalization of the middle class.[38] Most of these suggested changes appear to create increased opportunity for the use of analysis, but the relation of these changes to utilization is seldom stated, much less supported.

Long lists of contextual factors are too often presented without specification of their interrelation, or, again, without careful specification of their relation to utilization. Alkin, Daillak, and White list eight "crude categories" of contextual factors to serve as guides for further research. Scott and Shore identify nine factors that influence the president's utilization of social science research. Larsen acknowledges the need for a model of contextual conditions and presents six factors for consideration.[39] It is clearly easier to list potential significant conditions than to construct models that single out the most significant factors and relate them to the impact of analysis. Until the latter task has been undertaken, we will have little actual theory worth testing and will scarcely be able to advance knowledge.

A variety of hypotheses suggest that characteristics of the organizations that produce and utilize analysis influence utilization or impact, although there is little supporting evidence. Several analyses, for example, suggest that university-produced policy analysis is less likely to be utilized than that produced elsewhere. In part the reason is a minimal emphasis on dissemination, but in part it is also research that emphasizes disciplinary concerns. Merton relates the type of research agency (independent or incorporated in the operating agency) to the type of clientele (government, foundation, business, and so forth). He suggests that "the problems of utilizing applied social science research in policy-formation probably differ according to both the social position of the research agency and the client (or sponsor)." While a number of hypotheses follow Merton's analysis, much remains to be clarified. Dunn, for example, argues that knowledge is more likely to be used in organizations with profit incentives than in those that operate from other bases. He also identifies specific structural features, including hierarchical support for analysis, structural connections between research and operational units, and specific linking mechanisms that facilitate utilization.[40] These hypotheses are suggestive, but further testing is needed to assess their validity.

A more common theme is that organizational maintenance or self-interest conditions the utilization of research.[41] The concept of organizational self-interest invites consideration of a more general topic, the relation of politics to the use of policy analysis.

Although the effect of politics on utilization is sometimes ignored, it is more often deplored. Yet studies frequently find that politics, expressed in terms of power or conflict, shapes the application of knowledge.[42] Unfortunately, ongoing debate regarding the political structure of American society makes the effect of politics on the impact of research difficult to determine. If, for example, one adheres to the pluralist view of American politics and believes that power and resources are widely distributed among various competing groups, one is likely to view the partisan use of analysis as an inevitable contribution to a natural process of bargaining and compromise, benefiting all interests.[43] If, on the other hand, one considers elitist or Marxist theories to accurately reflect American politics, analysis is seen as a tool by which a ruling economic class maintains domination over subordinate classes within society and secures its

own interests at the expense of others.⁴⁴ A common pattern in the
literature is to assume, or on occasion explicitly to argue, that one of
these theoretical formulations accurately depicts American politics
and to argue accordingly regarding the effect of politics on the use
and impact of analysis. The discussion proceeds with little analysis
of politics apart from passing references to political forces that interfere with direct impact on decisions. In any case, we have a long way
to go in understanding the relation of political structures to the utilization of analysis before we are likely to reach any agreement.

In relating politics to the utilization and impact of analysis, we
may also consider the effect of the type of policy under consideration. Lowi has argued that social expectations regarding the impact
that policy will have on society tend to shape the political structure
and process within which particular issues are considered. He identifies three major functional policy categories—regulation, distribution, and redistribution—each with its characteristic pattern of
politics. In terms of our earlier discussion, he contends that regulatory politics approaches the pluralist model, while redistributive
policy is more in line with elite theory. A major difficulty with
Lowi's formulation is the classification of policy. As Greenberg, Miller, Mohr, and Vladeck have noted, many policy decisions are likely
to manifest some characteristics of each policy type. In addition, the
classification rests on perceptions of policy impact without any clear
indication of whose perceptions of policy count and without any
indication of how any variation in perceptions should be handled.⁴⁵
Nonetheless, the theory provides some interesting ideas for consideration. Particularly intriguing is the suggestion that the pattern of
interests engaged by policy questions shapes the politics that accompany their consideration.

The use and impact of analysis may also be influenced by value
conflict, or relative disagreement regarding the ends or objectives of
policy. Several studies have described the influence of politics in
such terms. Yet the relation of value conflict to the impact of analysis is seldom carefully specified or integrated with considerations of
the power and resources of participants in the conflict situation.
Horowitz and Katz, for example, argue that, "when a genuine broad-
based consensus exists, the social scientists perform major legitimiz-
ing and rationalizing services, but when a dissensus is present, the

social scientists can only serve to reflect that situation in the very polarities of their own professional writings and researches." Similarly, Wildavsky suggests that "acceptance of evaluation requires a community of shared values." Lindblom contends that, when "conflicts of interest are too great, the policy problem is not going to be given an analytical solution, but will be decided by political interaction."[46] Greenberg's criticism of Lowi's policy typology can also be applied to these claims. Whose values count? How is value conflict or consensus to be measured? How do the power positions of various actors interact with the level of value conflict or agreement? These issues need to be explored further. Value conflict, however, does seem to have the potential to provide a basis for integrating the various hypotheses.

Several process factors have also been said to influence the utilization and impact of analysis. Some of those frequently mentioned include communication or dissemination, timely presentation, advocacy, and interaction of researchers and clients or sponsors. Smith argues that careful communication of results to decision makers is very important. Barber notes that restrictions on the dissemination of information hamper utilization. In addition, Roberts and others suggest that presentation is seldom timely. Yet several studies play down the importance of communication or dissemination. Knott and Wildavsky, for example, argue that the ambiguous term "dissemination" serves as a scapegoat for nonutilization. The issues of advocacy and interaction between researchers and policy makers also suffer from mixed findings. Patton contends that the personal factor—the presence of someone who takes responsibility for communicating and pursuing the utilization of research—is crucial for utilization. Similarly, Weiss maintains that close interaction between researchers and policy makers increases utilization, but she suggests in a later study that close interaction appears not to be "an all-purpose panacea," as decision makers have great difficulty articulating their research needs.[47] Here again, contradictory findings preclude well-supported assertions relating process factors to the impact of analysis. In addition, there is little indication as to which of the many factors identified may be the most important for utilization and impact.

In the four categories of hypotheses that we have considered—

the knowledge specific, the two communities, the decision-production context, and the process—many obstacles to the utilization of analysis have been identified. In light of the full catalog of obstacles, it seems remarkable that research is ever used. Several researchers seem to aid this conclusion by simply enumerating their own long lists of obstacles. Perhaps the best example of the tendency to enumerate obstacles are Weiss and Bucuvalas, who mention thirty-five factors as hindering use across production, decision, and linkage systems.[48] Long lists of obstacles serve mainly to divert attention from the situations in which utilization and impact do occur and to obscure efforts to construct a general theoretical framework which promotes understanding without unduly complicating matters.

Failure to come to grips with the apparent complexity of the impact of policy analysis creates additional problems. Despite the seemingly undeniable range of hypotheses across the four broad explanatory approaches, every theorist has a favorite approach, and few attempts are made to integrate plausible hypotheses in a comprehensive model. A few exceptions are notable. Brewer suggests that the key to theoretical advance lies in exploring the interface of knowledge-specific factors and process features such as interaction between researchers and policy makers. Rich finds that the two-communities theory performs less well than bureaucratic explanations of knowledge use. Gouldner examines the relation of ideology to interests and suggests: "(1) To the extent that knowledge is grounded in interests its pursuit is *energized* and motivated by them and, at the same time, (2) knowledge is always *limited* by these same interests." While these efforts have not produced elegant theory, they have begun to link seemingly important explanatory factors in a productive fashion. Several quantitative studies also consider a range of factors. Caplan, Morrison, and Stambaugh examine the relative predictive power of three theories, the two-communities, the knowledge-specific, and the policy-maker constraint (their term). According to the analysis based on an additive model, the two-communities theory is the best predictor of nonutilization, but each of the other formulations has some explanatory power as well. Weiss and Bucuvalas found no statistically significant interaction of research characteristics and decision-maker attributes in their tests.[49] These studies are clearly atypical. Most research on utilization and impact of research avoids analysis of the interrelations among explanatory factors. Yet a review of the research indicates that interaction is plausible. Further theoretical advance may well depend upon the success of attempts to conceptualize and relate a range of factors in a comprehensive model. In another important sense, however, past research fragments important considerations.

Most studies focus on single dimensions of impact, usually direct impact on decisions or on one of several interests that benefit from the introduction of policy analysis. Rarely are these impact dimensions considered together, much less included in an analysis of impact on decision processes and individual belief systems. Yet evidence suggests that a range of impacts result from production, communication, and attempted decision use of policy analysis. The major dimensions of impact need to be brought together within a common framework. For greatest practical and theoretical significance, a full range of impacts should be related to a single set of explanatory conditions. Such an investigation would provide a base for a fruitful discussion of the normative and political issues involved in funding policy analysis. It is simply not adequate to rely on simple assumptions, for example that utilization is good and nonutilization is bad.

Value Judgments and Policy Analysis

Social scientists who adhere to a logical positivist approach have been taught to avoid making value judgments in their work; professional norms make it unscientific to address questions of value. Yet social scientists are seldom able to adhere fully to this norm, nor do they all desire to do so. On the other hand, social scientists often base their research on simple normative assumptions and beliefs without explicit reference to this fact. They subordinate normative concerns to empirical analysis and generally do not give such concerns careful attention.

The ideal of direct impact on decisions is a case in point. It is often assumed that policy analysis should be used for policy making; nonutilization is to be avoided. Much research is thus geared toward promoting utilization.[50] The basis for this assumption is examined less frequently. Why is decision use beneficial? What difference does it make? Why should we value this difference? Answers to these questions are seldom sought.

The general negative attitude toward political uses of analysis also reflects normative assumptions. Political uses are phenomena not simply to be explained but to be avoided or constrained. Why should this be the case? The implicit answer is often that politics is dishonest or tainted by selfish interest. Furthermore, political use does not harmonize with the ideal of direct impact on decisions. Yet this argument is rarely made explicitly or examined with care and precision.

Recent studies suggesting that policy analysis should serve an enlightenment function likewise imply value judgments. The implication is that policy analysis should be undertaken and funded even if it seldom exerts a direct impact on policy decisions. In other words, enlightenment alone justifies expenditures on policy analysis. Indirect impact on decisions, through a process of enlightenment, is a second-best solution to direct impact on decisions. Both are viewed as beneficial, and again, decision use is presented as an ideal. The possibility that analysis reinforces prejudice and myth receives scant attention, as it sours the favored outcome. Deliberate analysis of the full range of impacts and incorporation of these findings in value judgment are absent.

Explicit consideration of value and of the bases for any judgment should be preferred to value judgment through disguise and fragmentary analysis primarily because it furthers deliberation and reasoned choice. Value judgment entails careful consideration of the full range of impacts of analysis. Simple assumptions based solely on faith will not do.

3 Development of Explanations

✳

Before I present a plan of investigation, I must outline the analytic structure of explanations—my ultimate objective—so that there is as little misunderstanding as possible about my purpose. In describing the explanation I will be providing a justifiable set of standards by which the work may be judged. I will then discuss the development or creation of explanations before introducing a heuristic case study of the impact of analysis on attempts by the Carter administration to reform public assistance policies. This case illustrates the use of policy analysis in the formulation of policy.

The Structure of Analysis

My objective in this book is to develop an explanation or theory of the impact of the production and dissemination of policy analysis at the national level of government.[1] An explanation is an analytic construct which attemps to model or depict a real-world situation. The construct, a human product, is isomorphic to the real situation and thus makes that situation intelligible. The construct also provides the means for intervention to control conditions or situations by relating specific actions, or intervention strategies, to their consequences.[2] The basic characteristics of an explanation are discussed below. The diagram illustrates the basic explanatory structure.

$$[S_1, \quad . \quad . \quad . \quad . \quad S_n; \; V_1, \quad . \quad . \quad . \quad . \quad V_n; \; R_1, \quad . \quad . \quad . \quad . \quad R_n]$$

Specifying Conditions	Explanatory and Impact Variables	Rules that State the Relations among Units

An explanation entails a classification of events and specifies the context within which they occur. In addition, it depicts a sequence of events which relates changes in one or more variables to changes in other variables. The potential for intervention made possible by this feature distinguishes explanations from other analytic tools, such as classifications or predictions. The principal building blocks of an explanation are specifying conditions, explanatory and impact variables, and rules that describe the interrelation of conceptual components.

Specifying conditions are part of the overall description that an explanation provides. They set the parameters within which the explanation is valid. In other words, they describe a set of relatively invariant conditions that furnish the context of the events encompassing intervention action and its consequences. Cultural attributes of a social system, particular beliefs or values, and so forth, for example, provide relatively stable patterns of conditions without which many forms of social interaction would change. In different cultural systems the same action or intervention may have very different consequences. Specifying conditions are considered necessary conditions. At different levels of analysis (for example, small-group research), the relevant conditions will differ. Classification depends on the purpose of the research and therefore on those segments of reality that must be addressed. The conditions are expressed as a set of concepts each of which can in principle be measured or scored along a particular scale. Development of highly reliable and valid measures may follow the first stages of the development of explanations or may take place at the same time. Within a particular explanation, however, a range of values or scores is indicated for each condition. The set of conditions serves to differentiate between cases or situations in which the explanation holds from those situations in which it does not. A set of specifying conditions is illustrated below.

$$[S_1 \ (0-5), S_2 \ (1), S_3 \ (3-6), S_4 \ (1) \quad . \quad . \quad . \quad . \quad S_n \ (0-1)]$$

There is a set of concepts S, each with a range of possible scores or measures, shown in parentheses. Measurement may be made at nominal, ordinal, interval, or ratio levels. In some instances, indication of the presence or absence of a condition is sufficient (a score of 1 or 0), whereas with other explanations and sets of specifying conditions, greater precision may be required. Elaboration and refinement of the set of conditions, as well as the level of measurement, are contingent upon a continuous process of research and testing. Specifying conditions represent empirical situations; their characteristics depend on the purpose of the research with regard to the situation in question. Relevant specifying conditions for an explanation of increased teenage pregnancy in the United States, for example, are likely to differ significantly from those for an explanation of increased concentration of capital in multinational corporations. Specifying conditions nonetheless assume the general form given above and serve primarily as classifying devices.

Explanatory and impact variables form the conceptual backbone of the sequence of changes, actions, or events that comprise the explanatory sequence. They provide the means to describe events or changes in particular conditions. This book, for example, focuses on the production and dissemination of policy analysis and on the consequences or events (that is, the impact of analysis) that result from these initial actions. Explanations provide the means to control events, as they tie particular actions that may or may not be taken to a set of expected impacts or consequences. Government officials, for example, often have the option of funding or not funding a particular study or analysis. By taking either action, they promote a particular set of consequences—change or maintenance of the existing state of affairs. Explanatory variables describe actions that may be taken, while impact variables describe expected consequences or the impact of these initial actions.

A third set of variables within this set relates to the sequence of events and conditions between action and impact. These variables conceptually detail the process by which consequences unfold. The events following the initial action are all impacts of the action. Research generally focuses on one event in the sequence, however, and treats it as a final consequence or impact, when in reality additional consequences probably follow. The focus on a particular place in the sequential chain of course reflects a value judgment. These sequence and conditional variables also describe variations in conditions that produce variation in impact. A given sequence, for example, may include a mediatory condition that influences the pattern of impact. If the condition is present, the impact of taking a particular action in that situation may differ from the impact of the action taken in a situation in which the particular condition is absent or in which it takes on some other value.

The extent to which the explanatory sequence must be detailed also depends upon the real-world situation and the purpose of the research. It may range from a highly elaborate presentation, if the main objective is to understand the underlying process, to little delineation of the sequence of events, if the main goal is intervention or control. With the latter objective the primary requirement is to relate action and impact with some degree of confidence. A detailed description of the sequence of events between action and impact may promote accurate intervention, or may increase the probability that it will occur, but is not necessary to achieve the objective. This discussion of how explanatory structures differ in response to the objectives of research overstates the difference somewhat in order to emphasize the importance of the research's purpose (in this example social understanding versus social intervention) in determining the necessary analytic structure. Explanatory and impact variables provide the conceptual base for description of the explanatory sequence.

Rules that state the relation among the conceptual units of the explanation link the components in a unified, logical whole. The rules embodied within a particular explanation may be simple or complex. They may take the common form "A varies directly with B." They may be even more modest; for example, "When A is present, B is present." Alternatively they may take the form of complex mathematical equations, which tie incremental changes in one or more variables to particular values or scores of other variables. Regardless of the specific form, which depends on the empirical situation that one attempts to model or represent, rules provide a calculus whereby changes in specific components of a situation are translated into changes in other dimensions of the situation. Within the analytic construct, the rule itself is abstract. It forces a given result to occur as the rule is applied or as the calculation is made. Rules are nonetheless intended to be isomorphic to real-world situations. They represent in abstract form the interrelations of real-world events. The form and complexity of any set of rules within an explanation therefore depends on the nature of the situation to be explained.

The model of explanation that I present is a general framework that implies a set of analytic standards. There is considerable variation in the extent to which studies that share the objective of explanation meet standards. The development and testing of explanations, a difficult evolutionary process, may take long periods of time. Advances in the accuracy, generality, and usefulness of an explanation may come in small or large increments. The dynamic nature of real-world circumstances makes advancement problematic. Just as an explanation is approaching high standards, the world may change and may force the research community to start anew. This is to say not that accurate and useful knowledge is impossible to obtain but just that obtaining it is difficult. Explanations present a base for criticism which contributes to progress by defining standards for the inquiry. A series of studies and tests in any given area of inquiry will probably (but not necessarily) be required before the ideal is approached.

Retroduction

An analytic model or set of standards offers few instructions for the development of explanations or theories. Social science has given greater attention to procedures for testing theories or explanations than to the task of creating these structures. Some attention has been paid to methods of theory building, of course, but those who address the issue of discovery disagree about useful methods or techniques. Typical prescriptions are often the employment of inductive, deductive, or dialectical logic.[3]

Still, the paucity of elegant social theory, which can be attributed to the approaches that have withstood criticism and test, leaves unsettled the question of methods of discovery. Until evidence accumulates showing the superior effectiveness of any particular means of theory development, the investigator must follow his or her own judgment as to method, bearing in mind the purpose of the research and the present state of knowledge.

The present investigation adopts an approach to theory development that was expounded some time ago by the philosopher Charles Sanders Peirce. He suggested a sequence of procedures that combine aspects of inductive and deductive logic. He labeled the method abduction, or retroduction.[4]

The first step in Peirce's retroduction is the statement of a hypothesis which purports to explain some particular event. The hypothesis is an inference and flows from the full range of experiences the investigator brings to the situation. The hypothesis is used to structure an investigation of a particular case or situation. After the first round of inquiry, the hypothesis is modified or elaborated so that it more accurately accounts for actual observations. A process of deductive reasoning may follow, as additional implications of the evolving explanation are deduced. The reformulated hypothesis or set of hypotheses is then again used to investigate another case or body of data. The process may involve one or two cycles of deductive and inductive inference, or many such cycles may be needed. As additional cycles are completed, what began as one or a few related hypotheses becomes by degrees an elaborate explanation or theory. The retroductive sequence is terminated when the set of hypotheses seems accurately to reflect the series of empirical situations examined. At that time the development phase ends, and a period of testing is called for.

I chose retroductive procedures after assessing previous research and my own objectives. The literature presents numerous discrepant and incommensurable hypotheses, evidence of diverse research purposes and a labyrinthine field of investigation. The present inquiry aims for a plausible explanation, worthy of further development and testing. The results of future tests and attempts to develop the explanation will also provide some basis for assessing the retroductive approach.

In the present context, the first step in the retroductive process involved the statement of a series of hyptheses based on my review of past research. I subsequently used these hypotheses and the associated conceptual frameworks to investigate a particular case of social policy analysis which was designed explicitly as an input to the policy-making process.

The second stage of investigation focuses on the role of the Seattle and Denver income maintenance experiments and attempts to reform public assistance policies during the Carter administration. The experiment and the welfare policy process served as a heuristic case study which was designed to develop the initial set of concepts and hypotheses further. As a heuristic study it should not be considered a test of the fully developed explanation to which it contributes. Before describing the heuristic case study in more detail, I will discuss this particular use of the case study and alternative approaches, particularly comparative analysis.

Social scientists all too often view the case study as standing in stark contrast to comparative analysis. The two approaches are generally differentiated in terms of the range of the research, methods, reporting of findings, and research objectives. Comparative research is viewed as "extensive"; a large number of cases are examined in terms of a relatively limited set of variables. Case study, on the other hand, takes an "intensive" or detailed look at a single case. Comparative research is thought to adhere to a carefully constructed research design, whereas case studies are open ended, and any technique employed is used flexibly. Reports of comparative research are held to be analytic or theoretical, whereas reports of case studies are thought to be narrative or descriptive. Finally, objectives are thought to differ. Comparative study attempts to develop general theory, while case study tries to capture the unique aspects of the single case. While particular studies often fit the description that I have presented, no logical or methodological argument makes it necessary to choose between such contrasting approaches to study. There is no reason why case study cannot follow a rigorous design, be pursued with analytic vigor, or strive for general theory.[5]

The common view of the case study as inferior to comparative research also ignores the role that case study can play in the development of theory. Case study can serve as a heuristic device, as a means for developing theory, in addition to being a tool for testing theories. Comparative study may, of course, serve each of these ends as well. The choice of approaches clearly involves trade-offs, but these balance out in many instances. Case studies, for example, permit in-depth analysis, which can be valuable when dealing with complex causal sequences. Case studies are also valuable because they do not commit the researcher, early in the process, to a limited set of variables. They therefore increase the likelihood that critical variables and relations will be found. On the other hand, comparative study enables researchers to consider cases that show variation on key variables and increases the range of inference or generalization that may be warranted on the basis of any single study. These valid considerations must be weighed in light of the current state of knowledge in a given area and the availability of suitable or critical cases for study. In many instances, the number of cases to study should be determined on the basis of practical considerations— time, money, personnel, and so forth—rather than on methodo-logical grounds.[6]

If generalization and theory development are treated as entailing a series of studies across time, the apparent disadvantages of case study are mitigated. The next round of study always offers the opportunity to introduce variation that was absent in an earlier phase and counters the argument of uniqueness by actually testing this claim. Comparative study or a series of cases may be used to test the generality of any theoretical framework that arises from heuristic case study. The framework either can withstand such tests or can be found to apply only to a particular case. Testing is paramount. Aggregation from the bottom up, so that an explanation applicable to a single case is repeatedly exposed to a range of cases in an attempt to determine its level of generalization, overcomes the limitations of a narrow case study. Critics of case studies fail to take into account the ongoing, incremental nature of the research process.

Heuristic case studies are designed to stimulate thinking about significant theoretical problems and potential solutions or gener-alizations. They reflect the assumption that generalizations do not just come to the theorist's attention in some mysterious fashion but are creative events that spring from consideration of theoretical problems in the context of empirical inquiry. Such a case study is more highly structured than the common conception would indi-cate. Conceptual frameworks and hypotheses based on previous research and reflection are used to investigate the particular case. The objective is not to test these hypotheses in a rigorous fashion, however. Limited testing occurs only in the sense that hypotheses are compared with observed patterns of events in the specific case. More important, the hypotheses are used to probe unresolved ques-tions in hopes of uncovering new insights and ideas. As the inquiry proceeds, the initial framework and ideas that guide the investiga-tion are modified on the basis of specific findings and new hypoth-eses suggested by the research.[7]

The advantages of heuristic case study are best realized if particular kinds of cases are available for investigation. The most useful cases are those which present significant theoretical characteristics—that is, those attributes which, in light of previous research, appear to be important explanatory factors. These cases should also represent the types of situation for which generalization would be useful. In other words, they should share characteristic features with a range of other cases. If such cases are available, the prospects of fruitful inquiry are increased. If suitable cases are not at hand, comparative study or some other approach may be necessary.

These procedures coincide with the principles embodied in Peirce's method of retroduction. They reflect the sequential employment of deductive and inductive technique. The insight and creativity of the particular researcher is needed to integrate observation and to form generalized patterns. There is of course no guarantee that plausible theoretical formulations will follow the process, but other methods offer no such guarantee either.

The Program for Better Jobs and Income

Eight months after taking office, President Carter proposed substantial changes in public assistance policy, his program for better jobs and income (PBJI). The program sought integration of major ongoing cash and in-kind transfer programs—aid to families with dependent children, supplemental security income, and food stamps. It also proposed a significant increase in public service job programs and the stimulation of private sector job opportunities. In addition, the cash transfer and job components were to be united in a single program.[8]

The cash transfer section of the program was a modified version of the negative income tax, a policy alternative that had been the subject of debate for more than a decade.[9] President Carter thus sought to overhaul a set of social programs that many had considered in need of repair for some time.

As the president and the executive branch began to design their proposal, the findings of a major relevant policy experiment approached the final stages of analysis. Results of the Seattle and Denver income maintenance experiments, a test of the negative income tax, were reaching the administration in the form of a steady stream of reports. The Seattle and Denver experiments were the largest and latest in a series of four similar experiments that had begun in New Jersey and Pennsylvania in 1967.[10] The principal focus of the analysis was the labor supply response or work behavior impact of a negative income tax program, although other impacts were examined as well. Thus the administration had at its disposal data which indicated some consequences of adopting the negative income tax. It lacked experimental data, however, on the impact of a negative income tax program combined with a job program. As matters turned out, the administration, armed with the experimental data, adopted a proposal which included a negative income tax. The Congress did not go along. The administration's bill was reported out of a special House subcommittee, but it was not considered by the appropriate standing committees in either chamber.

The 1977 welfare reform process serves as a heuristic case study for this investigation. It provides a series of observations which assist the retroductive process of theory development. I selected the welfare reform case for study because it presented a fertile field for development of an explanation. The series of negative income tax experiments were a major attempt to provide analytic input to policy decisions. They cost $108 million and spanned more than a decade. The time and labor invested in the analysis made it difficult to ignore. The negative income tax experiments represented a pioneering effort, and several other large experiments have been undertaken since to inform social policy decisions.[11] If the trend continues, it will be useful to have theory which directly addresses this particular type of work. The experimental technique is also widely believed to be the most fruitful form of study for policy knowledge.[12] Results of experiments are not above criticism but provide stronger evidence than most other techniques. In addition, welfare represents a major component of redistributive social policy, an area in which much research has been done and in which it is likely to continue.[13] Furthermore, within the welfare domain there is a high level of value conflict, a dimension of the policy context that appears to be an important explanatory factor.[14] A major practical consideration is that, as the investigation began, major events in this particular policy process had occurred recently and were still fresh in the mind of participants. The welfare reform case thus appeared highly suitable for the purpose of this investigation.

The Seattle-Denver experiment and analysis based on its findings appear to have had a series of substantial impacts on the policy process, on participant belief systems, and on a distribution of benefits, if not on the final policy output. Case study procedures informed and helped explain this series of conclusions while offering stimuli for an investigation of the impact of policy analysis. In the next chapter I will give the explanation in detail. The following two chapters present the welfare reform case and examine the basis for the conclusions described above.

The case study relies primarily on analysis of published materials and interviews with key policy and research participants. The first step in the investigation was to examine published materials in order to gather observations and prepare for the interviews. The documents examined covered the history of the four negative income tax experiments, attempts to reform public assistance policies prior to the Carter administration, and President Carter's PBJI. I examined various sources: newspapers, books, journal articles, congressional documents, Harvard University case studies of President Nixon's family assistance plan, the Ford administration's little-known welfare reform attempt, and the PBJI. The congressional documents included both descriptive and background materials regarding the PBJI and testimony before various committees on this legislation and previous reform attempts. In addition, I searched reports presenting the findings of each of the four experiments.

Participants selected for interviews were close to the events under consideration and viewed them from a range of organizational positions. The interview schedules were based on the review of the welfare reform literature and the initial conceptual framework and hypotheses. As previously noted, the initial hypotheses evolved from assessment of the more general literature on the impact of policy analysis. The interview schedules were a balance of open-ended questions, to some extent tailored to the specific respondent, and structured-response items. Interviews took from sixty to ninety minutes. The objective of the interviews was to obtain data to assess the plausibility of initial hypotheses and to elicit the insights of participants. The interview first gave the respondents the chance to state their beliefs about the impact of the Seattle and Denver experiments and related analyses on the welfare reform process, in their own words, without the constraint of highly structured questions. Afterward both structured and added open-ended questions were used to probe further. The open-ended and structured questions thus supported each other. The interview questions tap respondent beliefs about the policy process and the impact of analysis. These beliefs may or may not reflect what actually transpired and may be challenged on that basis. A rigorous test of an explanation would necessarily rely on other types of data as well. Additional questions tested respondents' knowledge of the experimental findings and sought attitudinal information regarding welfare reform and the use of analysis for policy making.

Interviews were conducted with key participants having a range of organizational affiliations. A total of forty-three interviews were held: twenty-six were face-to-face encounters, and seventeen were conducted on the telephone. The interview mode was determined primarily by logistics; people in Washington were interviewed in person, and those elsewhere (California, Wisconsin, Georgia, and so forth) were interviewed by telephone. The telephone and face-to-face interviews were similarly structured. Interviews were held on Capitol Hill with congressmen, key committee staff, legislative assistants, and staff at the Congressional Budget Office (CBO). Within the executive branch, interviews were held at the office of the assistant secretary for planning and evaluation at the Department of Health, Education, and Welfare. Interviews were also conducted in the office of the assistant secretary for planning, evaluation, and research at the Department of Labor. In addition, members of the domestic policy staff at the White House were contacted. Eight interviews were conducted with members of various Washington-based interest groups concerned with welfare policy. Two reporters who covered the welfare reform process were also interviewed. Researchers not based in government, who played key roles in the negative income tax experiments, were also consulted. Twelve interviews were conducted with participants at Stanford Research Institute (SRI), Mathematica Policy Research, and the Institute for Research on Poverty at the University of Wisconsin.

The range of participants provided numerous perspectives and opportunities to cross-check various descriptions of events. The interviews also provided insight that often comes only from those fully involved in a series of events. Many respondents had given several years of their lives to a series of experiments or to attempts to reform welfare policy. It becomes readily apparent that some of the respondents would like to have the "final story" told a particular way; some such respondents have forgotten events that are strongly confirmed by other evidence and would seem hard to forget. It also turns up when respondents claim in response to penetrating questions that they "don't know" or have "no opinion." Such problems became puzzles to be solved.[15] They were probed in later interviews with people who were in positions "to know" or to "have opinions," and the public record provided a revealing account of events, which was used to cross-check responses. The procedures that I have described clearly differ from those used to test a set of hypotheses rigorously but fit well with my plan to develop an explanation.

4 An Explanation of the Impact of Policy Analysis

✳

The production and dissemination of policy analysis affect the distribution of benefits and costs across social groups. The resulting allocation of value may be collective—that is, gains and losses may be shared across a wide range of groups—but this is seldom the case. Frequently some groups or social interests benefit more than others. Patterns of allocation emerge over time and are tied to particular social conditions and events.[1]

The explanation of the impact of policy analysis that I present in this chapter is offered less as the final answer than as a tool for further investigation. Refinement and elaboration of the explanation will presumably come with further research and testing. My explanation proposes a novel approach for controlling and understanding the impact of policy analysis.

While I address the impact of analysis in advanced capitalist societies, my model was constructed primarily on the basis of evidence from the prototypical advanced capitalist society, the United States. I am concerned to provide grounds for the analysis of other times and societies, although the extent of applicability can be determined only by further empirical analysis. In this chapter I will begin by delineating and supporting the explanation in the most general terms, without reference to any particular society. In chapter 6 I illustrate the model with my case study of the impact of welfare policy analysis in the United States.

Policy analysis produced and disseminated with the intent of influencing public policy decisions at the national level forms part of a complex field of social forces and interrelationships. Seldom is analysis the dominant factor in the policy process; numerous other forces combine with it to affect public decisions. The influence of analysis varies across policy contexts. Part of the research objective is to separate social circumstances in which analysis plays a significant role from those situations in which it does not. Figure 1 illustrates the explanation of the impact of analysis presented in detail below.

Specifying conditions determine the background or social context for the explanatory sequence. The basic categories include conditions of culture, institutions, and social structure that describe basic aspects of the context and contribute to the overall classification of events. They also set the parameters within which the explanation holds. The explanation may be generalizable to a wider range of societies or specifying conditions, but I will not advance such a claim at this point. Further testing is required before any such judgment is warranted. At present the specifying conditions, which I will describe at greater length below, serve as partial statements of the social conditions, of advanced capitalist societies, and of the types of societies to which the explanation is presumed relevant. The statements are partial in that they identify only those contextual features that are most important to the impact of policy analysis.

Explanatory and impact variables comprise the remaining conceptual components of the explanation. I subdivide this set of concepts into sets of mediating, explanatory, and impact variables. Mediating conditions include value conflict and various dimensions of individual belief systems. These conditions vary across policy contexts and influence the impact of policy analysis. Explanatory and impact variables form a causal sequence of events; the chain begins with a set of interests that motivate the production and dissemination of policy analysis in order to influence further events. Control of production and dissemination provides some measure of control over subsequent events or consequences. As these actions are subject to individual and organizational choice, the consequences that flow from these efforts can be manipulated by the funders and producers of policy research. The series of consequences that follow production and dissemination decisions include impact on decision processes, on individual and societal belief systems

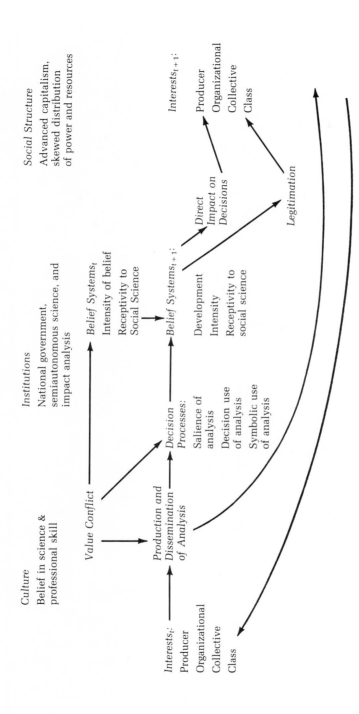

Figure 1 *The Impact of Policy Analysis. t* = present time period.

(the aggregate of individual belief systems), on decision or policy output, on legitimation of various ideas, and ultimately on specific interests (see figure 1). The interests responsible for undertaking policy analysis are likely to be some of the parties affected. All impacts are mediated or conditioned by value conflict and prior individual beliefs. That is, impact varies according to the specific set of conditions in the actual policy context. My research, then, considers a range of events and conditions affected by the production and dissemination of policy analysis, from impact on policy processes to gains and losses experienced by particular social interests.

The various conceptual units of the explanation stand in specific relation to each other. Value conflict, for example, is directly associated with the salience of analysis during the decision process. Alternatively, the intensity of prior belief is negatively associated with development of belief systems. In total the statement of relations among the conceptual units holds the framework together and provides its explanatory power. In the presentation that follows, I first define specifying conditions and mediating variables and then discuss them in detail. The analysis proceeds through the causal sequence and defines concepts and relations among the components. As a result there emerges a tentative explanation of the impact of the production and dissemination of policy analysis in a specific class of societies.

The Context of Impact Processes

Societies at a given point in their history may be described in terms of their cultural, institutional, and social structural dimensions. These basic attributes form the backdrop for ongoing social interaction. They condition or influence both the process and the outcome of that social interaction. Social theorists must consider these basic specifying conditions as they develop theory.

A general stragegy of developing explanations is to state specifying conditions narrowly at first. If the explanation is found through a period of testing to hold in the limited range of cases first specified, further research may be directed to expanding the range of social cases under consideration. The explanation can be tested under circumstances differing from those first stated. If the explanation still holds, the specifying conditions may be reformulated to take this finding into account. The outcome is a more general explanation— that is, it applies to a wider range of cases than it did in its first form. Attempts to extend the specifying conditions end when the explanation is falsified under the series of tests. Statements of specifying conditions, then, are important theoretical devices that present the range of social conditions under which an explanation holds.

The present study generalizes to policy processes at the national level of government in advanced capitalist societies. In so doing it specifies a set of basic cultural, institutional, and social structural attributes. The explanation may apply to subnational levels of government or to other group decision processes, but I do not advance these assertions at present. Similarly, I do not attempt to classify all aspects of these societies but identify only those elements essential to the proposed explanation. The classification presents a series of necessary conditions, attributes that any particular society must possess if the explanation presented is to apply.

Belief in Science and the Professions

Advanced capitalist societies place considerable value on scientific discovery and the development of professional skills (as do some other types of societies). Various scientific and professional groups may enjoy greater prestige than others across time, for different issues, and so forth, but the general tendency to value science and professional skill persists, although there are always some doubters. These beliefs have grown out of the Enlightenment and have become widely shared with the advance of industrialization, the application of scientific theory to social and physical conditions, and the growth of the professions within an increased division of labor in society.

Science has reduced the impact of previous traditions and ideologies in the course of rising to prominence in various social value structures. Whereas in earlier times individuals turned frequently to religion, folklore, or myth for an understanding of the human condition or for salvation, they now turn increasingly to science and to its corollary, technology. While religion and other traditions have not ceased to be powerful cultural forces, they now compete with faith in science as the dominant belief system. Science is thought to be a superior means of understanding reality, despite some persistent doubts and unanswered questions, and is also seen as a powerful way of controlling and shaping future realities.[2] There is an interesting paradox with the cultural beliefs in science and the professions. Although belief or faith in science and professional skill is high, there is widespread ignorance of scientific practice (a frequent lament of scientists) and overestimation of the scientific base of some professions (for example, medicine). Consequently people have exaggerated expectations, which approach anticipation of miracles, from science and the professions. These beliefs manifest themselves in many daily experiences. Science holds a place in educational curricula from early childhood education through postgraduate instruction, although it is often a weak or ineffectual component at many levels. Industries and government invest substantial resources in scientific research. The mass media extol the virtues of scientists in white coats, who develop a wide range of technical gadgets and cures for individual and social ills. Science has permeated the value structure of modern society.

Professionals are commonly valued for the skills they display in tackling a wide range of perceived problems or for other applications of expertise. In part professional skill is valued because of its perceived scientific or technological base. To take a clear example, the practice of medicine has reduced or eliminated the debilitating effects of many diseases, although the record on preventing sickness is at best mixed. The various engineering professions are also notable examples of professional groups with scientific know-how. These examples unite the values of science and skill in immediate social groupings. Many other skilled professions—artists, musicians, writers, and baseball players, for example—have little scientific basis but nonetheless share prestige because of the high social value placed on professionalism and skill.[3]

The general social value that attaches to scientific discovery and skill substantially conditions the impact of policy analysis. The social science disciplines may be regarded by some observers as less scientific than the physical or biological sciences, but they nonetheless share in the high value that society places on science. Without these strong beliefs, it is doubtful that analysis would have much impact or that it would even be produced. In this sense belief in science and skill are necessary conditions. Without strong general social support for these values, there is little role for analysis in policy making. Slight variations in belief do not alter the impact of analysis, although major shifts would do so. Events such as the dropping of the atom bomb, the nuclear mishap at Three-Mile Island, and the Project Camelot fiasco of the 1960s have shaken believers and have increased the uncertainty of future trends but have not substantially altered the general faith in science and, consequently, the impact of analysis. Belief in science and skill—societal attributes—specify conditions necessary for the consideration of policy analysis and for the consequences.

Governmental, Scientific, and Policy-Analytic Institutions

Several attributes of governmental, scientific, and policy-analytic institutions in advanced capitalist society condition the impact of policy analysis. As ongoing practices embedded in social and political processes and established organizations, these institutions are significant features of the policy context.

My focus on the national level of government has several significant implications. At this level large bureaucratic organizations, which utilize many professionals and experts, are concentrated. This is generally the case whether the political structure is unitary or federal. Scientists, engineers, lawyers, and numerous other professionals, dominate public agencies and the businesses and lobbies with whom they interact. Furthermore, scientific professionals have secured new positions on legislative staffs and support organizations as these have expanded in recent times.[4]

The professional and scientific makeup of national governments increases the likelihood that policy analysis will receive a hearing at this level. Where analysis plays a role in policy making, it competes with a range of considerations for the decision maker's attention. Nevertheless, there is a predisposition to consider analytic inputs at the national level.[5] While administrative organizations are generally more inclined than legislatures to take scientific information into account, both types of institutions tend increasingly to consider such input. There is also considerable variation in the predisposition to turn to analysis across agencies and subunits of the legislature. The tendency to consider research inputs is somewhat higher at the national level of government than at other levels.

Specific characteristics of the relation of scientific institutions, or the scientific estate, to the rest of society also condition the impact of policy analysis. Societies with a semiautonomous scientific profession are of particular interest. In these social systems, science is for the most part self-governing. Its governmental system includes some central authority but is largely decentralized and fragmented. At the lowest level, professional norms—value neutrality, disinterestedness, universalism, or organized skepticism—guide behavior to some extent. Professional associations and organizations of scientific professionals also contribute to the system of self-governance. Elites within the scientific professions allocate, or greatly influence the allocation of, major rewards—research funds, publication, and recognition—and thus help maintain adherence to common norms. Thus while the individual scientist has considerable control over his or her scientific activity, action occurs within a governmental system of norms, rewards, and sanctions which influence the behavior of scientists.[6]

The scientific profession is only semiautonomous as it remains linked to other major institutions, and its members often share the dominant social ideology. Since World War II, scientists have become increasingly dependent on government and industry for research funds. While the resulting relationships do not eliminate scientific initiative from inquiry, they certainly lessen the amount of research guided only by the investigator's curiosity. The researcher must increasingly address questions posed by industry and government if funds for large-scale projects are to be available.[7] If the research questions of sponsors coincide with the curiosity of the scientist, then a genuinely collaborative effort is possible. When sponsors dictate research questions and the investigator goes along, however, autonomy and initiative are absent, although the investigator's interests apart from curiosity may still be served. A wide range of sponsoring organizations and interests supply important counter tendencies to loss of autonomy. In addition, considerable research and inquiry is conducted without significant sponsorship, without much external funding. This research clearly differs in scale and character from that made possible by six-figure budgets; nonetheless, it serves to promote an autonomous science.

Scientific communities also generally share the dominant social ideology and in turn suffer a loss of autonomy. They adhere to widely accepted beliefs about the political and economic operations of the society and thus often limit inquiry to subjects and questions appropriate to the preservation of the given political-economic structure.[8] Malcontents challenge fundamental beliefs and assumptions occasionally, but this deviation does not significantly alter the general patterns.

A semiautonomous science, then, does not operate free from external checks and influences, nor does it surrender itself to complete control by government, industry, or any other force. It takes a middle position on the continuum. The particular relationship that the scientific institutions bear to the rest of society affects the impact of policy analysis.

Science prefers to be perceived as value neutral and autonomous, unbeholden to any set of values or interests beyond those associated with free inquiry. The scientific community has projected this image and has gained legitimacy and influence as a result.[9] The image is still widespread, although critics view science much differently. As science has established highly visible links with government and industry, its value neutrality has been questioned. Critics see science as the handmaiden of various interests, if only those of the scientist, but often those of organizations and social classes as well. If this belief spreads, science may lose influence, or the character of its influence may change. Science is increasingly seen as a forensic tool, a device to help make a point in the debate, whatever that point may be. Social science is particularly vulnerable in this regard, although other sciences are also perceived increasingly in this manner. When the handmaiden and value-neutral images of science persist alongside one another, the role of policy analysis in the policy process is subject to contradictory forces. As long as the scientific community remains semiautonomous, the pattern is likely to continue.

Most modern societies have institutionalized an increased capacity to produce policy analysis. Productive ability interacts with the elevated beliefs in science and professionalism to yield growth. Capacity is determined by trained personnel, organization, proven research technique, and analytic hardware such as computers. Each of these areas has seen dramatic advances within the last few decades.

A history of analytic input in policy processes leads participants to expect continued analysis and research input. The continuous communication of policy analysis to policy makers increases their tendency to make some use of the materials to which they are exposed. It may even lead them to seek out analytic input. The ongoing production and dissemination of policy analysis, then, condition its impact. As analysis enters the policy process, habitual or patterned responses develop over time. Responses will undoubtedly vary among individuals. Some will become more receptive to analysis, while others will become less receptive. Production and dissemination begin the chain of events that can be described as the impact of analysis. The patterns may change over time, but the repeated exposure promotes impact of some form, whether on the policy process, on individual and societal belief systems, or on policy decisions. In short, policy analysis feeds upon itself. It forms expectations that in turn influence the reception of analysis produced in the future. Ongoing institutional mechanisms increase the impact of policy analysis.

The relations of institutions to the impact of policy analysis are general tendencies. As will become apparent later, additional features of policy processes and personalities that vary from one situation to another may counter these general background features. Nonetheless, governmental, scientific, and policy-analytic institutions provide a framework in which specific patterns of the use and impact of research and analysis unfold.

Distribution of Power and Resources

Social structure is based on the distribution of power and resources, such as wealth, income, prestige, and position across individuals, groups, and classes within society. It is the last of the specifying conditions to be examined. The extent to which power and other resources are skewed toward one end of the social spectrum, or are unequally divided, varies to some extent across societies.[10] For those who possess them, resources such as wealth, income, prestige, and position contribute to the capacity to exercise power. They do not automatically translate into power, but they provide a capability that would otherwise be absent which is sometimes used to produce and shape policy analysis and also influences the reception of analysis in policy arenas.

This book generalizes to societies in which power is substantially skewed toward one end of the social distribution, a quite common condition. Advanced capitalism, a prototypical example of this social configuration is the focus of my theoretical attention. Marxist theorists emphasize disparity in power across capitalist and proletarian classes.[11] Others note within advanced capitalism a considerable unevenness in power distributions and important social implications but do not give economic class theoretical primacy.[12] Power within what may be seen as basic class units may be quite as uneven as it is across class units.

Equal distribution of power and resources has heretofore been primarily the stuff of social reformers' dreams. Even modern examples of what might be called state socialism have social structures characterized by highly uneven distributions of power and resources.[13] The gap may not be as great as with capitalist systems, but it is substantial and is important nonetheless.

Social structure both constrains and shapes the focus and content of the pool of analysis available to policy makers and the behavior of policy participants toward research inputs. The type of questions that analysis addresses defines its focus. Analysis may be concerned with problem definition, value judgment, estimation of impacts of alternative policies, or the effectiveness and/or efficiency of ongoing programs, to cite typical examples. Content goes beyond questions addressed to the method of research and concepts and theories employed. The focus or substance of answers given to the major research questions also represent an element of context. Typical behavioral responses to analysis include outright rejection, attacks on its form and content, and legitimation of decisions already taken. Less frequently analysis is considered for policy and decision purposes. The focus and content of analysis and behavioral responses to analytic products cannot escape the influence of social context.

Skewed distributions of power and resources influence the impact of policy analysis initially by limiting the focus and content of the pool of analysis available to policy makers. Studies that strongly challenge major social-structural conditions or that suggest major structural reform are much less frequent than analyses which address incremental policy changes that do not threaten dominant interests significantly. Seldom does analysis link social problems, such as unemployment or crime, for example, with a stable disparity of wealth and income, that is, with social structure. Policy analysis seldom suggests the overhaul of structural alignments or substantial redistribution of wealth and income as a means of solving persistent social problems. Ideology or common belief systems complement structure and also shape analysis. Researchers and analysts, like other members of society, adopt prevalent beliefs and values. Their analytic work is shaped by their views even as they vow that it will not be and attempt to keep it from being affected. Policy approaches that threaten dominant interests are in effect for the most part off the policy analysis agenda.

Under skewed structural conditions, analysis generally addresses narrow, technical issues of policy design. Technical analyses take accepted policy goals for granted or at most consider marginal changes. Analysis then explores and assesses alternative interventions or policies in terms of these already established criteria. A variety of tax policy changes, for example, may be compared for their contribution to capital formation. The relative importance of capital formation would likely be taken as an article of faith. Analysis does not often engage in wide-ranging exercises in problem definition or value judgment or move beyond a narrow range of acceptable alternatives in providing analytic input to policy makers.

Analysis involving ongoing programs or approaches to social problems tends to prevail over studies that counter dominant interests. Analysis of institutionalized policy approaches under skewed distributional conditions generally views social problems as an accumulation of individual deficiencies rather than as extensions of fundamental social or economic conditions. Unemployment, for example, is regarded as biologically rather than economically inspired. Drug addition, suicide, and mental illness are examined as human frailties rather than as products of economic and social alienation. Implied solutions or interventions, then, focus on the individual in a piecemeal fashion in attempts to address shortcomings, to reshape attitudes and behaviors. Transfer payments, substitute drugs, crisis intervention, and psychotherapy are provided. Analysts attempt to assist service delivery and program efficiency within the constraint of institutionalized interventions. Analysis of established policy approaches and other technical efforts promote the interests of dominant elements of society. They do so as they draw attention away from structural conditions and their connection to persistent social problems.

An overall result of constrained production of analysis is to stimulate the use of analysis for policy making. Use, however, is very limited. It is restricted to narrow, incremental policy changes where there is little at stake for dominant interests. When analysis does on occasion challenge dominant interests, it is unlikely to exert a direct impact on decisions, although it may have other consequences (it may, for example, legitimate particular ideas or change belief systems). While analysis is a source of power, it is insufficient in strength to alter stable distributional patterns. Social structure, then, delimits the range of issues for which analysis plays a substantial policy role. It tends to limit its impact to minor issues that do not alter significantly the distribution of power, wealth, income, prestige, and other valued resources.

Hypotheses Concerning Specifying Conditions

1.   The cultural values of scientific discovery and professional skill are positively related to the impact of policy analysis.

2.   As the decision arena shifts from subnational levels of government to national, policy analysis has a greater impact on decision processes, on belief systems, and on policy outputs or decisions.

3.   As perceptions of science as value neutral shift to perceptions of science as value laden, the impact of policy analysis on policy processes increases, while the impact on decision or policy outputs decreases.

4.   The institutionalization of policy analysis increases the

impact of analysis on policy processes, on belief systems, and on policy outputs.

5. Social structures with skewed distributions of power and resources limit the questions addressed by the majority of analyses to those that support or do not threaten dominant interests.

6. Social structures with skewed distributions of power and resources limit the range of policies that are directly influenced by analysis to those that do not counter dominant interests.

The Unfolding Process of Impact

Some discussion of mediating variables—value conflict and belief systems, including intensity of belief and receptivity to social science—is now necessary. Mediating conditions influence the sequence of events that follow the introduction of policy analysis. Unlike the cultural, institutional, and structural conditions that I examined above, which also influence this process, mediating conditions are subject to considerable variation across time, policy contexts, issues, and individuals. This variation is a key determinant of the impact of analysis. Mediating conditions differ across policy processes, so that wide disparities in the impact of analysis result. These disparities account for the seemingly inconsistent findings in the literature. To resolve the apparent inconsistency, variation in mediating conditions must be linked with variation in the impact of analysis and with the process that culminates in the impact.

Value Conflict and Belief Systems

Value conflict is disagreement within society over the ends or objectives of policy. It refers both to variation in preferences and to the intensity of belief in particular objectives or values to which objectives are linked. Value conflict would be very high, for example, when the society is polarized by diametrically opposed preferences or values. As value conflict lessens, a dominant or majority opinion grows. In some, but not all, instances, substantial conflict will persist alongside a decidedly majority position. At the other end of the scale is low value conflict where there is consensus or considerable agreement on the aims to be achieved by policy-guided action.

Value conflict remains fairly stable over short periods of time, although there is change at the margins. Social preference structures fluctuate over long periods or may respond to the sudden shock of events, but societies undergo rapid unheavals in value structures infrequently. Conflictual behavior that stems from value conflict may fluctuate much more rapidly than the beliefs with which it is associated. High value conflict in particular policy areas can be accompanied by relative calm. Those who disagree may see little potential for immediate gain by action, or their attention may be turned to other matters.[14] A sudden shock or event can alter the scope of conflictual behavior, which builds upon itself, during a period of contagion.[15] The swing in behavior appears before the backdrop of a stable level of value conflict.

"Belief systems" refers to the collection of valuational and cognitive elements and their interrelations that constitute individual knowledge. Social belief systems may be regarded as the aggregation of individual systems.[16] The relations among individual and societal beliefs are more complex than I have suggested, but this way of conceptualizing it suffices for the purposes of the present research. Particular emphasis is given to three dimensions of belief systems: development, intensity, and receptivity to social science. The belief systems of policy process participants and attentive individuals are of greatest importance in shaping the impact of analysis. Such people are most likely to be influenced by analysis, to be in a position to affect decision outcomes, and to transmit altered or confirmed beliefs to a larger audience.

Development of the individual belief system indicates the degree of elaboration or differentiation of elements in specific substantive areas and their interconnectedness. At one extreme, when the structure is undeveloped, there is an absence of belief in a particular area of an individual's belief system. At the other end, a rich set of elements, hierarchically ordered from abstract to concrete formulations, are interwoven in an integrated whole representing adaptations to environmental reality.[17]

To some extent individual belief systems reflect knowledge that has accumulated within the society over time, but there will always be substantial gaps in individual structures. They will be less developed than the accumulated understanding in many respects. The individual structure also contains values and beliefs, or knowledge, that may not be widely shared; some beliefs are peculiar to the individual. The extent to which beliefs are shared is likely to vary widely across areas of knowledge.

"Intensity" refers to the strength of particular beliefs. A belief may be only casually entertained or may be tentatively assumed to be valid. At the other extreme is an idea so strongly considered warranted, justified, or true that few or no events imaginable are likely to shake the conviction. Intensity is influenced by a variety of forces internal and external to the individual. An inner drive to maintain consistency of beliefs may yield heightened conviction with core or highly interrelated elements. The weight of supporting instances is also likely to affect intensity. A tendency to defend oneself from external threats or opposed viewpoints may in some cases become operative as well.[18]

Receptivity to social science is a willingness to consider the findings of social science and to accept scientific findings as relevant to policy decisions. Organizational, professional, and disciplinary affiliations are assumed to influence this predisposition. The two-communities explanation of knowledge utilization may be considered in part a matter of receptivity. People with scientific training that predisposes them to a particular view and approach toward worldly affairs are likely to be among the most receptive to analytic input. Receptivity will vary across individuals with scientific background, and interdisciplinary and other rivalries suggest the need for further qualification. Still, those with different formative experiences are more likely to display low receptivity. Policy participants schooled in the rough and tumble of political life—that is, those exposed to an experience widely different from those of scientific training—may be less receptive to science as a problem-solving tool than others of differing background will be. Here again, general patterns undoubtedly mask considerable variation. In addition, as I suggested above, broader cultural dynamics are likely to influence receptivity over time.

The discussion of receptivity to social science must also be qualified to take into account the quality of the analytic product.

People who are receptive to social science are predisposed to value rigorous research or research of high quality by scientific standards, although it is quite difficult to achieve agreement on the criteria. As a result, some individuals will not consider the most obviously deficient studies. With research that does not manifest blatant errors, judgments of quality become quite problematic and tenuous. People who lack scientific training or familiarity with scientific standards, regardless of receptivity, find it difficult to assess the quality of research.

The prior belief systems of policy participants and attentive individuals are important mediating conditions. Two structural elements—intensity and receptivity to social science—affect the impact of analysis on subsequent belief patterns. They affect the way in which individual beliefs are influenced by analysis.

Production and Dissemination

The production and dissemination of policy analysis in many cases begin a series of political events. If the analysis is publicly funded or is produced with the intent of influencing policy decisions, its political nature is apparent. Even privately funded research may constitute the beginning of a political process. Production and dissemination of analysis are political in that they affect the allocation of value for society. These actions confer costs and benefits on identifiable interests, for example, as particular ideas or approaches to perceived problems are advanced over others or as research funds are granted to a producer of analysis at the expense of competing organizations. Such impacts occur even when the research has little direct effect on decisions.

The production and dissemination of policy research do not occur in a political vacuum. Production involves the systematic analysis of definitions and alternative "solutions" or actions regarding perceived public problems. These activities are inherently political.[19] "Dissemination" refers to efforts to communicate the substance of policy analysis to participants in policy-making or decision processes. The purpose is to influence policy outputs and hence policy outcomes. Dissemination may occur without systematic or formal procedures. On occasion dissemination is systematic. Production and dissemination are undertaken with the intent of further-ing some particular interest or set of interests. Individual researchers may begin analyzing a particular issue with little motivation beyond a concern with informed decisions. While many people share this concern, the reason for undertaking analysis is generally more com-plicated. Analysis often flows from attempts to benefit particular interests—those who gain materially or symbolically from produc-tion and dissemination. Potential beneficiaries may be classified as producers, organizations, classes, and collectives. Producers are those who perform analysis and the professional organizations and associations to which they belong. Producers' interests are actually a particular form of organizational interest except in cases when a lone researcher is involved. Specific producer interests may include, for example, satisfaction of idle curiosity, improved professional repu-tation, career advancement, research expense accounts, and policy objectives. Organizational interests are objectives that inspire coor-dinated action to seek their fulfillment. Pertinent organizations in the context of this research certainly include government agencies, lobbyist firms and citizens' groups, and business corporations. Class interests are those that coincide with particular positions in the so-cial relationships that govern economic activity. In advanced cap-italist societies the major class interests are those of the capitalist and those of the working class. Collective interests are those shared by large groups of individuals, irrespective of class, which are not supported to any significant extent by organized action that fosters their achievement. The four categories of interests are necessary to express the full range of interests relevant to the explanation. No single category, whether expressed in class, organizational, or group terms, is sufficient to capture the complexity of the social context.

Analysis is produced and disseminated by individuals and orga-nized groups intent on advancing specific interests. In this sense analysis is a political tool; it becomes a means to further or to advance particular interests. On one level analysis may be under-taken solely to promote the professional career of the analyst. If the analyst works for a profit-seeking research firm, the corporate bot-tom line may be a prime motivator. In these situations further inter-ests are at stake, as someone is willing to pay for the research. Any

one of the other major interests—organizational, class, or collective—may motivate the research, or some combination of them may
be involved. Analysis intentionally deployed as a political tool may
strengthen arguments for a preferred policy alternative or may fortify
an attack against the proposals of opponents. A government agency,
for example, may undertake research to support a policy it has
favored for some time but has been unable to establish. The analysis may even be designed to produce the favorable information.
Intentional bias is not implied, however (although it is not ruled
out either), as research initiators may sincerely believe that favorable findings will result from an objective test. Conceptual and
research frameworks also often unwittingly delimit or bias research
in a particular manner. When there are mixed findings, however,
evidence and conclusions are often reported and emphasized selectively to support the desired political impact. While part of the
ritual use of analysis is to claim political neutrality and scientific
objectivity, the political underpinning of policy analysis should not
be ignored.

The extent to which values conflict in a policy or issue area also
influences the production and dissemination of analysis. The level
of conflict affects the character of the pool of analytic inputs available in a policy area. When conflict is low, studies focus on the
means of achieving agreed-upon values—that is, the studies become
technical exercises. The central objectives are to identify and assess
the effectiveness of various alternatives. While political dimensions
of production are not absent in these contexts, they are less pronounced and less salient than in other situations. The general agreement on the ends of policy encourages careful review of analysis.
Hence research reports are more technical than polemical; they
focus on relatively narrow issues of cause and effect rather than on
broad questions of value. Yet the general paucity of warranted policy
theory or analysis, together with a sometimes strong desire to
achieve shared interests, may result in highly limited or speculative
research reports as well.

When value conflict is high, the range of analysis widens, and a
diverse set of arguments unfolds. High conflict tends to generate
additional analysis. Representatives of major positions in the controversy consider it necessary to document their positions with analy-

sis, particularly if an opponent has already done so. It is also customary to produce reports that challenge or refute the findings of opponents if their own research appears to be advancing their cause.[20] The two tendencies produce a general profusion of analysis which grows with the magnitude of the stakes involved. The high-conflict situation also accentuates the polemical nature of the research products. It becomes apparent that the analysis is directed more toward establishing or refuting a preestablished position than toward yielding disinterested or intersubjective analysis. Research that adheres to strict scientific standards is only somewhat more useful in this regard than research which does not. Individuals who use analysis for legitimation or delegitimation purposes may respect scientific cannons, or they may violate every imaginable agreed-upon procedure. As the best studies are seldom immune to all valid criticisms, both high- and low-quality analyses are produced and subsumed in the escalating conflictual behavior. In addition, the body of research input may be so varied, and may be directed at so many cross-purposes, that as a whole it presents a formidable body of materials to be integrated and assessed. High value conflict, then, tends to lead to a highly diverse set of analytic inputs that cannot be compared.

In summary, production and dissemination are influenced by interests that use policy analysis as a way to secure their ends. It is also affected by the general level of value conflict in the particular issue or policy area.

At this point in the process, before decision processes or outputs have been affected, the producer's interests have already been served. Producers benefit to some extent, either symbolically or materially, from the mere act of production. Benefits may take the form of profit and reputational rewards to a research organization or may bring a reputation and career advancement to the lone researcher. If a particular analysis goes on to influence debate, to change minds, or to alter policy outputs, the gains to producers multiply. Without these further results, the production itself fosters a minimal allocation or distribution to the producers of analysis. The hypotheses regarding production and dissemination that I presented above are three.

Hypotheses Concerning the Production and Dissemination of Analysis

1.   As value conflict lessens, policy analysis becomes increasingly technical in its focus on means of achieving agreed-upon ends.

2.   As value conflict increases, the number and diversity of analyses increases.

3.   As value conflict increases, analysis is increasingly linked to specific partisan policy positions and interests.

Decision Processes

Research products influence decision processes or activity undertaken to define and "solve" (or deal with) perceived social problems. Research is only one of many influential factors, but it is nonetheless a significant element in many cases. A primary effect of analysis on the decision process is to capture the attention of the participants, that is, to influence salience. The salience of analysis is the extent to which policy analysis dominates the attention of participants and attentive individuals in the policy process. Attention given to analysis is in some instances a serious endeavor to inform decisions and at other times a ritualistic or symbolic gesture to the norms of rationality. In the former situations decision makers crave solid knowledge about policy questions or potential actions before them, although they may at the same time wish to limit access to some of this knowledge. The knowledge commodity is generally in short supply, particularly that which has a considerable evidential basis as compared with mere speculation or wishful thinking. Solid data are therefore a valuable resource sought by decision makers.

Symbolic use of analysis is intended to influence other participants rather than to inform oneself. Decision makers, given general social values, think they should appear to proceed rationally in an ideal sense by carefully seeking and weighing all policy-relevant information as they make decisions. They may well actually be making logical or rational calculations, but this is another matter. The perceived requirement may lead to symbolic displays of analysis.

Symbolic action is that which, intentionally or not, results in emotional or psychological reactions of assurance or perceived threat among witnesses.[21] Those who undertake symbolic action may be using a conscious strategy, or their action may have other intentions but may produce a similar result. Decision makers may appear to be weighing evidence, to be seeking further information, when in fact a decision has already been made. Such rituals or symbolic actions tend to reassure those who witness the process but are unaware that the decision has been made that careful consideration is being given to the policy issue and all relevant information is being gathered for the decision. Symbolic action may be taken to strengthen or add to policy coalitions as well as to give the appearance of rational action. It may itself be a sound or rational strategy. I do not mean to imply that individuals respond either emotionally or rationally to analysis. Most reactions are undoubtedly a mixture of both elements, although the mixture is likely to vary considerably among individuals and instances. I discuss this activity further below. With both symbolic and decision uses, then, analysis becomes salient in decision processes.

The salience of analysis in any particular decision process is influenced by several conditions. Characteristics of the pool of available analytic input are important. The greater the amount of relevant analysis at hand, the greater the salience of analysis during the decision process. In addition, if particularly large-scale studies have been undertaken, they are almost certain to receive attention. Furthermore, if there is a single study in an information-poor area, it may achieve considerable salience. Moreover, if particularly powerful actors, or at least those powerful enough to ensure some degree of access, possess analytic input, they are likely to promote its salience during deliberations. If the gathered body of analytic products represents widely divergent and conflicting findings and opinions, this incongruence is likely to force some attention to analysis. Salience of analysis during the decision process thus hinges on characteristics of the analytic input.

The level of value conflict in an issue area also influences the salience of analysis during deliberations. In addition, value conflict conditions the symbolic and decision uses of the analytic input. Furthermore, as value conflict increases, the salience of analysis increases. When value conflict is high, there is always the potential for a contagion of conflictual behavior, an acting out of disparate and intensely held beliefs. With general social beliefs in science and the institutionalization of policy research, analysis is often drawn into the conflictual activity. As research supporting one position in a controversy is made public, attacks upon its foundations and countervailing studies are invited. Research salvos may escalate into repeated attacks and counteroffensives. A very high salience of analysis results.

When conflictual behavior involving analysis spreads, symbolic actions displace decision behavior. In other words, symbolic use of analysis is directly related to the contagion of conflictual behavior. In high-conflict situations, analysis is more a symbolic device than a decision tool. The symbolic use goes beyond, but certainly includes, previously mentioned attempts to give the appearance of acting rationally. Analysis is used symbolically in these instances to reassure supporters and to build coalitions, but it tends to threaten opponents as well. Participants use analysis to strengthen support for their positions by attempting to reassure those in their camp and those uncommitted that their policy position is the preferable alternative. Participants may carefully weigh competing values and make a careful decision. They may also react emotionally to a dramatic display of research findings. More often these responses stem from both emotional and rational dimensions of personality. In these instances analytic findings are selectively presented and communicated in such a way that emotional responses are maximized at the expense of careful, fully informed deliberation.

In low-conflict situations the symbolic use of analysis is far less pronunced and certainly less pronounced than decision uses. There is also little basis for significant escalation of conflictual behavior. Research may still be salient, but it is more frequently used for decision purposes than for political posturing. When there is considerable agreement on the basic goals or objectives of policy, deliberations turn to technical issues. The search is more for policies and actions that promote agreed-upon ends than for analytic tools of coalition formation. There is of course some conflictual behavior and symbolic action even in low-conflict situations. Alternative policies directed at common ends may have spillover effects on other values that generate some antagonistic or symbolic behavior, but the symbolic use of analysis is considerably less in low-conflict situations than in high-conflict situations.

A major exception to these patterns of symbolic and conflictual activity occurs in certain high-conflict situations. When a single decision maker or small group is able severely to reduce the visibility of a decision process, little symbolic or conflictual activity may follow. Low visibility may be maintained because of a homogeneity of values within the group or because of institutional or other factors. Salience of analysis is also expected to be lower in this type of high-conflict situation than in others. Low-visibility decisions are likely to differ considerably from those that come to the attention of actors with disparate value orientations. While much of the following discussion pertains to these latter situations, I discuss low-visibility decisions again when I examine the direct impact of analysis on decisions.[22]

The production and dissemination of analysis, then, affects policy decision processes. Impact on these processes is mediated by the level of value conflict in the issue area. The impacts may themselves be of great concern to some parties. Increased salience of analysis and its symbolic uses may be viewed favorably or unfavorably. To the extent that the impacts coincide with or counter the values of particular social groups, they serve or harm their interests. The explanatory sequence does not stop here, however; other events and impacts follow. Some of the further impacts may be of greater political significance. The following list summarizes hypotheses involving decision processes.

Hypotheses Concerning Decision Processes

1. The greater the amount of analysis, the greater the salience of analysis during decision processes.

2. As the disparity of analysis reports present during decision processes increases, the salience of analysis during the decision process also increases.

3. As value conflict increases, salience increases.

4. As value conflict increases, symbolic behavior increases and decision use decreases.

5.   As value conflict lessens, decision use increases.

6.   As the visibility of decisions decreases, impacts on decision processes come to coincide with low-value-conflict situations (even if value conflict is high), that is, with lessening symbolic behavior and increasing decision use.

Belief Systems

An important juncture in the process of unfolding impact of analysis comes as individual belief patterns are exposed to decision process events. If analysis is to have a direct impact on decisions, it must shape the views of numerous policy participants or at least those in key positions. If analysis is to contribute to a process of learning or enlightenment, which might affect policy in the long term, it must have lasting impact on individual belief systems. In addition, various interests benefit by way of changes in individual beliefs, either through policy changes that occur or as decisions are legitimated. This chain of events takes the presentation further along the explanatory sequence than I can describe in detail at present, but it indicates the central place in the explanation of individual belief systems—the collection of valuational and cognitive elements and their interrelations that compose individual knowledge. Policy change and legitimation are considered in detail below. At present, the link between decision process factors and belief systems, as mediated by prior knowledge, is examined. While the direction of relationships among components is explored, the relative strength of these explanatory forces remains to be determined.[23]

Complex and poorly understood processes of cognitive and affective development may be simplified by reference to change and confirmation of beliefs. Change in the content and structure of beliefs occurs through the addition or differentiation of elements and the reformulation of links among components. Established elements may give way or be replaced. For the most part change involves effective adaptation or readaptation to surrounding circumstances. The process is governed by a reality constraint, a continual drive to move the belief structure toward compliance with actual conditions. Individuals may learn something regarding an issue about which they knew nothing previously. They may conclude that an earlier belief is now mistaken. Alterations or changes in belief systems involve both evaluative and cognitive representations.

Confirmation of images or beliefs already held occurs as additional evidence that supports or falsifies specific ideas accumulates. The intensity or strength of conviction regarding some propositions is altered. When the images held are confirmed, the amount of uncertainty regarding the validity of these claims lessens. In other words, the individual's beliefs or value judgments are intensified. What may once have been described as speculation or mere belief assumes the status of knowledge as confirming evidence increases. With changes or differentiation and confirmation or shifts in intensity of beliefs, areas or subsystems of the overall structure are said to develop.

The influence of analysis on decision processes was examined earlier. Attention now turns to the way in which variation in conditions of the decision process shapes change and confirmation of beliefs. Impact on belief systems is mediated by the individual's prior knowledge or belief patterns. Before I consider the mediating force of prior knowledge, I will examine the direct effect of decision process events (see figure 1).

The salience of analysis during the decision process is positively related to both change and confirmation of individual belief elements and structures. As salience increases, so does change and confirmation. The greater the exposure to analysis, and the greater the attention it receives, the greater the likelihood of impact on participants' thinking. Beliefs and values may be changed or may simply be confirmed.

With symbolic uses of analysis during the decision process, the result is quite different. As symbolic activity increases, the potential for change in thinking decreases. Political posturing and inflammatory rhetoric, or dramatic appeal, tend to evoke emotional reactions tied to basic ideological or philosophical positions. Participants are strongly predisposed to agree or disagree with the thrust of the symbolic gesture on the basis of these core beliefs. They are much less likely to change their pattern of thought, to alter beliefs or values. Thus when decision processes include much symbolic use of policy analysis, the primary effect is to confirm beliefs held prior to participation.

Attributes of already established belief structures join with the force of these decision process events to influence cognitive and affective responses. The extent to which experience changes or confirms the individual elements of belief systems depends on the intensity of the particular area of belief prior to the new experience and receptivity to social science.

Receptivity to social science is positively related both to change in beliefs and to confirmation. If participants value scientific input, and if they have favorable attitudes toward such input, they will generally at least consider relevant analytic material. They may or may not alter their thinking as a result. If participants are hostile to social science, and thus receptivity is low, there is little chance for even a hearing. Impact on thinking is thus likely to be minimal.

Intensity of belief, however, provides a more complex mediation with respect to change and confirmation. As intensity of belief or strength of conviction increases, the likelihood of change decreases and that of confirmation increases. Strongly held beliefs are unlikely to change in response to exposure to the thoughts or ideas of others. With intense beliefs there is a tendency to see confirming evidence in a sense everywhere, or toward selective perception. Intensely held beliefs, whatever their nature, are more often confirmed than altered by reference to conflicting thought patterns.

Intensity may increase with the weight of experience in support of specific ideas or with the importance of the element to overall consistency of the belief system. Value conflict in the social arena also influences the intensity of beliefs. The higher the conflict, the greater the intensity of relevant belief components. Thus value conflict travels two routes to exert considerable influence on individual thinking. It promotes a decision process event—symbolic use—that encourages confirmation and inhibits change. In addition, value conflict increases the intensity of prior beliefs, which has the same dual effect.

The process of change and confirmation of belief systems is normally called learning. Without proceeding any further toward impact on policy decisions, we have what many people would consider a valuable consequence of the production and dissemination of policy research. Analysis disseminated in an attempt to shape decisions may promote learning, the acquisition of warranted or adaptive assertions regarding social life. If, at a given time, the learning that has occurred fails to alter policy in any way, in the future it stands some chance of having that result. If changes in beliefs or values are long lasting, they will probably influence future decisions. Because placement of issues on political agendas is often cyclical, a number of opportunities to influence decisions generally arise. Knowledge, regardless of its use, may be valued apart from its impact on policy decisions.

The above analysis indicates, however, that change in belief systems is most likely to occur in situations where value conflict, and thus symbolic actions and intensity, are both low and where receptivity is high. With other situations or individuals, very little learning may occur. Even in these favorable learning situations, there is no guarantee that the changes in belief systems will take the form of valid or warranted assertions. The paucity of high-quality research means that lesser-quality products are at least as likely to promote change in belief systems. Erroneous ideas may be seized upon as well as those that warrant support. By doing a number of analyses and investigations it is possible to minimize the possibility to some extent, but this is no final solution.

If sponsors of policy analysis are willing to take chances in terms of expected policy consequences in situations most favorable to learning, they may be less inclined to do so in those situations that favor confirmation of established beliefs. If value conflict is high or beliefs are intensely held, analysis may do little more than strengthen polar beliefs and values. Neither position may entail a valid representation of the social issues under consideration. The quality of research or strength of support for its conclusions may be of little consequence. Under these conditions little learning takes place. In fact, something akin to ignorance may be promoted.

The present discussion highlights the complexity of cognitive and affective processes and the range of impacts on belief systems that flow from the production and dissemination of analysis. It cannot be assumed that learning, or the acquisition of warranted assertions, takes place automatically. It is more likely to do so in some situations than in others. Any assessment of the impact of analysis on beliefs must carefully consider the variations in impact that stem from variations in social contexts. Ignorance, or the acquisition of unwarranted propositions, may be the outcome rather than learning. It is doubtful that there are many situations in which society would value ignorance above learning or in which ignorance would justify the expenditure of scarce public resources on policy analysis. I list below the various hypotheses regarding the impact of analysis on the belief systems of policy participants and attentive individuals.

Hypotheses Concerning Belief Systems

1. As the salience of analysis during decision processes increases, so do both confirmation and change in beliefs.

2. As symbolic activity increases, change in belief systems decreases and confirmation increases.

3. As receptivity to social science increases, so do both change and confirmation of beliefs.

4. As intensity of belief increases, the likelihood of change in belief components decreases and that of confirmation increases.

Direct Impact on Decisions and Legitimation

A change in or the confirmation of beliefs among participants in the policy process may lead to changes in policy or to continuation of current provisions (even if the current policy is to do nothing). The policy output of the decision body may be altered in some manner, as the term "direct impact" indicates. Analysis need not be the only force in shaping policy—indeed it seldom is—for a direct impact to occur. "Policy" here means formal rules that guide the actions of administrators or implementors. It specifies actions to be undertaken in particular situations and may be informal or may be embodied in legislation and administrative regulation. As I noted in chapter 2, direct impact on decisions is the common definition of "utilization" and the most frequent meaning given "impact." Policy impact may occur as analysis influences proposals that are developed and later acted upon or as it affects adoption of particular policies. Research may have little or no direct impact on decisions, or it may have a very substantial effect on decisions. Whatever the direct impact of analysis on policy, there is another interesting decision impact or use. Research may serve to legitimate or justify a policy decision made on other grounds. In this respect the analysis follows or at least coincides with the decision rather than preceding it. With legitimation the decision output is not affected; there is no impact on policy output. The effect is primarily to influence perceptions of the decision process and to generate support for the result. Consequently the impact of analysis on belief systems may end there, or it may have a direct impact on policy or may serve legitimation purposes.

Direct impact on decisions depends on changes in individual belief systems. The greater the amount of change, both in terms of additions or deletions of beliefs and the number of individuals influenced, the greater the likelihood of direct impact on decisions. It is also possible to alter policy outputs by changing the thinking of a small number of key participants. The explanatory sequence suggests that low value conflict and low symbolic action, as well as certain attributes of individual belief systems, help bring about changes in thinking. When these conditions are absent, change in beliefs and policy decisions is less likely to occur. An exception mentioned earlier is when high-conflict issues are decided in low-visibility situations. In these cases analysis may provoke changes in the belief systems of members of the secluded group. During high-conflict, high-visibility episodes, other factors—political power, bargaining, and compromise—loom much larger in the policy decision than analysis.

When analysis is salient during the decision process but does not influence policy output, some degree of legitimation occurs. This consequence transpires in several ways. First, if policy is changed at all, analysis can be used to justify the change. Studies can always be found or manufactured for this purpose. Such analysis appears to demonstrate generally perceived beneficial consequences from the policy or action adopted. Second, if the policy decision is to keep the present policy or to continue to do nothing—that is, if there is no policy change—analysis can be used to support this result as well. All alternative policies can be found wanting in some respect. Or it can be argued that there is too little knowledge at the time to tackle the perceived problem. In either case analysis is used to support the status quo. A final mode of legitimation occurs as various interests, whatever the policy output, continue to use studies selectively to support or justify their positions on the issue. This strategy is an attempt to secure immediate symbolic gains and to influence future policy outputs rather than an effort to support current action or inaction. Again, if preceding events are considered, legitimation uses predominate when value conflict is high and when beliefs are intensely held.

Hypotheses Concerning Direct Impact on Decisions and Legitimation

1.   The greater the amount of change in belief systems and the number of individuals influenced, the greater the likelihood of direct impact on decisions.

2.   Direct impact on decisions increases as value conflict, symbolic action, and intensity of beliefs decrease and as receptivity to social science increases.

3.   As the visibility of decisions decrease, the relation of value conflict to direct impact on decisions no longer holds.

4.   As salience increases, legitimation increases.

5.   As value conflict and intensity of beliefs increase, legitimation increases.

Allocation of Value

At the outset of the explanation, I considered various interests that influence the production and dissemination of policy analysis. It is now time to examine the interests that benefit from production and dissemination across a range of situations. The impact of analysis on belief systems yields two major results—legitimation and direct impact on decisions. There may of course be no impact, but when impact does occur, it takes one of these forms or some combination of the two. Each output results in a different allocation of value to social interests.

When analysis has a direct impact on decisions, gains accrue primarily to research producers and collective interests. Producers gain considerably beyond the benefits that stem from production activity. If policy analysis survives the policy process and influences the decision output, the producers of the report gain prestige and recognition. This is the principal reward of scientific work and is highly valued in itself. In addition, future benefits are likely to flow from such a successful analytic effort. In this usage "success" refers to perceived impact of policy analysis on policy processes. Foremost are the grants and contracts for analysis that follow successful performance. The organized interests that support analysis seek successful research producers and are eager to gain legitimacy for their analytic input by having it conducted by highly respected researchers or research organizations. In some instances the continued profitability of the research organization is at stake. At least there is some impact on future profits. Gains to researchers do not imply deceit or any other questionable behavior (although on occasion such conduct may be present) but necessarily accompany analytic performance.

Collective interests benefit, together with producers, from the direct impact of analysis on policy decisions. My earlier discussion emphasized the important mediating effect of value conflict on the impact of analysis. In addition to its effects on the production and dissemination of analysis, I argued, value conflict fosters the symbolic use of analysis during decision processes and hence the confirmation of beliefs rather than change. For change in beliefs to occur and for there to be a direct impact on decisions, value conflict must be low. Low value conflict implies value agreement or shared interests. Thus in situations where analysis has a direct impact on policy, it acts in support of widely shared or collective interests. Research in these cases is largely a technical tool used to assess various approaches toward achieving agreed-upon ends. When it influences policy and is accurate, it furthers the agreed-upon ends. Analysis in these situations thus comes as close to the ideal of policy utilization as in any other context.

A major qualification of benefits to collective interests through direct impact on decisions concerns the accuracy of the analysis. If the analysis correctly demonstrates the relation of policy to shared values, collective interests are served through the direct impact on decisions. If the analysis is inaccurate or faulty, however, entirely different interests may be affected, either favorably or adversely. Actual policy consequences may differ in unpredictable ways from the projections of the original analysis. As a result, when inaccurate analysis influences policy decisions, there is no way of predicting which interests will ultimately be served. This difficulty suggests the need for institutional mechanisms to guard against the use of faulty analysis for decision making. At best such structures can reduce the instances; we cannot, given the the state of social science, realistically suppose that unforeseen consequences can be eliminated.

The major exception to the generalization expressed above concerns high-conflict policy issues and low-visibility decisions. Under such circumstances analysis may have a direct impact on decision output without benefiting collective interests. The allocation of value in these situations depends on the normative or valuational constitution of the low-visiblity decision makers. While such decisions, whether or not they are influenced by analysis, might benefit collective interests, they might just as well further class or organizational interests. The impact in terms of interests served cannot be predicted without reference to the specific group or individual decision maker.

When analysis is used to legitimate policy decisions or the viewpoints of various participants in a controversy, there is a similarity on one point with situations in which analysis has a direct impact on decisions. Producers enjoy prestige and recognition as their analysis is used to legitimate various decisions, just as they do when analysis has a direct impact on decisions. This result is particularly strong if the research in question supported the winning position, whether it is a policy change or maintenance of the policy status quo. The legitimation process increases the salience of analysis and thereby the recognition of its producers. The recognition is likely to pay handsomely in future support for research. When analysis does not support the winning position, it may still be used in attempts to legitimate various losing positions. This activity does not, of course, confer as much recognition as legitimating the winning position, but it may nonetheless involve some added recognition and gain to the producers.

Producers are not the major beneficiaries of such legitimation, however. Dominant classes, coalitions, and organizational interests benefit highly from the use of analysis to legitimate or justify their favored policy positions. The previous analysis suggested that legitimation outputs are most likely to occur in high-conflict situations. In these situations the policy process is characterized by symbolic uses of analysis and confirmation of previously held beliefs. High value-conflict situations may involve class, intraclass, or non-class-based conflict. Research does not influence the policy outcome in these situations. When class conflict involving significant threats to the capitalist class arises, analysis may be used to justify policy outputs that favor the dominant class. It does not affect the outcome of these struggles, however. With intraclass and non-class-based conflict, a dominant coalition wins the policy dispute through a process of bargaining, compromise, and logrolling. On the other hand, a negative coalition that blocks policy change may prevail. Research helps to justify the winning position. It attempts to demonstrate that the policy which strongly benefits the dominant class or coalition is in the interest of the entire society. Rather than promoting learning or enlightenment, analysis in these situations serves to obfuscate and mystify. Governmental and nongovernmental organizations take positions in accord with various class and group interests. As they do so they may be said to benefit through legitimation as well, although they gain primarily as agents of the respective interests that they represent. The list below summarizes these points.

Hypotheses Concerning the Allocation of Value

1. As direct impact on decisions increases, so do gains to producers and collective interests (if the analysis is correct and the decision process visible).

2. As the legitimation use of policy analysis increases, so do the gains to producers of analysis.

3. As the legitimation use of policy analysis increases, so do the benefits to dominant coalitions and social classes and related organizational interests.

5 The Negative Income Tax: Experiments and Proposals

✳

In contrast to the 1960s, which were characterized as the decade of "tireless tinkering with dependent families," the welfare policy agenda took a sharp turn in the 1970s.[1] The decade witnessed repeated failures at major reform. A series of attempts to achieve comprehensive welfare reform began with President Nixon's family assistance plan (FAP) in 1969 and ended with President Carter's second legislative attempt, the social welfare reform amendments of 1979.[2] These bills submitted to Congress, and a series of proposals between 1969 and 1977, all incorporated aspects of a negative income tax, a policy alternative that had gained widespread support during the decade of tinkering.[3] The 1970s were primarily years of struggle over comprehensive reforms and over the negative income tax.

A series of experiments with the negative income tax paralleled the proposals for comprehensive reform. The first experiment in New Jersey and Pennsylvania, launched by the OEO and external collaborators in 1967, was followed by similar undertakings in Gary, Indiana; in Iowa and North Carolina; and in Seattle and Denver.[4] HEW assumed the OEO's supervisory role after the latter agency's downfall, but the focus of the research stayed the same. Each experiment emphasized the effect that cash transfer payments to households would exert on their members' work behavior, or labor supply response. The findings of these experiments, and analyses based on them, permeated the reform attempts. The findings thus helped keep the idea of a negative income tax alive and played a significant role in various policy deliberations. They had other consequences as well.

This chapter examines the popularization of the negative income tax, the experiments, and various proposals which followed popularization but which nonetheless contributed to its continuation. It will provide the background information necessary to understand the welfare reform attempt during the Carter administration. I trace events from the early 1960s to 1977.

The Negative Income Tax and the Series of Experiments

Support for a negative income tax alternative to welfare policy grew steadily throughout the 1960s. Milton Friedman's call for a tax-based reform in 1962 and Robert Theobald's call for a negative income tax in 1963 set the stage for popularization of this idea and for development of executive branch support.[5] Friedman's argument was to supplement "the income of the poor by a *fraction* of their unused income tax exemptions and deductions."[6] Similar ideas had been put forward previously, but this time support for the proposal mounted rapidly.[7] The proposal later developed into a more general income transfer scheme featuring a guaranteed level of income and a marginal tax rate, which applied to earned income. Increased economic efficiency and individual freedom, and reduced welfare stigma and bureaucracy, were some of the benefits thought to result from the negative income tax. The negative income tax was viewed as a simplified cash transfer program that emphasized individual incentives.[8] The suggested efficiency gains, a primary economic value, steadily won economists over to the concept. In 1968 twelve hundred economists signed and published a petition urging Congress to adopt "a national system of income guarantees and supplements," a move which symbolized their shift to the front of the welfare reform debate.[9] By this time, however, a lesser number of economists had allied themselves with the OEO and HEW in support of the negative income tax, or the more general guaranteed-income concept, and the New Jersey and Pennsylvania experiments were under way.

The OEO, in conjunction with economists at the Institute for Research on Poverty (IRP) at the University of Wisconsin, began

crucial steps to further the negative income tax with formal proposals for such a policy change in 1965 and 1966.[10] The IRP had been
funded by the Office of Economic Opportunity as a poverty research
institute in 1966.[11] The early proposals came out of the Office of
Research, Plans, Programs, and Evaluation at the OEO as part of the
newly instituted programing, planning, and budgeting process. Once
it became apparent that funds would not be available for a proposal
as expensive as the negative income tax, a fallback strategy developed. Experimentation was viewed as a first step toward the negative income tax, as a method of keeping the alternative alive. With
the assistance of Heather Ross, Mathematica Policy Research, a New
Jersey research organization, offered the OEO a research proposal. In
1967, at the OEO's request, the Institute for Research on Poverty
joined with Mathematica to launch the first income maintenance
experiment.[12]

During this period, support for a negative income tax also developed at HEW. Staff members in the assistant secretary's office for
planning and evaluation, in conjunction with OEO personnel, with
whom they had close relations, offered their own internal program
memorandum in support of the negative income tax in 1966. Political appointees at HEW, primarily Undersecretary Wilbur Cohen,
were hostile to the proposal and squelched further advances of the
alternative at that time. Cohen helped draft the social security legislation in the 1930s, which provided the basis for welfare programs
that a negative income tax would have replaced. The planning staff
remained supportive and later assumed a greater role in the negative
income tax research and policy process.[13]

As support within the OEO and HEW grew, debate over the
negative income tax continued among academics and their colleagues in government. Despite the strong support for a negative
income tax, the policy approach had outspoken critics. James
Vadakin, for example, argued that, as there was no political consensus on the appropriate level of income guarantee, it was premature to
advance proposals.[14] Alvin Schorr thought that any potental stigma
from the current categorical aid program was a small price to pay for
continuance of adequate aid to the poor.[15] Christopher Green's 1967
study indicated that a universal negative income tax, with a guaranteed income at the poverty line and marginal tax rates that were low

enough to maintain work incentives, would be quite expensive. The policy implications were that either the guaranteed income level or work incentives would have to be sacrificed to bring any proposal within what Congress would be willing to spend on such an unpopular policy as welfare.[16] Furthermore, during this period the Congress and the public were generally against the negative income tax. The OEO received angry letters from opponents.[17] The income maintenance experiments, however, promoted continued support for reform, despite the prevalent objections, and ensured that the debate over a negative income tax would continue for some time.

In 1967 the OEO negotiated contracts with the IRP and Mathematica to conduct the first negative income tax experiment. The IRP was placed in control of the research design, and Mathematica was to supervise the fieldwork. The decision to fund the experiments and to join the effort of the nonprofit and profit-making research organizations resulted from a combination of circumstances: initiatives from both research organizations, the OEO's support for the negative income tax, personal ties between the organizations, and the desire of Sargent Shriver (director of the OEO) to protect the OEO, given its political vulnerability.[18] Initiation of the most ambitious social experiment ever undertaken in the United States required careful political maneuvering. The experiment had no basis in legislation or executive order, and the funding had to be squeezed out of the Community Action Program budget.[19] The OEO took on the responsibility for the experiment and its funding in part because no other organization was willing to do so.[20] By the time the experiment had been completed, some $7.8 million had been spent and twelve hundred families had participated.[21] To the surprise of some observers in the OEO, the research did not generate a political storm. Congress seemed to approve or at least was indifferent to the research, and several key members encouraged further research.[22] Negative income tax advocates and researchers lost little time once they had been given the green light. Within a few years three additional experiments were undertaken.

After the New Jersey experiment started, the research team became aware that it would not provide all the answers sought by proponents of a negative income tax. Changes in New Jersey's public assistance program after the experiment began created problems.

After New Jersey had been selected as a research site, in part because it had no provision for unemployed fathers in its aid to families with dependent children (AFDC) program, the state decided to add such a provision. Families in the least generous experimental treatment groups left the experiment for AFDC participation. The new program also altered the effective net guaranteed income level and marginal tax rates for the families who stayed with the experiment. In addition, the New Jersey and Pennsylvania sample was considered inadequate for generalization of the findings to the national level.[23] While researchers were learning about experimentation, there was also a change of administrations, which presented the OEO with a hostile president determined to dismantle the agency at the front line of the War on Poverty.

After HEW contracted for a comprehensive plan for future income maintenance research with the IRP, the OEO continued its support for income maintenance research, and a series of experiments got under way. With the second experiment in rural Iowa and North Carolina, the Ford Foundation contributed partial funding, and the IRP again performed as lead researcher. The third experiment, conducted in Gary, Indiana, engaged the research efforts of the Urban Institute and Indiana University. For the final experiment, by far the largest, the OEO contracted with Stanford Research Institute for work in Seattle and Denver.[24] When the OEO was abolished in 1973, HEW assumed responsibility for supervision of the ongoing experiments and analysis. By the time all of the contracts had run their course, more than $108 million had been spent. Much of that sum had gone to the researchers, and nearly nine thousand families had participated.[25]

Each of the four experiments sampled quite different populations. The plan was to accumulate data on all relevant groups in order to simulate the effects of a nationwide program. The New Jersey–Pennsylvania and Iowa–North Carolina experiments focused on male-headed families in urban and rural areas, respectively. The Gary experiment centered on nonwhite, female-headed households. Finally, in Seattle and Denver, female- and male-headed families were combined in a single experiment.[26] As learning about experimentation continued and proponents of a negative income tax multiplied, a relatively bold but small experiment in

New Jersey and Pennsylvania expanded into a series of expensive research projects.

The earliest research and policy participants indicate that the experiments were primarily political actions designed to advance the negative income tax. Some participants were motivated primarily by their scientific interests. They were nonetheless swept into a political thicket. In 1967, with economists the main supporters of the negative income tax proposals, the alternative stalled within the Johnson administration. The Vietnam War cut into the domestic budget and made a major overhaul of public assistance programs impossible at that time. In addition, early discussions of the negative income tax prompted concern that recipients of a guaranteed income would cease to work or would drastically curtail their efforts. Advocates of the negative income tax considered this expectation a major political hurdle for enactment of the legislation. The work-response question was particularly crucial, as the program would extend coverage to the working poor. Cross-sectional economic studies and microeconomic theory suggested some drop in labor supply with a negative income tax program, but the magnitude of the effect was uncertain. Advocates believed that the labor supply response would be negative but minimal. If they could gather rigorous evidence in support of this belief, they thought that political opponents would be mollified. In addition, as research scientists they were more inclined to introduce research as a political mechanism than to overcome opposition by other means.[27]

The political need to build support for a favored policy proposal through the study of labor supply coincided with the professional disciplinary interests of the economists, whether or not they were supporters of a negative income tax program. The labor supply response question represented an important part of microeconomic theory, which had not been fully elaborated or demonstrated empirically. In the language of the discipline, the magnitude of the income and substitution effects of altering the labor-leisure trade-off, through a program of cash transfers, was unsettled. Microeconomic theory suggests that, by raising family income, the negative income tax makes families better off and therefore able to work less while maintaining a higher standard of living (the income effect). Consumption of normal goods (those of which people buy more as their income rises), for example leisure, increases. The marginal tax rate associated with a negative income tax (usually in the range of 50−70 percent) reduces the net wage from work and therefore lowers the price of not working (that is, the price of leisure). This substitution effect also suggests that labor supply drops in response to a negative income tax. The experiment offered an attractive opportunity to address these important theoretical questions in a rigorous fashion which was unlikely to be otherwise possible. Discipline-focused economists found it easy to join hands with their policy-focused colleagues in the experimental efforts. Each group had interests at stake. Both of these interests were of course shared by some of the participants. It is difficult to assess the relative strengths of the scientific and policy motivations of the participants, but both were clearly operative in the research process.

As the proposal for a negative income tax gained momentum, the experiments started, and as analysis staffs at the OEO and HEW pressed for policy change, economists became the lead actors in the welfare policy field. The proposals by Milton Freidman and others, along with the petition by economists, put the dominant position within the discipline on record. The research offices at the OEO and HEW also included many economists, a fact which furthered their lead role.

> Both offices had many of the key spots in their hierarchy manned by people coming directly from the academic community, and a number of other staff persons whose backgrounds made them peers with social science community researchers. The head of the analytical offices in the period under study were quite similar in backgrounds. All four were well trained in economics; had spent most of their time in prestige research institutions as opposed to universities (three at Rand, one at the Brookings Institution); were reputable members of the academic community with good, if not outstanding, reputations, particularly in the policy areas; and were working-level practitioners of their discipline rather than distinguished methodologists. In a very broad sense all four had a similar policy-oriented economist's approach to the problems they faced.[28]

The disciplinary focus at the IRP was quite similar. Its series of directors were also economists, and economists made up the majority of the appointments at the institute.[29] The negative income tax alternative found a comfortable home in these organizations. The question of whether to proceed with a negative income tax proposal was not seriously questioned. Rather, a subtle process of increased attention to design details within this framework occurred. Rein and Peattie note the ease with which such a focus develops under these conditions:

> In the process of drawing on academic research for program design it is not so much the research findings that are crucial as the cast of mind of the researchers. They grasp from a discipline an essential insight that is converted into a program. In the example of academic interest in income distribution, the comprehensive means-tested negative income tax, ideally administered through the tax system, served as a prototype. Whatever its origin in the academic disciplines, the negative income tax is now a reform in the political realm, and poverty research is inspired by an effort to work out the design problems presented by the conception with the analytic tools of economists.[30]

The advance of the negative income tax proposals to the policy experimentation stage symbolized the dominance of economists in the welfare policy subsystem. This trend was also aided by a series of commissions, task forces, and legislative proposals.

Commissions, Task Forces, and Proposals

A series of task forces and commissions late in the Johnson administration preceded President Nixon's family assistance plan in 1969. The legislative proposal placed the experimental researchers in a difficult position. Neither they nor the earlier advocates of a negative income tax had expected a legislative proposal so soon. As a result, although the research played some role in the policy process at this time, it had not progressed far enough to provide the kind of support for the negative income tax that the advocates had anticipated.[31] The FAP ran into legislative difficulty in Congress and was eventually abandoned, but the experiments continued, and further proposals surfaced in 1974, before the Carter administration took its turn at reform.[32]

Joseph Califano, special assistant to President Johnson, appointed a task force on income maintenance in July 1968. The task force included a number of OEO and HEW supporters of the negative income tax. Its chairman, Merton Peck, from the Council of Economic Advisors, managed to forestall a report supporting a negative income tax in favor of a series of recommendations which were intermediate steps toward a negative income tax system. These measures included national eligibility and benefit standards (primary components of a negative income tax plan). Shortly after the task force report had been completed, President Nixon was elected president, and Califano and acting HEW secretary Wilbur Cohen rejected the recommendations of the task force.[33]

As a parting gesture President Johnson appointed the Heineman Commission, headed by Benjamin Heineman, Sr., to consider the recent public assistance debate. The commission's report, issued late in 1969, put the Democrats on record as supporting a negative income tax. It called for the replacement of "AFDC, Food Stamps, and similar programs with a single, national income maintenance plan."[34]

While the Democrats had been at work with their commissions and task forces, the incoming Nixon administration had been doing its homework. Richard Nathan headed a task force for the president-elect that did not push for a negative income tax but, like the first Johnson task force, called for incremental reforms moving in that direction. The Nathan task force called for national standards for all aid categories, the protection of high payment states, and fiscal relief for states and localities.[35] At this time few welfare policy regulars expected the Republican administration to offer a dramatic departure from past policy, but it came in the form of the FAP, modeled after a negative income tax.

President Nixon's 1969 decision to propose the FAP is explained in part by the persistence of negative income tax advocates within the executive branch. The policy analysts at HEW, including Johnson administration holdovers, persuaded a key presidential adviser, Daniel P. Moynihan, to accept a negative income tax plan.[36] Moynihan had previously favored granting an allowance for family or for children in place of the negative income tax. Nonetheless, he became a forceful advocate of the FAP, which was prepared at HEW.

Eventually—I am making a long and somewhat complex story much too short—President Nixon accepted the proposal. The orginal plan called for a guaranteed income of fifteen hundred dollars (later raised to sixteen hundred dollars) for a family of four and incorporated a 50 percent marginal tax rate. It was to be administered by the Social Security Administration and included a strong penalty for able-bodied recipients who did not work.[37]

The FAP passed the House in early 1970 with majorities in both parties and the hardy support of Wilbur Mills, chairman of the Committee on Ways and Means.[38] Soon thereafter it stalled in the Senate Committee on Finance and finally in November 1970 was defeated there by a vote of 10 to 6.[39] The Finance Committee story is long and complex. The legislation found itself in a hotbed of value conflict, and neither Chairman Long nor ranking Republican Senator Williams would support the bill. HEW personnel were given rough treatment in committee by Senator Williams, who brought to everyone's attention the fact that the FAP did not fit very well with other assistance programs. The combined effect of simultaneous participation in several programs created a "notch" effect where marginal tax rates at certain levels of income approached 100 percent and in some cases exceeded this level substantially. Families who participated in several aid programs (for example, the FAP, Medicaid, and food stamps) and whose incomes approached the eligibility level stood to lose hundreds or thousands of dollars of benefits from working more and earning just a few more dollars income. The legislation failed, but even so, its submission by a Republican president jolted those who just a few months earlier had doubted that legislative action on a negative income tax proposal stood any near-term chance. Given the continuation of the negative income tax experiments, and ongoing dissatisfaction with the existing policy system, additional proposals lay not too far ahead.

Consideration of the FAP by Congress put the New Jersey income maintenance research team and the OEO in an awkward position. Congress was considering a proposal similar to their experimental treatment, but the effort was barely under way, and substantial analysis had not been conducted. Under pressure from the OEO and other parties, the New Jersey team released data to the OEO. The OEO wrote a brief in favor of the FAP which concluded,

"Fears that a Family Assistance Plan could result in extreme, un-usual, or unanticipated responses are unfounded." The research team also testified to much the same effect before various commit-tees. Problems arose when a General Accounting Office report sug-gested that "OEO had not conducted sufficient analysis to support any conclusions," and that the report was premature. The early data were later found to present a more favorable response than the final analysis. The OEO and the research team survived the embarrass-ment of the moment, but these events were not forgotten by the Carter administration as it used analysis from the Seattle and Denver experiments to support the program for better jobs and income.[40]

In 1974 two additional proposals emerged. A subcommittee of the Joint Economic Committee issued what became known as the Griffiths plan, after its chairwoman, Martha Griffiths. The plan was based on the negative income tax and included cash allowances and tax rebates. It was a comprehensive proposal that would have replaced aid to families with dependent children, supplemental security income, food stamps, and the income tax personal exemp-tion and standard deduction.[41]

The second proposal came from HEW. Work on the income supplement program (ISP) within HEW crossed the Nixon and Ford administrations. In 1973 President Nixon and Secretary Weinberger were interested in incremental reforms, given the perceived faults of the welfare system and the earlier experience with the FAP. After eight months of interaction with staff and aids, both proponents and opponents of the negative income tax, Weinberger surprised his con-servative colleagues by adopting the ISP despite its $3–5 billion price tag. Supporters of the negative income tax, which was clearly reflected in the proposal, had once again persevered and had won a policy dispute. As in the past, however, opposition, this time from President Ford, put a stop to the matter.[42]

My brief and incomplete history of the negative income tax and its embodiment in experiments, reports, proposals, and legislation demonstrates the difficulty of killing proposals that are well anchored in influential sections of the executive branch. The experiments and continued advocacy of the negative income tax by researchers and analytic staffs kept the anchor in place. After another change in administrations, the negative income tax resurfaced.

6 Income Maintenance Experimentation and Policy Decisions

✳

Welfare reform events during the Carter administration will serve to illustrate the explanation presented in chapter 4 and are intended to show its plausibility rather than to test individual hypotheses or the overall structure rigorously. I took all quoted statements in this research from transcripts of interviews conducted between August and October 1980.[1]

The Context of Impact Processes in the United States

It is necessary to consider the social context within which the Carter administration's welfare proposal was formulated and acted upon. The United States during the period under discussion can be characterized as possessing the cultural, institutional, and social structural attributes of an advanced capitalist system.

Ascendant Beliefs: Science and the Professions

Belief in science and professional skill became a dominant part of the popular ideology in the United States after World War II. A gradual process of acceptance of these beliefs had been ongoing for many decades. In 1919, for example, Thorstein Veblen argued that a "machine-made" preconception of inquiry with emphasis on "efficient causes" had permeated the technological sciences and threatened the humanistic fields.[2] The rise of behavioralism and logical positivism in the social sciences exemplified the ascendancy

of the belief in science in those fields that concerned Veblen. Technological outgrowths of physical laws of nature (automobiles, airplanes,
telephones, radios, and so forth) contributed to the belief system. As
the twentieth century progressed, the general cultural trend toward
belief in science and technology became most pronounced.

The ideology of science displaced the previously dominant
force of religion. As Feyerabend suggests, "the assumption of the
inherent superiority of science has moved beyond science and has
become an article of faith for almost everyone. Moreover, science is
no longer a particular institution; it is now part of the basic fabric of
democracy just as the Church was once part of the basic fabric of
society."[3] As belief in science and the professions has secured a
dominant position in the popular mind, individual behavior and
governmental action have been affected.

Belief in science and technology led to the rapid growth of funds
allocated to scientific research and to the development of technology
following World War II. Machlup found that total research and
development expenditures grew at the rate of 17 percent to 18 percent per year between 1954 and 1958. In 1958 these expenditures
totaled $10.9 billion. At the same time expenditures on social re-
search also increased tremendously. When the National Science
Foundation began its social science program in 1958, the initial
appropriation was $750,000. By 1965 the amount had risen to $10
million.[4] The belief in science and technology, coupled with the
efforts of scientists, resulted in substantial allocation of resources to
scientific activities.

Beliefs in science, technology, and professional skill are also
exemplified by career preferences in the United States. A 1973 Gallup Poll found that 65 percent of the U.S. population would first
recommend a professional career as a doctor, lawyer, engineer or
professor to a young man who sought its advice. Similarly, a 1974
survey of college students found that 67 percent of the sample
planned careers in teaching, medicine, business, law or research and
science.[5]

Belief in science and professional skill permeates the culture of
the United States, although knowledge of science is generally very
limited. Science and the professions have become articles of faith
which guide human activity. The public expects science and tech-

nology to provide solutions to the growing problems of industrial society. Individuals seek the assistance of professionals to help solve their personal problems. On occasion the belief is brought into question, and doubters persist in their skepticism, but beliefs in science and professional skill have a prominent place in the prevalent ideology.

Institutionalization of Science and Policy Analysis

The government or state sector in the United States experienced rapid growth during this century until very recently. The growth in government has increased the positions available for scientists and other professionals. Total expenditures in current dollars for all levels went from $0.8 billion in 1890 to $10.7 billion in 1929 to $408.0 billion in 1973.[6] By 1980 the figure had again doubled to $869.0 billion. From 1929 to 1980, expenditure as a percentage of gross national product went from 9.9 percent to 31.1 percent. Expenditures have concentrated at the national level, with the national government spending $602.0 billion, the states $148.2 billion, and local units $128.5 billion in 1980.[7] A different picture emerges when employment is considered. From a total of 16.7 million government employees, only 3.0 million work at the national level, and employment at this level has risen only about 25 percent since 1955. During the same period, state and local government employment has risen from about 4.7 million to 13.7 million employees—an increase of nearly 300 percent. Grants-in-aid from the national to state and local governments as well as divergent program concentrations across levels help account for the mismatch of expenditures and employment. Grants from the national to state and local governments rose from approximately $2.3 billion in 1950 to $105.9 billion in 1985.[8] The national government has increasingly become a disburser of funds to the state and local levels and a supervisor of multilayered programs in a complex federal system.

As the national state sector has assumed supervisory functions in the federal system, there has been an increased professionalization of the work force at the national level. In the four-year period from 1961 to 1965, the percentage of professional positions in the national-level state sector went from 46.7 percent to 52.4 percent.[9] The national level of the state sector has grown considerably through the twentieth century. With this growth has come an increasingly professional and specialized work force operating within a fragmented context of executive departments and semiindependent agencies and commissions.

During the twentieth century in the United States, a semi-autonomous scientific institution developed through a system of internal governance based on a system of shared norms and ideology. Merton identifies an ethos of science, an "affectively toned complex of values and norms which is held to be binding on the man of science. The norms are expressed in the form of prescriptions, proscriptions, preferences, and permissions. They are legitimized in terms of institutional values." The major values he identifies are universalism, communism (common ownership of scientific findings), disinterestedness, and organized skepticism.[10] Science relies on internalization of these norms by practitioners to ensure decentralized self-governance of the scientific community.

The professional norms take on the character of a more general ideology when coupled with other belief structures. Greenberg argues that the scientific community is bound together by a twofold ideology: "first, a desire for society to support, but not govern, science; and second, for the community of science to exist as a loosely organized entity—meritocratic anarchy may best describe it—in which hierarchy and tables of organization bear little relation to the realities of power." The scientific community believes that it deserves public support for research but that it should be free to handle its internal affairs. Its belief structure incorporates the ideal of a semiautonomous science. The norm of pure science—disinterested, objective analysis—inspired by the quest for knowledge supports the semiautonomous position. Merton argues that the norm of pure science serves "to preserve the autonomy of science," to eliminate or depreciate the norm subjects science to "the direct control of other institutional agencies and its place in society becomes increasingly uncertain."[11] Science has its own ideology or system of norms that help govern or pattern scientific activity. The norms are by no means universally accepted, and some would argue that as standards they are impossible to achieve. Nonetheless, they are incorporated in individual belief systems and help maintain the semiautonomy of science.

The government of science includes associations and networks of scientific elites that assist in the overall governance of scientific activities. Professional associations and elites, which permeate state-sector agencies, influence the allocation of professional rewards and research funds to the scientific community. Through the power to reward and sanction scientists, the scientific elite helps ensure adherence to professional norms. As Greenberg suggests, "what must be joined to this recognition of the freedom that does prevail in pure science is the realization that the laissez-faire system takes place within the bounds of an intricately constructed, subtly functioning system of government that, in effect, defines the possibilities of science by governing the availability and use of resources."[12] Science has its own institutional structure that guards the relation of the scientific estate to the rest of society.

While science maintains a considerable self-regulating apparatus, it becomes increasingly subject to external forces and demands as it accepts research funding and support from external actors. The amount of support has increased dramatically since World War II. Total support for scientific research and development from the national government has gone from $7.6 billion in 1960 to $49.5 billion in 1985, with $33.4 billion of the latter amount devoted to defense research and development. Support for social research and development has risen from $0.3 billion to $10.7 billion from 1953 to 1979. It is estimated that two-thirds of university-based research and development comes from the national state sector.[13] This figure indicates the dominant role of the state in support of scientific research. While scientists influence the distribution of these funds, some loss of autonomy ensues as the state in part determines research priorities. The same loss of autonomy follows industrial support of scientific research.

In addition, loss of autonomy results from the scientific community's acceptance of the prevailing political and economic structures. Scientists are unable to detach themselves completely from the institutional structures and historical events that they have experienced. Acceptance of social structures and institutions reduces autonomy. Scientists share basic beliefs about social and economic relationships that influence their behavior. Acceptance of these basic cultural attributes limits the autonomy of the scientific community.

Another important institutional development is the multiplication of organizations and professions that increase capacity for the production of policy analysis. A series of organizations have developed over the last several decades that have increased production capacity substantially. National agencies have created units such as HEW's office of the assistant secretary for planning and evaluation, the DOL's office of the assistant secretary for policy, evaluation, and research, the Department of the Interior's office of the assistant secretary for policy, budget, and administration, and the Department of Housing and Urban Development's office of the assistant secretary for policy development and research. Agency-level units have also often developed research, policy, and evaluation units. The Occupational Safety and Health Administration's Office of Regulatory Analysis and the Consumer Product Safety Commission's Bureau of Economic Analysis are two of many examples.[14] Other central units include the Congressional Research Service, the Office of Technology Assessment, the Congressional Budget Office, and the General Accounting Office.

These executive and legislative branch organizations perform brokerage functions and often conduct and supervise a great deal of analysis themselves. As brokers they link policy makers with researchers in an attempt to produce policy-relevant research. These units often possess a significant analytic staff to conduct their own research. Central analysis units also serve as supervisors or monitors of contract research performed by profit and nonprofit organizations. While some of these units have long histories (for example, the Department of Agriculture's Economic Research Service), many of the units were established in the 1960s when President Johnson ordered domestic departments to implement the Department of Defense's planning, programing, budgeting system.[15]

A large number of academic and nonacademic (profit and nonprofit) research organizations have also increased the capacity for the production of policy analysis. Organizations such as the Institute for Research on Poverty, SRI International, Mathematica Policy Research, the Urban Institute, the Brookings Institution, the Institute for Policy Studies, Abt Associates, the American Enterprise Institute, the Rand Corporation, the Hoover Institute, the Heritage Foundation, and the Institute for Contemporary Studies are just a few of the many analysis organizations that have created additional production capacity.[16]

The numerous analysis organizations have raised many interesting questions about the organizational requisites of effective production capacity. For the most part these questions remain unanswered.[17] Clearly, however, production capacity has increased and a history of analysis conducted for policy-making purposes has been evolving for some time. The continuous input of analysis is likely to influence the expectations of policy participants and ultimately the impact of analysis, although the full effect of ongoing institutional practices is unclear. It may be that analysts have generated overly optimistic expectations for policy analysis. This is certainly true in some cases. While some potential users of analysis have learned of the gap between promise and performance, many others have a great deal to learn about the adequacy of policy analysis as currently practiced.

Distribution of Power and Resources in the United States

Skewed distributions of power and related resources characterize the United States in the late twentieth century. Income, wealth, position, and power all tend to be disproportionately concentrated among the few. The remainder of this section considers these structural characteristics and examines their implications for welfare policy research.

Market forces in the United States distribute income quite unevenly. In 1984 the top fifth of American families received 42.9 percent of the nation's money income, with the bottom fifth receiving 4.7 percent (the middle quintiles register 24.4, 17.0, and 11.0 percent). Not only is there considerable unevenness, but the overall distribution is remarkably stable. The top fifth of U.S. families received 40.9 percent of income in 1970, 41.3 percent in 1960, and 42.8 percent in 1950. The lowest quintile registered 5.8, 5.2, and 4.5 percent of income during the same years.[18] The growth in redistributive programs in the decades after World War II, as important as it has been for those on the bottom of the economic ladder, has been insufficient to alter basic distributional patterns substantially.

In addition to income, wealth is distributed in a highly unequal manner in the United States. In fact, the distribution of wealth is much more uneven than that of income. In 1983 the average financial assets of families earning $50,000 and above was $125,131. For those earning less than $5,000, average financial assets were $3,254. A middle category, with income of $15,000 to $19,999, exhibits a very slow rise in wealth as one moves up the scale. Families in this bracket had financial assets of only $12,021 on average. Wealth may also be examined across categories of net worth. Wealth holders possessing less than $250,000 total net worth held a total of $122 billion in 1982. Those with more than $1 million had a total net worth of $1,122 billion, almost ten times that of the lowest category.[19] People of wealth in the United States clearly have great wealth. The distribution across social groups is quite uneven. The pattern also holds with specific forms of wealth, such as stock ownership.

Possession of stock in corporations is highly concentrated. Only one family out of six in the United States owns stock in a corporation, and two-thirds of all stockholders own less than $10,000 in stock. Ownership is highly concentrated, with less than 10 percent of stockholders holding 80 percent of all stock. In 1969 more than half of corporate stock was owned by only 1 percent of the U.S. population. Expressed differently, the top fifth of households in terms of net wealth owned 76 percent of the wealth in the United States.[20] Although wealth is not equivalent to stockholdership, ownership of stock is the major category of wealth in the United States. Concentrated ownership of economic resources provides a considerable power base.

Concentration of economic resources within large corporate enterprises in the United States yields considerable market power. Over the last thirty years, mergers have resulted in the rapid growth of corporate enterprises. From 1955 to 1970 the total assets of the top five hundred mining and manufacturing corporations nearly doubled. The top one hundred corporations account for 35 percent of merged assets. The growth of corporations through mergers and other means results in considerable market power. In many industries a few firms dominate production. In 1970, for example, two firms accounted for 90 percent of metal container production; in the drug industry four firms accounted for 80 percent of production; in heavy electrical equipment two firms accounted for 80 percent of production, in photographic supplies one firm produced 75 percent of total output; and in computers one firm accounted for 90 percent of production.[21] These are just a few examples of the market dominance of one or a few firms across industries in the United States. They clearly indicate the prominence of large corporations in the American economy and the uneven distribution of power and resources among economic actors.

The controversy over theories of political power and policy making within political science has hardly subsided in recent years. Yet to most students individuals and organizations seem clearly to translate income, wealth, position, and other resources effectively into influence over public decisions. Charles E. Lindblom, for example, argues that large business corporations dominate decision making in important governmental and nongovernmental public arenas. Lindblom suggests that the business community has a "privileged position" over other particular interests as well as collective concerns in the state sector: "Businessmen generally and corporate executives in particular take on a privileged role in government that is, it seems reasonable to say, unmatched by any leadership group other than government officials themselves." The wealthy or owners of capital do not always agree on policy, nor are they always free from competition from others to influence policy, yet as Robert A. Dahl puts it, "existing patterns of participation tend to enhance the relative influence of the already advantaged strata."[22] Other interests make demands on government and on occasion their demands are met.

Ongoing mechanisms and processes translate resources into policy and protect the vital interests of dominant social groups. Electoral politics, consultation, interest group activity, financing of political parties, and public relations or propaganda are the most frequently studied means. Lindblom again states the case succinctly: "All citizen groups compete in politics with the use of their members' own incomes and energies. Except for businessmen. They enjoy a triple advantage: extraordinary sources of funds, organizations at the ready, and special access to government." When business interests are uniform—when protection of private property, promotion of profit accumulation, and stable patterns of income and wealth distribution are at stake—there is no match for corporate interest in securing governmental assistance.[23] When other issues are at stake, lesser interests fight among themselves for any favors they can get from government.

When conflict arises within classes over particular interests, or when conflict has little economic or class basis, there is greater competition among groups to shape policy. At this level of politics, there is a fragmented system of shared and overlapping powers in which a large array of organized interest groups compete for influence on public policy. Power in the United States is shared to some extent among competing interests, but that competition is often severely limited, and specific interests are often represented ineffectively in areas of great concern to them.[24]

Uneven distributions of power and resources in the United States influence policy analysis. They do so primarily by shaping the focus and content of analysis and by affecting the reception of particular analyses in policy arenas.[25] In short, structure conditions the production and use of policy analysis; it is not the only influence but the most basic. I will examine the relation to production further before considering the matter of utilization.

Policy analysis in the United States is generally linked to ongoing policy and program activity that does not threaten established interests substantially. A recent National Research Council study of 180 national agencies found most social research and development to be "mission oriented" and to have "followed, rather than preceded, the policy and program commitments that specify the agency's purpose and responsibilities—its mission." Poverty research commonly adopts institutionalized policy perspectives. Analysis tends to concentrate either on direct public distributions of aid to recipients or on work and the impact of these interventions on poverty. These focuses flow from academic traditions centered on established policy and from immediate program concerns.[26] A lesson of the income maintenance experiments frequently mentioned by research participants is the striking similarity of a negative income tax to existing cash transfer programs. At base each consists of an income-guarantee level and a marginal tax on earnings. Although tax rates differ considerably, guarantee levels are not very different. Public assistance adds qualification criteria absent a negative income tax and fails to establish national benefit standards, but these differences are marginal rather than fundamental. The influence of the established policy perspective on analysis was so subtle that years of research were needed to make participants grasp the similarity of the negative-income-tax-based reforms to institutionalized policy.

In addition, structure affects production negatively: analyses are seldom produced that challenge dominant interests. The poverty arena again provides instructive examples. Consider alternative policy options geared to alleviating poverty. Instead of guaranteeing income, policy could conceivably guarantee jobs. The Carter administration did not have an analysis of a major jobs alternative as it sat down, in the president's view, to overhaul the welfare system, nor did it have an analysis addressing smaller-scale jobs programs or combined cash and jobs programs similar to the proposal it finally formulated. Given public sentiment in favor of work over cash transfers, the contribution of earnings to the alleviation of poverty, and the typical analytic prescription to consider alternatives, such an analysis would have been appropriate. Maintenance of labor markets for low-wage, "dead-end" jobs is clearly important to the continuation of structural inequality. A partial explanation of this analytic focus in the welfare arena comes from this basic economic structural reality. A guaranteed-jobs program is anathema to the structurally advantaged in the United States, and policy analysis of such an option was therefore not forthcoming. A related point involves the income-guarantee levels incorporated in income maintenance experiments. The politically charged nature of guarantee levels was foremost in the minds of the first income maintenance researchers and sponsors. Indeed, the experiments (see below) were an attempt to discredit the view that labor supply would drop precipitously in response to a guaranteed income. The experiments thus embodied benefit levels that were in large part below the poverty level. Political feasibility was recognized. Analysis calling for benefits that would bring recipients out of poverty ran too far against ingrained structural interests to be considered seriously.

The influence of structure on the focus and content of analysis promotes the utilization of analysis for policy making. It shall be argued below that the Seattle and Denver income maintenance experiments (SIME/DIME) shaped several minor features of the Carter administration's reform proposal, such as the income accounting period and tax reimbursement provisions. Analysis had such influence precisely because minor policy issues were involved. Incremental policy changes are much more likely to receive widespread support than are radical departures from established approaches. Thus when the focus and content of analysis lends itself to questions of minor policy revisions, as it often does, and when this analysis appears well founded, it is likely to shape policy.

The Impact of the Seattle and Denver Income Maintenance Experiments

Advocates and Social Scientists Take Over

The Seattle and Denver income maintenance experiments and the three previous experiments were motivated by specific interests. Those who advocated a negative income tax were the major force. A second group was more interested in scientific investigation and specific theoretical questions of importance to particular disciplines than in advancing the cause of the negative income tax. These group interests overlapped in some individuals.

A small group has maintained open advocacy of the negative income tax since the concept took hold in the 1960s. Members of this group thought the experiments would further their policy cause in future policy debates. Some 85 percent of the respondents interviewed in this research, including numerous participants in the early events, considered the experiments an attempt to legitimate the negative income tax. Two responses from OEO personnel are typical:

> Yes, it [the New Jersey–Pennsylvania Experiment] was an attempt to remove any doubt. It was thought if a 5% labor supply response can be shown that a NIT [negative income tax] could easily be had. There is no question about it. All the planner participants were predisposed to a NIT.

> I don't know if I should be concerned with the attempt to use the experiments to legitimate a single policy approach. It is a hard question to answer in retrospect. At the time we certainly had

no problems with what we were doing. OEO was very above board in its advocacy.

Proponents of the negative income tax alternative to welfare policy thought the policy change would advance various values which they held.[27] Most of the advocates were economists, and the primary value they sought to advance was allocative and technical efficiency. Allocative efficiency involves structuring policy or market alternatives in such a way that individual preferences are maximized. With a negative income tax, welfare recipients are given cash transfers and may spend the money as they see fit to better their condition. With in-kind transfer programs, such as food stamps or housing allowances, the scope of individual choice and hence economic efficiency is reduced.[28] Individuals are constrained to accept specific goods or services if they are to receive any assistance. Economists also believed that excessive marginal tax rates (sometimes exceeding 100 percent) on earned income, with the present welfare system, further impair allocative efficiency by interfering with individual work and leisure decisions.[29] With high marginal tax rates, individuals would work less than they otherwise preferred to work, as the income benefits from work are minimal. In some cases recipients would lose more in welfare benefits than they gained in income.

Technical efficiency results when a good or service is produced with the minimum expenditure of resources. Many economists view the executive agencies that administer welfare policy as inefficient mechanisms. Administrative costs of food stamp programs, for example, are about 11 percent, whereas for social security administrative costs are about 3 percent.[30] If administration of redistributive policy could be simplified and expenses reduced, a greater amount of resources would be available for redistribution. The negative income tax was thought to be just such a method of reducing overall administrative costs. It would combine various assistance programs and would achieve economies of scale. A simple income test for eligibility was also thought to be much less costly to administer than the complex regulations and standards that guide current programs. For those who favor less reliance on the public sector to promote human welfare, the negative income tax also proved attractive. A range of program changes that would accompany a negative income tax were thought to yield substantial efficiency gains.

While technical and allocative efficiency gains are the major values that economists sought to promote through a negative income tax, other values are involved. Many of these values associated with a negative income tax counter perceived problems with current welfare programs. The negative income tax was favored by some who saw it as an effective means for altering the distribution of income or for increasing equity among social groups. Major beneficiaries in this case would be the working poor and married couples with low income in the twenty-four states that do not have an AFDC program with a provision for unemployed fathers.[31] These families and other low-income families that did not qualify under one of the existing categorical programs would also become eligible for assistance for the first time. A negative income tax was also thought to be less demeaning and less stigmatizing than current welfare programs. Those who believed strongly in the need to reduce the negative psychological consequence of welfare joined the ranks of advocates of the negative income tax.

A series of values served to motivate the negative income tax advocates. They sought to advance these interests in an altered welfare policy by promoting the experiments at a time when their proposal had stalled in the policy process. An OEO staff member made the point:

> Most of the people involved thought the chance of getting a NIT into policy was very remote. Therefore, we emphasized a strong design. We did not think time was crucial. We thought that the research would revive a stalled debate. The advocates had hit a stone wall in the Johnson administration.

Social science researchers had much at stake in the initiation of the experiments apart from the policy interest in a negative income tax proposal. Participation in large social experiments offered a series of potential benefits to research organizations, researchers, and the disciplines from which they came.

Research contracts are the lifeblood of profit and nonprofit research organizations. They are beneficial to the careers of individual researchers as well. The $108 million in research contracts for

negative income tax experimentation provided a significant opportunity to the research organizations that participated.[32] It enabled
them to increase or solidify their status in relation to competing
organizations. Not only was a lot of money at stake, but the opportunity to move to the forefront of a new approach to social inquiry—
large-scale social experimentation—proved attractive. In response
to a question about beneficiaries of the experimental effort, several
respondents emphasized the gains to individual researchers and
their organizations:

> Policy analysts, SRI, IRP, Mathematica, etc., all benefited. Policy
> people were kept busy and paid well. They were addressing
> important questions, but Congress was not overly concerned.

> In a callous sense, the researchers involved benefited the most.
> But who knows, maybe Watts [New Jersey–Pennsylvania co-
> director] would be better off today if he had done something
> different. It was a real gold mine for research-types right on
> down the line. It made Mathematica. It was a small fledgling
> organization before the experiments. Perhaps it helped the IRP,
> but I'm not sure how much.

Academic disciplines benefit from participation in policy analysis.
The labor supply focus of the Seattle and Denver experiments gave
economists the chance to examine a significant aspect of economic
theory empirically. This scientific interest or research orientation is
emphasized by an early participant who identified the potential policy implications but was primarily motivated by the research question:

> Everyone brings with them a complicated set of interests. My
> views were that important evidence was lacking for any type of
> welfare reform. For example, what would be the effect of in-
> creasing the support level or for expanding coverage? I saw the
> labor supply response question as central to various types of
> welfare reform. It was an important empirical question. The
> experiments were a rigorous attempt to address this question.

The experiments also fostered increased attention to economic
issues in social research. Labor supply has become a major concern

in a policy area where the original objective was to ensure subsistence-level income to families with children. Children seem to have given way to labor supply as a focus for recent discussion. Significant but lesser research opportunities also went to sociology as the experiments addressed a series of sociological questions. Research organizations and social science disciplines had much to gain by encouraging the negative income tax experiments.

Individual researchers saw the experiments as an opportunity to advance their professional careers. The experiments provided an avenue for many research publications, the *sine qua non* of a successful social science career. Several research participants have noted that a "massive number of papers" were written on the experimental methodology and findings.[33] In addition, there is the straightforward matter of jobs for research professionals and financial assistance and training for graduate students. The negative income tax experiments boosted the careers of many of the research participants.

In summary, the interests of negative income tax advocates, social science researchers, their organizations, and their disciplines inspired the experimental efforts. A series of policy analyses were thus produced and disseminated. The aforementioned interest groups, however, were not the only forces affecting the production and dissemination of analysis.

Value Conflict Over Welfare Policy

The level of value conflict in the welfare policy area proved crucial for the production and dissemination of the negative income tax research. Welfare policy is a high value-conflict issue. Beliefs regarding the preferred ends of welfare policy are diverse and are often intensely held. Many students of welfare policy have commented on the highly conflictual nature of the policy area.[34] Public opinion polls spanning the 1960s and 1970s also reflect the value conflict among the population regarding welfare goals and programs.

Public opinion polls have indicated relatively consistent disapproval of ongoing welfare programs. In 1965, 43 percent of a national sample had a "favorable" impression of current programs, while 45 percent had "mixed feelings" about ongoing policy, and 6 percent wanted to do away with the programs altogether. A 1977 national survey found that the most frequently desired change in welfare was the institution of better screening procedures (52 percent) to cut down on fraud and to eliminate ineligibles from the welfare rolls. Similarly, according to a 1979 poll, 36 percent of the sample thought that one-half or more of those on welfare received more assistance than they are entitled to.[35]

Welfare programs add to the value conflict in the policy area, as they counter fairly explicit public preferences. The public has generally favored programs that emphasize work or job creation, while the majority of program efforts favor cash or in-kind transfers to recipients. Support for work-related programs is consistent across income groups. A 1965 survey found that 84 percent of the entire sample and 85 percent of the lowest income group thought that all able-bodied men on relief must "take any job offered which pays the going wage." In 1979, 79 percent of a national sample favored requiring able-bodied women welfare recipients with children thirteen and over to take "any full-time work available."[36] This favorable response came from virtually all income groups. Support for the jobs approach has resulted in modest efforts, but these programs remain subordinate to cash and in-kind transfer. The favorable attitudes toward work programs not only keep welfare officials on the defensive but are a major obstacle to those who advocate a negative income tax.

Public support for a guaranteed income or negative income tax has been small except for a brief favorable shift when President Nixon proposed the family assistance plan in 1969. In 1965 a survey found 19 percent in favor and 67 percent opposed to a negative income tax. A 1968 survey found 36 percent in favor of and 58 percent opposed to a guaranteed annual income of thirty-two hundred dollars for a family of four. Similarly, in 1969 a national survey found that 32 percent favored a guaranteed income of thirty-two hundred dollars, but 62 percent still opposed this proposal. With the latter two surveys, support for a guaranteed income decreased as income rose. The 1965 survey found that 26 percent of respondents with incomes of more than ten thousand dollars favored the plan (68 percent opposed), while 47–48 percent of the respondents with income of five thousand dollars or less favored the guaranteed-income concept (45–48 percent opposed). The 1969 survey found 24 percent of those with income of more than ten thousand dollars in favor of a guaranteed income for a family of four and 40–43 percent of those with incomes below five thousand dollars in favor of such a plan.[37]

The policy, research, and interest group participants interviewed in this research reflect the value conflict among the public. Respondents are more likely than the public to favor a negative income tax but are nearly evenly split. When respondents were asked how they felt about a negative income tax, 50 percent found it preferable to current welfare programs, and 50 percent thought the opposite. A similar balance was found on the question of nationalizing administration: 42.9 percent believed that welfare should be centralized, and 42.9 percent disagreed. The sample of respondents was overwhelmingly in favor of maintaining welfare expenditures (100 percent), reducing inequity in payments (92 percent), and emphasizing work (85.7 percent). The sample, then reflects general support for improved jobs programs and for reducing inequities. Respondents differ, however, on the issue of spending; no one agreed with the public's opinion that welfare costs should be cut. These findings cannot be taken as accurately reflecting the population of welfare policy and research professionals, because the sample was not drawn randomly from that population. Nonetheless, they add to the description of value conflict over welfare policy objectives.

The general public thus shared a distaste for current welfare programs with negative income tax supporters. The public, unlike the advocates, thought the answer to the welfare program was work and jobs and more effective administration. Welfare reform means different things to different people. A large majority of the population with similar majorities across income groups seems to favor jobs programs. It is likely, however, that the results of questions regarding jobs programs would differ if program costs were included, as there is little support for the required increased spending. A 1974 survey found that 34 percent of the sample favored reducing spending for "social programs such as health, education, and welfare," with higher support for reduction from those with incomes of more then twenty thousand dollars (39 percent) and from Republicans (40 percent). [38] Evidence is not available, but differences in preferences among income groups probably increase with the cost and generosity of the income transfer program. At the same time, however, a group of social science professionals strongly favors a negative income tax. This result suggests that there is a high level of value conflict over welfare policy. To some people, welfare reform means spending less, putting recipients to work, and cutting back the rolls. To others welfare reform means equalizing benefits and raising them in at least some cases, expanding coverage to all those below some income line, and consolidating and simplifying program administration. Such wide disagreement over the ends of welfare policy mediate the production and dissemination of welfare policy analysis and its impact on the policy process.

The Effect of Value Conflict on Production and Dissemination

High value conflict over welfare policy had several effects on the production and dissemination of analysis. The discussion above suggests that the high value conflict affected the advocates' decisions to push for the experiments. They thought the experiments would lessen the value conflict over welfare policy. Additional effects of high value conflict include the focus of the analysis, the number and diversity of reports generated, and the polemical nature of production and dissemination.

Research produced throughout the policy process was more of a political than a technical exercise. That is, there was not a series of reports concerned with the best or most efficient means of obtaining agreed-upon objectives. High value conflict kept a series of technically oriented analyses from being produced. There was simply not enough agreement regarding the ends of policy (low value conflict).[39] The income maintenance experiments dealt with the technicalities of a negative income tax, but the research was not directed toward agreed-upon goals, nor was a range of program alternatives examined. The experiments did test the effect of various program options on labor supply response, but the options tested were only variations of the basic ingredients of a negative income tax (marginal tax rates and guarantee levels). Alternative programs designed to promote labor supply were not studied, as there was no agreement that labor supply response was the primary objective of welfare policy. Labor supply response was simply a political hurdle to be dealt with and a question of interest to economists. Research on jobs programs, for example, has been undertaken only recently; a jobs program might influence labor supply response. The experiments focused on the labor supply response to a negative income tax, not on the labor supply response to job training programs or to any other type of program. The experiments were more of a political effort to support a particular policy and reduce a political obstacle than a technical exercise, which analyzes a range of programs in terms of agreed-upon criteria.

The number and diversity of the analysis reports both increased as a result of high value conflict. This pattern took a peculiar form, given the scale of the experiments and the conflictual behavior between the DOL and HEW. Analyses multiplied as each department sought to make the best use of the experimental findings for its own purposes. Several respondents close to the process report this use of analysis:

> Esoteric social science warfare was at the heart of the DOL-HEW squabble. The research community is now in policy positions and therefore tends to dominate the controversy. In this case it leads to a typical liberal solution—provide jobs. It appears that DOL has appropriated the welfare term. They have gained some turf as they now have welfare reform and income maintenance staff.

> I remember a meeting some of us had with the Labor and HEW people. Not much came out of it, but the experiments were discussed at length. DOL and HEW each used them to support their own point of view. So the findings weren't exactly disregarded, but the results were not that clear cut. We had the old, on the one hand, but on the other, type of discussion.

HEW initially had control of the data base and the simulation model it developed. The DOL sent numerous requests to HEW for analyses that would support its view. The DOL requested cost and caseload estimates for a large number of program variations. In addition, the DOL asked for estimates of the proportion of additional program costs needed to pay for the decreased labor supply of recipients. The results showed that from 25 percent to 50 percent of the increased cost, depending on the specific program alternative, went to compensate for labor supply reduction. This politically sensitive expression of the labor supply response was quite harmful to HEW's position. HEW had been generating reports which suggested that the negative labor supply response was small in an attempt to cast its favored alternative in the best possible light. HEW's report on the Seattle and Denver mid-experimental findings, for example, suggests that husbands work "only *slightly* less—6 percent fewer hours—and that, although wives work 17 percent fewer hours and female heads of households work 12 percent less, "the absolute decline in their hours was *small* [emphasis added]."[40]

Analyses external to the executive branch added to the analytic input. The CBO was asked to analyze and to estimate the cost of the administration's PBJI. Its cost estimate differed considerably from that of the administration, and a controversy over the actual cost of the program ensued. The administration estimated $2.8 billion in additional costs, while the CBO issued a figure of $13.9 billion. Beneath the dispute over the cost analyses lay the highly conflictual issue of how much to spend on welfare. Another example of value conflict affecting analysis production stems from Senator Moynihan's interest in the use of welfare reform to provide fiscal relief to states and localities. He requested an analysis from the Congressional Research Service that showed the redistributional impact of the administration's proposal on the states.[41] There might have been an even greater number of analyses if the experiments had not been so large in scale. The number of analyses generated and the diversity of the reports that accumulated were nonetheless considerable.

The high value-conflict condition also contributed to the polemical nature of the analysis. As had been indicated, much of the analysis was directed at political objectives—gaining support for or attacking a proposal. Comparison of the various reports and analyses reveals the outlines of the intense conflict under way. Examples include the divergent cost estimates of the administration and the CBO and reports that draw attention to single policy impacts, whether it is labor supply response, marital stability, or fiscal relief.

Dissemination of information based on the experiments was also polemical. Information was carefully sifted before being released. Some findings were emphasized, while others were ignored. A midexperimental labor supply response report by HEW, for example, presents the figures for only those groups with the smallest negative response (wives and husbands in intact families) and omits those with larger responses (secondary workers). The department was also less than energetic in disseminating the marital stability finding.[42] Seattle and Denver treatment families split apart from two to three times more frequently than control group families. The result was known in the professional community but was deemphasized in policy deliberations and did not receive general exposure till the second legislative attempt. As one legislative staff member remarked,

> HEW suppressed the results in terms of entering them into the policy process, but they did not hold them out of scholarly circles.

A marital stability researcher added:

> I can see the outsiders' perspective on it. In retrospect it appears that it would have been better to handle the findings differently. HEW intermediaries have admitted to me that they did not push them. They weren't going to put themselves on the line. Several of them said this to me.

The damaging potential of the finding was not lost on HEW. It was difficult for those in the assistant secretary's office to say much about the finding, however, when HEW secretary Califano and the president were making public statements that PBJI would stabilize families. One researcher attributed cautious dissemination to the earlier experience with experimental evidence and the FAP:

> There was an incredible amount of stalling, attempts to prevent the SIME/DIME results from being released. . . . They didn't hold back on the labor supply findings. The FAP experience, however, affected their actions; they were somewhat gun-shy with the Seattle-Denver experiment. So on the marital stability finding the researchers felt pressure to keep quiet, to be careful about what you say. There was definite pressure.

A White House aide who had worked for HEW notes the limited dissemination of the marital stability finding:

I did not know of the finding prior to the November 1978 hearing [Moynihan's public assistance subcommittee]. In the policy discussion it never came up. The finding did not threaten any legislation prior to November 1978. I was at HEW during 1978–1979. At that time Barth [director, income security policy] and Aaron [assistant secretary for planning and evaluation] were very concerned about how to defend the legislation against this charge. The finding caught them by surprise. I don't really know if HEW handled themselves well throughout this. At most I saw a few things in the papers and was present just enough to catch the concern at HEW.

The marital stability finding presented HEW with quite a dilemma. It was a potential deathblow to the negative income tax. In addition, although there was no evidence, there was a theoretical basis for expecting the same type of effect from the jobs component of the PBJI. Administration officials therefore carefully limited their efforts to disseminate the results.

This section has illustrated the role of group interests and the effect of value conflict on the production and dissemination of policy analysis. Advocates of the negative income tax, social science researchers, their organizations, and their disciplines stood to benefit from the conduct of the income maintenance experiments. The former group found the experiments a useful vehicle to keep their proposal alive and even at the top of the welfare reform agenda. The latter individuals and organizations received considerable symbolic and material benefit from participation in the experiments. At this early stage in the policy process, a significant allocation of value had occurred. A series of policy objectives held by specific groups had been advanced. In addition, substantial benefits had been allocated to the social science participants and their organizations.

Decision Process: Forensic Social Science

High value conflict during the PBJI formulation process influenced the impact of the analysis on this decision process. Major divisions arose over whether it was best to provide the needy with jobs or with cash transfers. The final proposal combined the two approaches but not before a protracted battle between the DOL and HEW had taken place. Another major issue concerned the amount of money that should be spent on the program. The president initially called for a zero-cost program, a program that would replace existing programs but would not spend additional funds. At a March 25, 1977, meeting, President Carter told department officials, "I want you to take all the money that is now being spent on welfare programs and redesign the whole system using the same amount of money. Then show what you can do, adding new money in $1 billion increments." Many administration officials (and probably the president) thought that an improved welfare system would cost additional money.[43] Increased aid to the welfare recipients, however, countered strong public sentiments that welfare reform meant removing chiselers from the rolls and spending less.

On August 8, 1977, President Carter unveiled the program for better jobs and income with a suggested price of $2.8 billion in additional funds. The five months that the administration took to formulate the bill were dominated by an executive branch struggle between the DOL and HEW. While this process did not attract widespread national attention, the value conflict across the society was represented by the departments, other officials of the executive branch, and the external organizations that became involved. Numerous disputes arose over details of the basic jobs and income components. Organized labor was concerned about the wage scale for the public service jobs that would be created. Governors were concerned about administrative relations with the national government and feared central administration. There was also conflict over benefit levels, which some groups believed were not high enough. Agricultural interests also opposed the elimination, or cashing out, of food stamps.[44]

The Seattle and Denver experimental findings and analyses based on them served a dual purpose during the decision process. The primary function was symbolic; the major adversaries used the analysis to push for their preferred alternative and to attack their opponents. A secondary use occurred as a simulation model was employed to cost various program alternatives and as minor features of the plan, for example the income accounting period, were directly influenced by the research findings.

The PBJI debate began in March 1977 with Assistant Secretaries Arnold Packer (DOL) and Henry Aaron (HEW) pushing opposed welfare strategies. Packer adamantly argued for a jobs-based strategy, while Aaron fought for HEW's favored negative income tax alternative. The battle between labor economists and income maintenance economists was under way.[45] Meanwhile, the president urged the agencies to work out their differences and to put together a zero-cost proposal.

Staff at HEW argued that the negative labor supply response was relatively small and should not prevent the administration from going ahead with a negative income tax program. Comments from HEW staff reflect thinking within the department:

> The labor supply response, or disincentive was not that bad, not striking. On the whole the research did not provide many striking findings at all. There was not that much there.

> Labor supply response was clarified. We have precise estimates for the income and substitution effects. There was not an enormous withdrawal from the labor force.

Analysts at the DOL and Assistant Secretary Packer pointed out that the negative labor supply response was much higher for wives and secondary workers (teenagers and young adults). Statements from the DOL respondents reflect this position:

> The labor supply findings were important and distressing. It was important to have the response quantified. SIME/DIME is the only creditable study, the figures for youths were particularly troublesome.

> All four experiments were fairly similar. The labor supply response was the biggie. Here we found a 10% to 15% negative response.

Therefore, the DOL argued that a jobs strategy was the most appropriate policy. Each side used the research findings to support its position. The statements above indicate the different manner in which the findings were viewed at the two departments. HEW's initial control of the data gave it the upper hand at first. The two departments were engaged in a fierce turf battle over welfare policy.

The jobs-versus-cash-transfer conflict was a zero-sum struggle over dominance in the welfare-policy field. At this level the analysis was used for its strength as a tool of symbolic politics. Those close to the process describe the events as follows:

> The Department of Labor used the research to strengthen its position that the NIT should be dropped.

> Each side used the research to support its own arguments. This made the President and Eizenstat [assistant to the president for domestic affairs and policy] think they could not give much weight to the research if it could be used this way.

> HEW was trying to use SIME/DIME as support, but it backfired. The conservatives picked it up and used it.

The analysis served to bolster an agency's position or to attack its opponents. There was no careful deliberation over several policy alternatives. Each side had predetermined positions. The analysis was little more than a weapon in the battle.

In stressing the minimal nature of the negative labor supply response, HEW emphasized the response of the groups that decreased their work effort the least. Male heads of households reduced their work effort from 5 percent to 11 percent and female heads of households from 9 percent to 15 percent. The findings for wives and secondary workers were considerably larger. Wives worked from 18 percent to 25 percent less, while the negative response for sixteen- to twenty-one-year-old individuals who were not heads of households ranged from 28 percent to 68 percent. These findings proved useful for the DOL in arguing that the negative income tax was inadequate. In addition, the striking and unexpected finding of increased marital instability among experimental treatment families provided ample symbolic ammunition against a negative income tax plan and a jobs program that included women heads of households. Treatment families were found to split apart in some sample subsets more than twice as frequently as control group families.[46] The marital stability finding was not used symbolically at this time, however, as the finding, if faithfully represented, would have weakened the positions of both the DOL and HEW. A negative income tax and a public service job both offer family members a means of attaining economic security outside the family that may affect decisions to continue marriages. Neither side, therefore, sought to use it politically. Considerable doubts about the finding, along with its politically damaging potential, also led the departments to downplay the result.

The analysis was highly salient to the analysis staff at the two departments and to legislative staff and interest groups active in the welfare policy subsystem. The analysis was less salient or well known to those outside the departmental research units. Numerous respondents report the salience of the analysis to executive branch personnel and staff members on the Hill:

> Barth and Aaron [HEW] were very interested in the experiments.

> There were a number of key insiders—Aaron, Barth, Packer [DOL], and Todd [HEW] who all knew of the results and cared about their implications.

> As academics Bowler [House Special Subcommittee on Welfare Reform] and Primus [Committee on Ways and Means] were predisposed to consider research. Other staff may have considered the research for similar reasons, but perhaps not to the same extent.

A staff member of the Senate Finance Committee commented:

> I followed the experiments somewhat. I was interested in them.

Those outside the administration and Congress had heard of the experiments indirectly and were not highly knowledgeable about them. Several respondents who participated in the welfare-policy process could not list any of the experimental findings when asked. One respondent reports indirect exposure to the findings:

> I didn't follow them too closely, so what opinions I do have are derived through my staff.

Although there was some variation in salience across participants, most of those involved in the welfare policy process knew of the experiments and could cite particular experimental findings.

The salience of the analysis at the assistant secretary and staff level stemmed from several factors. The scope of the research, HEW's investment in the experiments, value conflict, and the disparate findings across experimental subgroups all led to an increased salience of the research among a major portion of the welfare policy subsystem. Although knowledge of the experiments varied considerably, most of the participants interviewed knew of the experimental research. The scope of the research effort and the intentions of the initial sponsors played a key role. The Seattle and Denver projects were unprecedented in size and expense in a social policy field. After the OEO was disbanded by President Nixon, HEW was given supervisory responsibility for the experiments. HEW received the series of research reports that arrived steadily during the mid to late 1970s. The department was predisposed to a negative income tax program all along and had hoped that the findings would bolster its position. The research findings reached HEW at a time when welfare had again reached a new president's policy agenda. There was little chance that HEW would reconsider its advocacy of the negative income tax. The scope of the research, although narrow by some standards, was wide enough to provide some findings of symbolic value to opponents of the HEW position. Despite such troublesome findings as the labor supply response of the sixteen- to twenty-one-year-olds and the marital stability findings, HEW continued its advocacy of a negative income tax.

The high level of value conflict represented by the DOL and HEW, and the Office of Management and Budget, with their concern for program costs, also promoted the salience of the analysis. The departments each stood to gain or lose considerably from the policy outcome. The president, who sought to be considered a fiscal conservative, and the Office of Management and Budget, as well as other politicians, were concerned about the overall cost of welfare reform. The Seattle and Denver experimental findings made possible construction of a complex simulation dubbed the "KGB model" after its developers, Kasten, Greenberg, and Betson at HEW. This model was used to cost various program options and predict caseload sizes.[47] The critical nature of the cost issue led to increased salience of the analysis through continual cost simulations of program variations. Several respondents described this process:

The research played a major role in estimating costs.

We worked eighty or ninety hours a week building the simulation model. There was no capability like this until 1977. We built the labor supply findings into the simulation.

As various interests strove to have their values or interests embodied in the policy proposal, participants and those close to the process chose to utilize the research findings to strengthen their position. The analysis became more salient.

The high value conflict tended to foster symbolic uses of analysis and to prevent substantial decision use of the findings. Participants were caught in an ongoing process of conflictual behavior, which emanated from disagreement over welfare policy goals. Discussions of policy within the administration at times resembled fights more than careful deliberations. Several participants summed up the process:

> In the early months of the welfare reform process there were two points of view expressed—HEW's and DOL's. The people at HEW had the horses. Their staff had greater technical expertise and they had the data. But the DOL people clobbered HEW. The data didn't do much good. There was a predisposition to go with jobs at the White House and there was the personal clash between Packer [DOL] and Aaron [HEW].

> There were conflicting pressures within the administration. The research was used straight at first. Later, after decisions were taken it shifted to brief writing, the use of what information you can get to support your position. Everything happened so fast this was all we could do.

> The programs were in an advocacy stance. There was no disinterested analysis. The White House was the brokerage unit. The President saw this, he did not get objective analysis. He did not have options to chose from.

Research became engulfed in a forensic process and was used to persuade the few who had remained uncommitted and to discredit opposing sides.

On May 2, 1977, the president publicly announced a series of principles that would guide the final drafting of a welfare proposal. The principles included statements supporting a combined jobs-and-income approach. Individuals close to the president suggest that he had envisioned a combined strategy all along. A member of the domestic policy staff at the White House commented:

> There was agreement from the beginning on an integrated plan. We always knew we would have both jobs and cash transfers.

A White House aide concurred:

> We were predisposed to combining cash and jobs from the beginning. It was HEW that tried to argue against this. Of course, they failed. President Carter and others always favored a combined program. He had said so publicly during the campaign.

Nonetheless, President Carter's statement clarified the administration's policy goals somewhat. The DOL was pleased with the president's statement, while HEW felt that it had lost the battle. In the next three months, efforts were devoted to forging a combined jobs and income program. Conflictual behavior lessened as the broad outline of a program was established by the president. Conflict remained, however, on the allocation of scarce resources between jobs and cash transfers. The analysis played an increased decision role at this time. The decision use centered on integrating jobs and cash transfers and on the costing of various alternatives. Political decisions, however, restricted the scope of technical decisions that were subject to analysis. The overall cost decision and the setting of the maximum benefit level at 65 percent of the poverty line (a limit determined historically by southern politicians), for example, left little room for fine-tuning of the proposal through analysis, although some such activity did occur. Once allotments had been made to the DOL and HEW and the guarantee level had been determined, the marginal tax rate automatically followed. The cost and guarantee decisions determined the outcome. Imposition of program goals by the president reduced the symbolic use of analysis somewhat and opened the door for a slight increase in decision use on narrow technical issues. Two HEW participants report, for example, that the research influenced (1) decisions over a tax reimbursement provision, (2) adopting of a six-month income accounting period, and (3) the setting of federal subsidy limits to states at 75 percent of the poverty level.[48] These decisions amount to minor program details necessary to keep the program within the cost constraint. The analysis achieved high levels of salience throughout the formulation period among those attentive to the welfare-policy subsystem.

Change and Confirmation of Belief Systems

The salience and symbolic use of analysis during the decision process influenced the belief systems of policy participants. Beliefs may be changed or confirmed. With change comes increased differentiation of belief elements and/or shifts in relations among components. Confirmation leads to greater intensity of belief or conviction. Individual patterns of belief prior to exposure to the decision process, however, mediate the impact of decision process events on current beliefs. As we will see, the analysis suggests that during the PBJI formulation process many participants confirmed prior beliefs, particularly concerning the overall acceptability of negative-income-tax-based reforms. For some individuals and in the case of less central beliefs, however, conditions were such that considerable change in belief systems also occurred.

The high salience of the policy analysis during the decision process promoted both change and confirmation of individual belief systems. Most of the participants knew of the analysis, and a significant number of participants were very familiar with the research. Of the respondents in this research, 87 percent were able to state specific findings of the experiment with considerable clarity. Those who knew little of the findings prior to the formulation process became aware of them as events unfolded. The public attention paid to the marital stability result increased the salience of the research among those who had previously been unaware of it. The many illustrations of changed and confirmed belief systems that follow indicate the influence of salient research on the thinking of attentive audiences.

The high symbolic use of the analysis during the early phase of the decision process also promoted the confirmation of beliefs already held by participants and inhibited changes in belief systems. When asked whether the experiments had influenced their thinking about welfare, 46 percent of the sample commented specifically that it had confirmed prior beliefs. In response to a similar question regarding influence on thinking about social experimentation, 35 percent of the sample indicated clearly that prior beliefs had been confirmed. As symbolic use of the analysis lessened somewhat after the president's May 2 statement of welfare principles, the tendency for further confirmation lessened, and the possibility of some change in thinking increased. To a considerable extent, however, belief systems had already been confirmed. Decision process events, then, exerted influence primarily to promote confirmation. Some individuals, however, changed belief systems in response to the analysis.

The prior beliefs of policy participants had a dual influence on subsequent patterns of change and confirmation of belief systems. That is, some belief elements were conducive to confirmation, furthering the confirmation impact generated by decision process events, while others favored change. I will provide examples below as I consider particular belief areas.

Receptivity to the use of social science for policy purposes was generally high among participants, although there was some variation. Many of the actors within the administration were social scientists with histories of employment in policy and research position. The high receptivity tended to promote both confirmation and change, as it increased the likelihood that many participants were highly aware of the analysis and would at least consider the experimental findings. Policy participants on each side of the issue of social science's usefulness for policy making had their beliefs confirmed by the experience with the use of research during the policy formulation process. Those skeptical of the fitness of social science research for informing policy decisions often found that belief strengthened. A number of the respondents saw experimentation as a very limited tool and had this predisposition confirmed:

> The Seattle-Denver experiments confirmed my belief in the difficulty of experimentation. It is hard to isolate particular effects, or to explain certain results. For example, what about the marital stability finding—who knows? They are a conservative force that is likely to stymie planners.

> The experiments reinforced my previous views. You need to

remember that they are only experiments. There will always be shortcomings and the need to qualify the findings.

I have never been a gung-ho supporter of experiments. I was drug into the New Jersey thing somewhat kicking and screaming. Experiments have a role, they can answer some questions. There are drawbacks though. They take a long time, are expensive, and hard to analyze. Just witness the NIT experiments.

Those who value policy analysis as an aid to decision making or as valuable for other reasons for the most part found their beliefs confirmed in the welfare policy process. These respondents reacted much more favorably to the experiments:

Seattle and Denver certainly have not made me think experiments should not be done. Before the experiments we had no such welfare research. I always thought experiments were a good idea. New Jersey and Seattle-Denver provided some interesting findings. I still think they are important to do.

The experiments are worthwhile to do. You can learn a lot from them. They pretty much confirmed my prior beliefs in this instance.

The experiments confirmed my belief in the value of experiments. You need to remember that I am a research scientist at heart. The experiments highlighted a few important issues.

Receptivity to social science, then, is a belief element like any other in that it may be confirmed as a result of exposure to analysis. Although the examples given above illustrate the predominant confirmation outcome with receptivity to social science, changes in this belief also occurred. I examine them below, after discussing the confirmation of central belief elements involving welfare reform.

Confirmation is greatest with those belief elements that are relatively intensely held. Confirmation as well as change is buttressed by high receptivity to social science. With the income maintenance experiments and welfare reform, one of the most intense beliefs involved the acceptability of negative-income-tax-based reforms. For the most part, both supporters and opponents had firm convictions. Affective or valuational belief elements regarding labor supply response were tied to overall judgment regarding reform strategy. People highly concerned with labor supply tended to see withdrawal of labor as "high" and therefore as supporting their opposition to negative-income-tax-based change. Those who regarded labor supply as relatively less important, or who had less intense beliefs, saw the same level of withdrawal as "low" or "moderate" and thus had their conviction regarding the acceptability of this reform strategy confirmed. In addition, reactions to the finding that marital dissolutions would occur were closely tied to the intense overall judgments of acceptability.

The Seattle and Denver experimental findings and analyses based on these results strongly confirmed prior views on the overall acceptability of negative-income-tax-based reforms. Those who, prior to the research, thought that the negative labor supply response would be large and opposed the negative income tax generally retained these beliefs and found them reinforced. Typical responses follow:

> The experiments confirmed my earlier belief in the need for a jobs approach. I had changed my mind towards a jobs approach early on as I became convinced that bigger gains in income would come from jobs.

> I am not a NIT advocate. I have been opposed to it since Green and Ross pointed out some of the problems with trade-offs. I saw in the 1960s that you cannot meet the three objectives at the same time. So the experiments have strengthened my prior beliefs. I feel the way now that I felt before the experiments.

Those who initially held the opposite position also found their beliefs confirmed by the experimental results. Several early participants illustrate this pattern:

> The people who inaugurated the experiments were by and large favorably disposed to a NIT. They wanted the results to come out in a certain way. By the way, this is not atypical of scientific work. I was one of this group. I was predisposed to the NIT and I still favor the approach.

> The experiments have not influenced my views a great deal. I

still strongly favor a simple NIT. I've always been against any type of work test.

Categorical programs are inferior to noncategorical programs. I haven't been disabused of this idea. That's the only influence the experiments have had on my thinking. I saw nothing that would make me a fan of work requirements.

Thus the same set of analyses confirmed opposing views. Participants saw in the research findings the results they wanted to find.

Preconceptions concerning the direction and magnitude of labor supply response interacted with the marital stability finding (which I examine below) to strengthen overall judgments on reform. In the case of labor supply, participants came to the policy process with somewhat intense beliefs. Most participants, on the basis of microeconomic theory, anticipated a negative labor supply response. Previous cross-sectional studies had supported this belief. In addition, many of the participants thought that the labor supply response would be small, but the evidence was not as compelling on this point. Typical responses among those who confirmed labor supply response beliefs follow:

The experiments showed what was expected. Secondary workers reduce their time working. Also, overtime workers drop some hours. But in the main there was not much effect.

I was not surprised at the labor supply response finding. It could have been used to buttress the conservatives position. It would not, however, have changed the minds of any liberals.

The basic finding, which was confirmed after Seattle-Denver, was that we had confirmation of our original labor supply response hypothesis. It is always possible to argue about what is large, however. But the main effect, or large response, is with secondary workers.

These comments suggest instances of confirmation of empirical beliefs regarding labor supply response and also indicate the difficulty of suspending evaluation of behavioral results.

The research provided support for quite disparate judgments on the importance of the labor supply response. The participants manifested major differences in the intensity of normative beliefs concerning labor supply response. A Senate Finance Committee report using the New Jersey results for illustration notes a tendency among participants to react quite differently to the same empirical findings:

> The conclusions drawn from the data produced by the studies have not always obtained universal acceptance. For example, the summary report on the New Jersey experiment published by the Department of Health, Education, and Welfare states: "The most striking feature of the findings is that the observed changes in labor supply in response to the experimental payments were generally quite small." By contrast, the data from the same experiment led John F. Cogan of the Rand Corp. to comment: "The central finding of an analysis of the labor supply response of while male heads of households in the New Jersey-Pennsylvania Negative Income Tax Experiment is a large, statistically significant labor supply withdrawal."

For some a negative labor supply response was thought to be a small price to pay for other expected beneficial consequences of the negative income tax plan. To others, who seemed to place more emphasis on the work ethic, any decrease in labor supply was disastrous. A staff member of the Senate Finance Committee succinctly stated the dilemma:

> Some say −10% [labor supply response] is small. In the Finance Committee it would have been viewed as huge. They are looking for +10%.

In fact, some had expected increased work effort from welfare reform. This belief also had its origin in the FAP period. In fact, the OEO released a report based on very preliminary results of the New Jersey experiment which indicated that the experimental group worked slightly more than the control group.[49] Rhetoric during the Nixon administration had suggested that the FAP would alter incentives to work in such a way that the work effort of welfare recipients would increase. A domestic policy staff analyst presented the argument:

> Across the 1970s the popular idea was that a NIT would produce

an increase in labor supply response. This was based on the talk at the time of FAP and the argument that a NIT would provide smaller marginal tax rates than the current system. So, there should be an improvement over current programs. There would be an increase in net take home pay. The idea was to have the poor work themselves off welfare. The Nixon and FAP rhetoric made this argument—in so many years we will eliminate welfare, and so forth.

Negative and positive normative beliefs regarding labor supply response and the negative income tax in general were often quite intensely held. Thus evaluative judgments interacted with empirical beliefs about labor supply response to strengthen prior conceptions on the acceptability of negative-income-tax-based reforms.

Predispositions to particular reform strategies were critical to participants' reactions to other research findings as well. The Seattle and Denver findings showed a substantial and statistically significant destabilizing effect on families. Treatment families split apart two to three times more often than control group families. Reactions to the finding varied according to prior beliefs. Those who were strong supporters of the negative income tax either rejected the finding outright as an artifact of experimental procedures, something that would not occur with an ongoing national program, or discounted the result of some other basis. Note the reaction of two HEW officials:

I talked with Aaron and Barth and they said the marital stability finding could be a problem. However, they said the results were shaky and not to worry too much. I asked them if they would change the program as a result, and they said no. The findings could have been a problem if they were conclusive, but they weren't. So it was not a real problem.

When I first came to HEW in 1974 the first reports were just coming in. In fact, I was asked to critique the early report. I found the research to be solid as did the conference we called on the issue. It was the best research I have seen in a long time. But prior assumptions—that stability would be promoted—are hard to shake. HEW people would not let go of this assumption.

An early experimental researcher was even more adamant:

> There is a statistically significant finding, but it is not clear that
> it stems from a NIT. With the experiments there was no penalty
> for backing out of a relationship like there is with the present
> system. Yes, there may be some income and independence
> effect, but it is not clear that there is a long term impact like SRI
> says there is. SRI has extrapolated the findings to the middle of
> the Gulf of Mexico. There is no basis for the projections they
> made.

In addition, some of the negative income tax advocates began to
develop evaluative beliefs or to see marital instability as a positive
outcome. A researcher notes this tendency at HEW:

> HEW's attack or approach to critics centered around two ques-
> tions. They would ask, is the result correct and is the result good
> or bad? They argued against release because of the political
> liability and because the result is not really a bad result.

A nongovernmental welfare researcher notes:

> There are unanswered questions about the marital stability find-
> ings. In the final analysis if families break, it is too bad, but so
> what? Do we give up other goals because of this? Come on, there
> is still a real need for equity.

Those who were opposed to the negative income tax either
thought the finding further demonstrated the inadequacy of a negative income tax or, along with some of the negative income tax
supporters, rejected the finding. A negative income tax opponent
notes the serviceability of the finding:

> The marital stability finding was a deathblow if one was needed.
> There is no doubt it had an effect on people's thinking. The
> impact and publicity certainly had impact on those basically
> opposed. It strengthened their position.

An HEW analyst suggests:

> As politicians found out they used it as ammunition somewhat.
> Moynihan was just about the only intellectual on the Hill and he

recognized the finding. His prior belief was affected. The Department of Labor used the finding to justify the inclusion of jobs. It was a powerful argumentative tool in this regard.

Seldom did the marital stability finding alter a persons' value judgment regarding the negative income tax. Together with reactions to the labor supply results, it served to strengthen or intensify prior position.

The general thrust of the influence of receptivity and intensity was thus to promote confirmation of prior beliefs about the negative income tax. Participants were receptive to social science research and had developed beliefs, often intensely held, about labor supply response and the negative income tax. Intense feelings had already developed on both sides of these major issues prior to any examination of policy analysis during the formulation process.

In some belief areas, however, high receptivity, combined with low development and intensity, paved the way for change in belief systems. Some of the most pronounced changes came with beliefs about marital stability, variation in labor supply responses, educational and health effects of a negative income tax, and use of experimental method for policy analysis.

The marital dissolution finding had more than the confirmation effect that I examined above. It did change many people's beliefs. It brought to their attention for the first time the possibility that a destabilizing effect might occur. The following comments are typical of the reactions from individuals who learned or changed belief systems in response to the marital stability finding:

> The experiments alerted me to the family stability problem, but this did not alarm me.

> The research helped me formulate my views. My eyes were opened to the family stability question. It is a tricky issue.

> I was surprised at the marital stability finding. I am more cautious now.

> I should say that I was surprised by the marital stability finding.

The marital stability finding also contributed to the formation of value judgments regarding this consequence. When changes in value judgments occurred, those affected generally tended to see marital instability in a more favorable light. The argument was that, if economic necessity is the only bond holding a family together, it is a good outcome for the family to split apart. Several respondents supported this argument:

> I don't think the marital stability finding should be given much weight. The explanatory theory is cloudy and on a value basis I am not against the result.

> Family stability is not that important. Should we hold families together for economic reasons?

Of course some rejected this argument and found a negative predisposition toward marital instability confirmed by the finding. Nonetheless, the marital stability finding did lead to changes in some dimensions of individual belief systems.

Changes in belief systems occurred beyond those relating to marital stability. Those close to the experiments learned about variations in response across subgroups and were often surprised by the large size of the negative labor supply response among secondary workers. A research participant comments:

> We learned a great deal about different groups. Each group may respond differently to a NIT. In addition, we learned a great deal about income dynamics. They are greater than we thought.

A CBO analyst concurs:

> What bothers most of us, however, is the work response of secondary workers. There was a very high withdrawal—30% to 40%—among housewives. This was higher than we wanted to see.

Large labor supply withdrawal among housewives and secondary workers had generally not been expected. Change in belief systems also occurred regarding program administration. Several respondents made this point:

> We have learned about administrative features of welfare programs that affect targeting, efficiency, etc. These findings have

revolutionized proposals for administrative reform. Monthly reporting is an example.

Remember the kernel of the reform idea: (1) the NIT, (2) simplify the process, and (3) reduce stigma of participation. Two and three are just naive. You can't really accomplish much simplification and stigma cannot be eliminated. There are too many exceptions and problems. It is hard to be humane in the face of cheaters. Welfare reform is extraordinarily complex.

In addition, there were interesting findings regarding family education performance, nutrition and infant birth weight, and various other noneconomic impacts. Some participants thought these were the most important findings:

> I'm more convinced of the importance of noneconomic impacts of the NIT. For example, I'm more concerned about the issue of stigma than I once was.

> We also found that a more generous payment would result in broad based improvement in family life. It would lead to less dependence on welfare. It would lead to investment decisions and so forth. The evidence here is not overwhelming, there are some contradictions, but there is a general trend that supports this conclusion. One of the most dramatic findings was on children's birth weight. This could help break the poverty cycle. Birth weight is an effective indicator of child and adult health.

> There was a significant increase in the weight of children born to some participants. There was also better performance in school by some children. I think these are some of the most important findings of the experiments.

Many of these findings developed or changed belief systems. The findings came in areas where the belief system was undeveloped and beliefs were not intensely held.

Substantial learning about social experimentation also took place. While many participants had prior beliefs confirmed, others seemed to have considerable changes in belief systems. Typical responses follow:

> I think a heck of a lot more time should be given to design

questions. Experiments are more difficult than I thought. The control device is somewhat slippery. Perhaps we tried to do more with ANOVA [analysis of variance] than is possible. The control group is complex in and of itself. We need to understand better what we are up against when we design the next experiments.

We have learned a lot about experimental design. We have developed an entirely new area of research capability.

Experiments are relatively expensive in relation to other types of social research, but not to other types of R and D. We should pursue less expensive methods if they can solve the questions at hand.

A few individuals became somewhat less sure of the value of large-scale social experimentation for use in policy decision. Perhaps their overall receptivity to social science suffered as a result. For the most part, these respondents became aware of the limitations of experimental research:

> I was at OEO early on and was attracted to social experimentation. The negative income tax experiments have made me less enamored with experimentation than I once was. It took millions of dollars to eliminate a small amount of uncertainty on several parameters. It just was not cost effective. And also, there were crucial errors with the early experiments.

> The experiments have influenced my thinking. I am somewhat more negative to experiments than before. Timing is a difficult problem. It is difficult to produce results when they are needed. It is also hard to ask the right questions, to anticipate the political process.

Perhaps one of the more significant shifts in belief systems came in the area of jobs programs. Some of those who had previously opposed such an approach gradually began to see a jobs strategy differently. Typical comments follow:

> The experiments led me to be more sympathetic to a jobs approach. It definitely changed my mind here.

I now think that jobs are more attractive. I have seen what they can do to the income floor. They can have a much stronger effect than a straight NIT.

I now think that work requirements are necessary, whereas before I was against them. So I don't favor a NIT as much as I did before, although I still support it in principle.

It is uncertain just when these changes in thinking among advocates of a negative income tax occurred, but they probably received an assist from the president's decision to go ahead with a combined jobs-and-income plan. Despite the considerable confirmation of prior views the experiments brought about considerable change or development in individual belief systems.

The impact of the analysis on belief systems, then, entailed both confirmation and change. The preconceptions most strongly confirmed involved labor supply response and overall attitudes toward a negative income tax. This important confirmation effect resulted from high value conflict, salient analysis, symbolic use of analysis, and intensely held prior beliefs. Changes in thinking came with less central concerns such as marital stability, variation in labor supply response across subgroups, educational and health impacts, program administration, and the use of experiments for policy analysis. In each of these instances value conflict was less than with central issues, or beliefs were less intense due to lack of development or lack of substantial support for them.

Direct Impact on Decisions

The confirmation impact prevented the analysis from having any significant effect on major program formulation decisions. That is, there was little direct impact on decisions, apart from that relating to a few minor issues, at the formulation stage. The research simply did not change many people's minds on the key issues, which might have had a cumulative effect on decisions. With opposed parties to the conflict each drawing upon the research to support their views and attack their opponents, those less directly involved in the fight gained the impression that the analysis could be of little decision use.

The major features of the PBJI were the result of political decisions made by the president and his advisers, unaffected by the experimental findings. Value conflict prevented the DOL and HEW from reaching agreement on their own. Analysis could not overcome the basic division. The president had made early commitments to a comprehensive program, which combined jobs and cash transfers but spent little additional money. Once overall cost limits had been set and a guarantee level of 65 percent of the poverty line had been reaffirmed, there were few major decisions to be made. Besides some impact on a few details of the PBJI, the analysis exerted little direct effect on decisions.

Legitimation

The analysis did perform a considerable legitimation function, however. As noted above, the analysis was at first used by the DOL and HEW to legitimate their preferred policy alternatives. After the president's May 2 statement of his major principles, which settled in large part the jobs-versus-income controversy, a subtle shift in the legitimation use of the research occurred. Gradually it was suggested that the analysis would support a combined jobs-and-income strategy, whereas it had previously provided grounds for supporting and attacking the two options individually. The proponents of a job strategy may have gained more through legitimation than their main adversaries; if so, this result could have significant implications for future policy. The analysis proved to be quite flexible as a legitimation tool.

Allocation of Value

As the experimental analysis had primarily a legitimation impact at the proposal formulation stage, a particular configuration of interests benefited. Producers of the policy research and analyses, organizational participants who legitimated their ideas and proposals, and classes who secured economic interests all gained through the use of analysis.

Those who conducted the Seattle and Denver experiments and those who performed related analyses gained considerably from the legitimation function that their products served. Additional benefits beyond the substantial gains secured solely from production followed the legitimation outcome. The attention given the analysis as various actors used it to legitimate their positions focused attention on the producers of the analyses. SRI International as the major contractor for the Seattle and Denver experiments benefited the most, whereas organizations central to the three previous experiments received some recognition but much less attention. SRI added to its professional reputation an image of a research organization capable of performing large-scale social experiments. More generally, SRI became known to individuals and organizations for the first time. No doubt some individuals who learned of SRI's capability will request its research services at a later date. The professional reputation of SRI was augmented by the salience of its research effort in the welfare-policy process.

Individual members of the research team also found their professional reputations enhanced as the research they conducted caught the attention of policy participants and other individuals. Those who worked on the marital stability analyses probably benefited the most, as this aspect of the research eventually received the most publicity. Public interest in the researchers' work certainly extended to the disciplines and affected prestige and recognition there. Individual analysts at the DOL, HEW and the CBO also benefited to various degrees as their research was used for legitimation purposes. The operative process was similar to that described for other producer beneficiaries. The attention paid to their work benefits their professional reputation and promotes career advancement. Legitimation use added to the initial producer gains that stemmed solely from production.

A series of organized interests gained from the legitimation use when the proposal was being formulated. The largest beneficiaries were the DOL and those constituents who favored a jobs approach. Individuals who took this position from the beginning rarely changed their minds. In addition, the jobs strategy seemed to gain the most supporters through conversion. For significant numbers of people, the jobs strategy became a legitimate option to the welfare dilemma. It can be argued that the public was already behind such a strategy and that other forces contributed to growing support for work solutions to welfare. Nonetheless, the boost given this trend by the research is unmistakable. Of those interviewed in this study the only ones who changed preferences moved from support of a negative income tax to support of a combined jobs-and-income program, to a straight jobs program, or to some form of work requirements with cash assistance programs.

Although HEW appears to have lost ground in the short term, the experimental analyses served a legitimation function for the negative income tax as well as for a jobs strategy. Many who preferred the negative income tax strategy prior to the research found their beliefs confirmed or intensified as the analysis was used in an attempt to persuade a larger audience. Some of the most favorable findings from the standpoint of the negative income tax advocates—gains in infants' weight at birth, improvements in educational performance, reductions in stigma, and nutritional advances—have received little attention thus far. If and when comprehensive reform of public assistance hits the political agenda again, these findings will have strengthened the position of individuals who favor a negative income tax. If the jobs approach wins immediate policy gains, not everyone on welfare will prove able to work, and it will clearly be difficult and expensive to find or create jobs for those who can do so. Eventually the policy agenda will return to the need to reform cash transfer policy, at least for some groups of aid recipients. When this occurs, the Seattle and Denver experiments will be found to have legitimated policy changes in the direction of a negative income tax. A large comprehensive program may be impossible for a long time, but incremental steps toward that ideal are more likely. The Seattle and Denver experimental findings and the analyses yet to be performed will legitimate arguments for incremental changes toward the negative income tax plan in the future.

Thus far benefits to producer interests and organizational interests stemming from analysis of welfare policy alternatives have been examined. Structural or class interests also gained as a result of policy research, however. I have already examined the tendency for analysis to be constrained in focus and content by social structural forces and thus to limit policy deliberation. The income maintenance experiments and analyses based on them had such a conservative influence. Research and analysis helped channel discussion of reform to alternatives that posed a minimal threat to labor markets and to the distribution of income in the United States.

A negative income tax has the potential to disrupt labor markets critical to advanced capitalism by reducing the availability of labor and by raising its cost. Political objections based on these potential consequences had in part inspired the entire experimental effort. A ready supply of low-cost labor is vital to the economic health of producers of goods and services, particularly those that face strong foreign competition. In addition, other things being equal, it is in the interest of employers to secure labor as cheaply as possible; the lower the price paid to labor, the greater the economic gain to employers. A negative income tax threatens labor markets, as it provides workers an alternative means of subsistence that could lure them away from employment. Labor market disruption varies with the attractiveness of the income maintenance alternative to work, which depends on the income guarantee level, marginal tax rates, and work provisions. If the guarantee makes nonwork or leisure appear too favorable, the pool of labor necessary for production is threatened. If there are no policy provisions that force people to work, workers will be tempted to collect the guaranteed income. In addition, as leisure along with a guaranteed income becomes relatively attractive in comparison to work, upward pressure on wages is generated as the supply of labor decreases. Employers are forced to pay higher wages to secure the required work force, and in the end profitability is reduced.

The overall force of the income maintenance analysis was to focus attention and limit policy deliberation to alternatives that posed little substantial threat to dominant economic classes. This result is somewhat ironic, however, as the experiments contained the seeds of more substantial and threatening change. SIME/DIME considered alternative income-guarantee levels of thirty-eight hundred dollars, forty-eight hundred dollars, and fifty-six hundred dollars for a family of four in 1972 dollars (92 percent, 116 percent, and 135 percent of the poverty line, respectively). By the time the PBJI was drafted, the guarantee level had reverted to 65 percent of the poverty line, or forty-two hundred dollars in 1978 dollars for the same family of four. Thus the experiments were considerably more generous than the final policy proposal. What led a relatively generous policy alternative to shrink to such a minimal level? The experiments provided the seeds of their own undoing. Labor supply response find-ings indicated that the relatively generous program configurations would be very costly within a national program. A negative income tax with a guarantee at 100 percent of the poverty line in 1975 and a 50 percent tax rate on earned income was found to cost $27.61 billion more than the current system.[50] A zero- or lesser-cost plan could be crafted by substantially reducing the guarantee, increasing the tax rate, or adding work requirements. The PBJI incorporated a reduced income guarantee and work requirements. The experiments pushed discussion away from relatively generous alternatives that ran coun-ter to structural interests in stable labor markets and income dis-tribution to the rather meager benefit level of the PBJI. This scaled-down proposal still could not gather sufficient political support to move very far within Congress. Analysis thus aided conservative interests and contributed to the preservation of the status quo.

7   Whither Policy Analysis?

✳

In chapters 1–6 we took a careful look at policy analysis and governmental decision making. My first objective was to describe and explain the impact of policy analysis on a series of events that make up the governing process. A second objective was to consider the policy implications of the research findings. National policy for policy analysis funding is at best fragmented, often ambiguous, and, even in some quarters where it should be otherwise, nonexistent. Research funding policies of various quality and sponsors grappling with policy making for policy analysis can nonetheless be found. This chapter examines the policy implications of the explanation developed and illustrated in the previous chapters. It should be remembered that the explanation is untested and may later be wholly or partly falsified. The discussion that follows assumes that it accurately reflects reality. Policy implications generally raise normative issues or matters of value judgment. A few of these hard questions are also explored. I comment on the future of research on the impact of analysis to end the chapter.

Policy Implications for Policy Analysis

The explanation of the impact of policy analysis presented in chapter 4 raises a series of issues that the public and policy makers in advanced capitalist societies must consider. It related variations in the impact of policy analysis on decision processes, belief systems, policy outputs, and interests served to each other and to important mediating conditions, value conflict, and prior beliefs. The explanation can assist individuals who must decide when to fund policy analyses in their efforts to understand the consequences of their actions. The explanation tells the policy maker what analysis can and what it cannot do—that is, it generates expectations of the impact of funding policy analysis under a range of circumstances. The projected impacts can be compared with the purposes that the policy maker wants the analysis to serve and can thereby assist policy making. The public may also want to consider the ends to which their tax dollars are put.

The explanation emphasized the critical influence of value conflict and prior belief systems on the impact of policy analysis. Before the policy maker can reasonably and accurately anticipate the impact of producing and disseminating analysis, the level of value conflict and prior beliefs of policy participants and attentive individuals must be known to some extent. The difficulty in obtaining this information will vary with the issue area and the policy-participant audience. In some cases answers need not be precise and are easy to come by. In 1966, for example, staff members at the OEO had little doubt that welfare policy was a high value-conflict area. If they had understood the impact of policy analysis, they would have seen the futility of their political strategy of experimentation. Surveys and everyday experiences of welfare policy officials reflect the high conflict. In addition, it was not difficult to discern developed beliefs about labor supply response. With other issues it may be much more difficult to ascertain the nature of the mediating conditions. Still, they can be measured through surveys of the general population and of the subset of policy participants. The costs of the surveys are justified when millions of dollars' worth in policy analysis contracts are being considered. When small-scale analyses are being considered, it is less advisable to undertake the expense of surveys prior to research funding. Nonetheless, value conflict and the belief systems of policy participants must be considered when the consequences of funding policy analysis are being projected.

The most significant lesson to be learned from the explanation is that analysis should not be funded for short-term policy-making purposes in high value-conflict issue areas where belief systems of policy participants are highly developed. Analysis will not affect

decisions under these circumstances. There will be more confirmation or intensification of prior beliefs than changes in or development of belief systems. Policy coalitions will form nearly as they
would without the introduction of analysis. The policy output will
reflect the strength of the various parties to the conflict and will be
unaffected by the analysis.

The capacity of analysis to influence decisions may be severely
limited. There is a certain amount of value conflict regarding all
public issues. It might even be suggested that most public issues are
high-conflict issues. The extent to which there is variation in conflict needs to be examined. The analysis has oversimplified the discussion by referring to either high or low value-conflict situations
when a continuum of value conflict would have been more accurate.
Empirical research can determine the levels of value conflict that are
critical for decision impact.

It may, however, be advisable to undertake policy analysis when
value conflict is high if the objectives are other than short-term influence on policy output. The negative income tax experiments showed
that analysis can contribute to belief development even in high
value-conflict situations. Unexpected findings and findings in areas
where belief systems are undeveloped are often unintended consequences of analysis. Belief development may thus result. In addition, a subset of the attentive audience with developed belief
systems may score low on intensity. These individuals are prone to
changing or developing belief systems in response to policy analysis.
Learning can still occur, then, although it is unlikely to affect immediate decisions. The learning that does occur in these situations may
be highly valued in and of itself, and it may justify the expenditure
of scarce resources on the analysis. It may also have long-term policy
impact by influencing thinking about social problems or by altering
the level of value conflict in the long term.

A great deal has been said about the benefits that accrue to
policy analysts and to the social science community from participation in the production of policy analysis. These benefits flow in high
as well as low value-conflict situations. This result may be viewed
favorably or unfavorably. Individually it is a matter of value judgment. Collectively it is a political decision. Social scientists are certainly not at the top of the list of beneficiaries of government

expenditure, although a few of them do very well. It can be argued, however, that the benefits that accrue to policy analysts and their organizations help improve the capacity to produce effective analysis in the future. Yet it must be admitted that the extent to which these benefits contribute to improved capacity for effective analysis is unclear. Policy analysis is a fledgling attempt to apply scientific technique to practical problems, to people's attempt to cope with each other and the physical environment. At this point in the effort, policy analysis is long on promise and short on performance. If society thinks the potential of analysis is considerable, research in high value-conflict situations may be justified by the contribution made to developing analysis capacity as well as by additional learning or long-term policy impact that may occur.

The converse of the first lesson of this research is that policy analysis can have direct impact on decisions in low value-conflict issue areas. When there is agreement on policy objectives, analysis can take on a technical focus and examine the effectiveness and efficiency of alternative means of achieving agreed-upon ends. In this respect analysis can improve the quality of policy and program performance. The byproducts of analysis production, development of belief systems or knowledge and improved production capacity, are also likely to follow the production of analysis in low value-conlict situations. Analysis here serves collective interests as it advances or contributes to the achievement of widely shared policy objectives.

An implication of direct impact on decisions in low value-conflict situations is that in some cases policy analysis may be fruitfully employed in established public agencies. When public programs involve low-conflict issue areas, policy analysis can be effectively used for program decision making. Ongoing programs involve low value-conflict issue areas to probably only a limited extent, but it is possible through further research to determine which policies and programs involve the lowest levels of value conflict. Policy analysis and program evaluation may be useful decision input in these situations. Current program or policy efforts can be evaluated and alternative mechanisms analyzed. When low conflict exists in particular program areas, advantages follow from analysis tied to ongoing program efforts. The Hawthorne effect of social experimentation is reduced as analysis occurs within the context of actual programs. There is less of a tendency for participants to perceive themselves as part of a temporary experimental process. Analysis is therefore likely to be more effective and to represent more accurately the process and impact of real programs. A secondary result is that a major critique of experiments is eliminated. Critics can no longer make warranted assertions that the analysis examines an artificial process. They can no longer charge that the findings of analysis do not apply to real programs.

Hard Questions?

Policy decisions often involve complex normative issues or value judgments, especially as the action guided by policy results in a diverse set of consequences or impacts. Value judgments involve assessments of the sets of consequences that follow alternative actions. Inaction is always one of these potential alternatives. Policy makers who wish to make reasoned choices must compare the sets of consequences that follow viable alternative policies and actions. Decisions to fund or produce policy analysis may be of little consequence if they entail small-scale efforts. General policies for funding analysis or for undertaking large projects such as the negative income tax experiments are another matter. As this research suggests, significant consequences follow large-scale analytic efforts. It is beyond the capacity of this research to examine fully the myriad normative issues raised by the developed explanation. An undertaking of this magnitude would require a lengthy book. Limitations of space make it possible for me here to consider briefly only a few significant normative questions that a full exposition would necessarily consider in detail. My aim here is solely to provoke thought about critical issues.

It has been suggested that the dissemination of policy analysis involving high value-conflict issue areas may confirm or intensify opposed beliefs and changes or may develop belief systems. These consequences occur with different groups and depend on their prior beliefs. The confirmation or intensification of opposed beliefs, however, is generally more frequent in the high-conflict context than the development or change that occurs with other individuals. The normative question is whether or not the gains in knowledge outweigh the negative consequences of polarization in belief systems. This question is not easy to resolve. Those who value learning and the development of beliefs or knowledge highly would probably prefer to accept this trade-off and would fund policy analysis in high-conflict situations. Those who are greatly concerned about the polarization of social groups and its potential consequence for societal stability would not consider the increments of knowledge worth the projected long-term cost.

There is also the issue of support for the social science and policy analysis communities and what may be considered the trade-off involved. Are the gains in knowledge and analytic capacity worth an obvious loss of autonomy for the scientists and analysts as well as the polarization effect noted above in high value-conflict situations? Social science knowledge may be highly valued but should nonetheless be considered as only one of various consequences that flow from support channeled through the mechanism of policy analysis. Autonomy and academic freedom are highly valued by many scientists. They are ignored by others. They are often viewed as requisites of scientific activity, although it is uncertain to what extent this is true. There have been scientific achievements in social systems where autonomy and freedom are lacking (for example, Nazi Germany and the Soviet Union). To what extent can autonomy be diminished while science is maintained? To what extent has autonomy already been compromised? To what extent can autonomy be maintained within a framework of policy-analytic activity? The normative questions raised necessarily open up additional empirical issues that are unsettled. The trade-off involving support for research and autonomy is, nonetheless, a significant issue.

With low value-conflict situations, similar normative issues arise. Are the expected gains in program performance with program evaluation, in terms of effectiveness and efficiency, worth the allocation of scarce resources to policy analysis? Do these efforts threaten scientific autonomy to the same extent as support for analysis in high value-conflict situations?

Perhaps the most fundamental normative issue concerns the legitimation of policy positions of dominant economic and other interests in advanced capitalist societies that flows from much of the analysis conducted. To what extent can this be obviated? To what extent should it be prevented? Is this a consequence that the society wishes to promote? To those who accept the current political-economic system, legitimation of dominant classes and interests is surely an acceptable consequence among the many that flow from the production of policy analysis and is not a cause for alarm. To those who think otherwise, the price of stabilization of a political-economic system that they disapprove is often considered much greater than any consequence of policy analysis that they may view favorably. Those who criticize policy analysis for its legitimation function in effect are denouncing policy analysis in the context of advanced capitalist societies rather than policy analysis per se. Within a different social structure, legitimation may be entirely acceptable to critics of analysis in the current context of advanced capitalism. Should policy analysis be continued if a major consequence is to support the inequities of advanced capitalist societies?

Future Research

A series of normative issues and additional empirical questions have been raised. While several points of view have been expressed, no attempt at reasoned answers to these difficult matters has been undertaken. These normative issues are worthy of detailed exploration. A careful analysis would contribute to future public discussion and perhaps to policy deliberations. For these reasons alone these questions warrant further consideration. Many of the questions, however, hinge on the accuracy of the analysis undertaken in this research. Empirical research to make such determinations is, therefore, required. Several avenues for future research are examined.

The overall explanation deserves a rigorous empirical test in the United States. We need to develop ways of making the concepts operational. While this task has not been undertaken here, I have formulated concepts with measurement considerations in mind. Several different approaches are available for testing the overall framework. Either a series of case studies that examine the sequential impact process under different combinations of mediating conditions (value conflict and belief systems) or comparative study that includes a range of mediating conditions is required. As I have already suggested, the decision regarding the approach to be pursued depends on practical considerations, the relative time and expense involved in comparative and case study, and the availability of a suitable case or cases for examination. Either approach provides a basis for testing or attempting to falsify the overall theoretical structure.

In addition, it would be useful to test the explanation in other advanced capitalist societies. The theory may also be fruitfully applied to subnational governments in any of these societies or to decision processes in corporate enterprises.

When it is not possible to undertake projects of the magnitude that I suggested above, analysis of individual hypotheses or sets of hypotheses would also contribute to an assessment of the empirical adequacy of the overall framework. It should prove useful, for example, to examine the production of policy analysis and test the hypotheses relating value conflict and interests served to production. Content analysis of policy analyses could be used to determine the types of analyses that are undertaken and the interests represented by these efforts. The research might also examine the effect of value conflict in particular issue areas on the focus and content of the analytic products. A series of issues that vary in terms of value conflict would help us assess the hypotheses relating value conflict to production. This example focuses on the initial events in the causal sequence that the explanation details. Comparable opportunities for research lie at each stage of the process. Much research needs to be done to adequately assess the explanation and to develop it further.

8 Postscript

✳

The Program for Better Jobs and Income Flounders in Congress

The Carter administration's PBJI lacked enough political support to do more than clear the lowest hurdle in the House of Representatives, the Special Welfare Reform Subcommittee. Chairmen of key committees, Congressman Al Ullman of the Committee on Ways and Means, and Senator Russell B. Long of the Senate Finance Committee, both opposed the proposal. Additional chairmen in the House, Thomas S. Foley of the Agriculture Committee and Carl D. Perkins of the Labor and Education Committee, were not supportive either. Because the PBJI affected food stamps, jobs programs, and tax provisions, it had to clear all three of the House committees mentioned: Ways and Means, Agriculture, and Labor and Education. During special subcommittee deliberations Chairman Ullman noted:

> The administration has fallen into an old trap. . . . It is convinced we can make poor Americans happy and secure by giving them a guaranteed annual income based on family size and income. To accept that concept is to perpetuate the "welfare syndrome." I don't think there is the time or the climate in Congress to push through a massive all-or-nothing welfare program this year.[1]

After casting a negative vote on the PBJI in the special subcommittee, Agriculture chairman Foley suggested that the bill that cleared the committee "cannot pass the Congress or the House in anything like its present form."[2] Senator Long and Congressman Ullman each had alternative ideas about the proper way to reform welfare. Senator Long can be a formidable opponent for any president. Opposition to the PBJI, however, was broader than a discussion focused on powerful chairmen indicates.

There was little support for spending $20 billion to raise benefits for public assistance recipients and to add families to the assistance rolls (even if some are eliminated as they would have been with the PBJI). Public opinion surveys indicate that a considerable proportion of the public wants to reduce spending and shrink the welfare rolls. The public also wants welfare recipients to go to work but is unwilling to support expenditures necessary to subsidize jobs in industry or to create public service jobs. Given the public sentiment, it is not surprising that the Congress halted before spending large sums of money on welfare reform.

The president's relationship with the Congress and his lack of political acumen did not help the PBJI. The White House's difficulty in establishing effective relations with the Congress is well known and need not be documented here. Several crucial presidential decisions, commissions, and omissions warrant consideration, however. First, the president wanted a comprehensive proposal that would consolidate established programs: food stamps, supplemental security income, and AFDC (Medicaid was left for the national health insurance legislation). This idea made passage of any related legislation most difficult. By combining programs in a single bill, the administration automatically involved a number of standing committees in each chamber. The president was advised of the difficulty of comprehensive welfare reform but still chose to take this route. Second, the administration proceeded to formulate a bill but did not closely consult with Senator Long and Congressman Ullman. This was a grave error. The White House must have thought that these chairmen could be brought around to an administration bill at the legislative stage. It would have been possible to do so with some reform packages, but it should have been clear that it would be most difficult with the type of proposal the administration was assembling. Senator Long's and Congressman Ullman's views of welfare reform were on record. Perhaps the administration thought that Chairman Ullman would come around and they would take their chances in conference committee with an undoubtedly very different Senate bill. Early signals of opposition from these key chairmen did not receive the attention they deserved. Third, the decision to let HEW and the DOL fight a jobs-versus-cash-transfer battle for five months, when a combined program had been decided upon from the outset, was clearly counterproductive. The bureaucratic turf battle dampened departmental support for the legislation. In addition, the bureaucratic squabble led to a more expensive bill. As HEW won more funds for cash transfers from the White House, the DOL sought to make the jobs component more attractive, and thus the bill grew increasingly expensive. In the end neither department could support the proposal wholeheartedly. It was not a bill for which either agency worked tirelessly. Finally, the president placed several major issues on the congressional agenda—welfare, taxes, national health insurance, and energy—at the same time. Most of this legislation had to be considered in whole or in part by the Senate Finance Committee and the House Committee on Ways and Means. The list of legislation was too long and too politically volatile to push through the Congress barring a domestic crisis atmosphere. Enough legislation to keep many sessions of Congress busy reached the ninety-sixth Congress at more or less one moment in time.

In early 1978 the president began to realize that he had to establish priorities; he could not have all the legislation he wanted. Welfare reform dropped from the president's list of priorities. The bill had probably already died when an appropriation for it was not included in the fiscal year 1979 budget early in 1978, and when the president had eliminated it from a list of priority legislation given to Speaker O'Neill in early 1978. Major welfare reform may have been achievable in 1977 or 1978, although it would certainly have been difficult under the best of circumstances. The president and his administration turned a difficult task, passage of welfare legislation, into an impossible assignment.

The PBJI did, however, pass the Special House Welfare Reform Subcommittee chaired by Congressman James C. Corman (Democrat, California) on February 8, 1978, by a vote of 23 to 6.[3] The efforts by the chairman were more responsible for reporting the bill out of subcommittee than any favorable shift in thinking as a result of the experimental findings or policy analysis. Congressman Corman strongly favored increased benefits to recipients and reduction of inequities across states. These commitments he made prior to exposure to the policy analysis input. The analysis played little part in his support of these objectives and in his support of the PBJI. Those who supported the bill in the special subcommittee ran little risk of political damage. It was clear to those involved that the legislation would not travel further in the legislative process. Indeed, none of the three standing committees in the House with jurisdiction over the bill formally took it under consideration. Chairman Ullman's inclination not to do so was clear from the beginning. In fact, his response during special subcommittee deliberation was to offer a considerably different piece of legislation of his own. As the special subcommittee rejected his proposal by a narrow margin of thirteen to sixteen, the opposing parties locked in a stalemate position. The program for better jobs and income was dead in the House. Meanwhile, Senator Long was unwilling to take up the bill in the Senate and extend its life. The House was not moving, and the proposal was much too different from his conception of what welfare reform should be.

The negative coalition that thwarted the president's proposal found plenty of ammunition in the policy analysis input to make its inclinations legitimate. The projected cost of the bill, which HEW worked feverishly to estimate and then argued about at length with the CBO, was all the justification anyone needed. The negative labor supply response could certainly have been invoked to justify inaction if it was needed. The marital stability finding could have been used to deal a crushing blow if by some quirk the fight remained close. There was not much need to use the research to support rejection of the PBJI, however. There was so little support for improving the material conditions of welfare recipients and of the working poor that opponents felt little pressure to justify their position. Still, the analysis legitimized inaction. It demonstrated the potentially high political costs of supporting the PBJI when Congressmen had little reason to do so. Inasmuch as support for the legislation was minimal, there was no need to bandy about policy analysis that was regarded by many as damaging in order to justify the decision not to take positive legislative action.

Notes   Bibliography   Index

Notes

1 Introduction

1 "Policy research" is generally defined more broadly than "policy analysis." It denotes the use of scientific methods to examine a broad range of empirical and normative questions related to public policies. "Policy analysis" focuses on the impact of established or proposed policies on members of society. I use "analysis" and "research" here synonymously.

2 For a detailed discussion of this concept of policy and its implications, see Eugene J. Meehan, "Science, Values, and Politics," *American Behavioral Scientist* 17 (September–October 1973):53–100.

3 For further exploration of this line of thought, see Sanford A. Lakoff, "The Third Culture: Science in Social Thought," in *Knowledge and Power: Essays on Science and Government*, ed. Sanford A. Lakoff (New York: Free Press, 1966), pp. 7–10.

4 Ibid., pp. 14–19.

5 Mary O. Furner, *Advocacy and Objectivity: A Crisis in the Professionalization of American Social Science, 1865–1905* (Lexington: University of Kentucky Press, 1975), pp. 1–7.

6 Ibid., pp. 8–9.

7 David M. Ricci argues that the discipline of political science suffers from long-standing contradictory pursuits—development as a scientific community and promotion of democracy. See *The Tragedy of Political Science: Politics, Scholarship, and Democracy* (New Haven: Yale University Press, 1984).

8 A noted example is John Kenneth Galbraith, whose writing may receive greater attention from lay audiences than from his fellow economists. Of his many publications, see, for example, the *Affluent Society* (New York: New American Library, 1958).

9 Gene M. Lyons, *The Uneasy Partnership: Social Science and the Federal Government in the Twentieth Century* (New York: Russell Sage Foundation, 1969), pp. 27–31.

10 Robert A. Scott and Arnold R. Shore, *Why Sociology Does Not Apply: A Study of the Use of Sociology in Public Policy* (New York: Elsevier, 1979), pp. 115–118.

11 Lyons, *The Uneasy Partnership*, pp. 27–31.

12 Ibid., pp. 27–43.

13 Ibid., pp. 47–49.

14 Ibid., pp. 53–54.

15 Ibid., pp. 64–75.

16 Robert S. Lynd, *Knowledge for What?* (Princeton, N.J.: Princeton University Press, 1939).

17 Lyons, *The Uneasy Partnership*, pp. 77–78.

18 Ibid., p. 99.

19 Ibid., pp. 91–123.

20 Ibid., pp. 81–82.

21 For a concise summary of recent changes in university research production, see Raymond G. Hunt, "The University Social Research Center: Its Role in the Knowledge-Making Process," *Knowledge: Creation, Diffusion, Utilization* 2 (September 1980):77–92. For more general discussions of the tension and conflict that developed between science and government, see Don K. Price, *The Scientific Estate* (Cambridge, Mass.: Harvard University Press, 1965); Daniel S. Greenberg, *The Politics of Pure Science* (New York: New American Library, 1967); and James L. Penick, Jr., Carroll W. Pursell, Jr., Morgan B. Sherwood, and Donald C. Swain, eds., *The Politics of American Science, 1939 to the Present*, rev. ed. (Cambridge, Mass.: M.I.T. Press, 1972).

22 See, for example, Penick et al., *The Politics of American Science*, pp. 14–34.

23 Lyons, *The Uneasy Partnership*, pp. 126–130.

24 Penick et al., *The Politics of American Science*, pp. 22–27.

25 Fritz Machlup, *The Production and Distribution of Knowledge in the United States* (Princeton, N.J.: Princeton University Press, 1962), pp. 370–374.

26 Ibid., p. 396.

27 Penick et al., *The Politics of American Science*, pp. 38–41.

28 Lyons, *the Uneasy Partnership*, pp. 146–160.

29 Ibid., pp. 234–240.

30 Abraham L. Davis, *The United States Supreme Court and the Uses of Social Science Data* (New York: MSS Information, 1973).

31 See, for example, Lauriston King and Philip Melanson, "Knowledge and Politics: Some Lessons from the 1960s," *Public Policy* 20 (1972):83–101; and Daniel P. Moynihan, *Maximum Feasible Misunderstanding* (New York: Free Press, 1969).

32 Henry J. Aaron, for example, contends that commitments to direct national policy at social problems during the 1960s led or preceded reliable social research rather than following it; see *Politics and the Professors: The Great Society in Perspective* (Washington, D.C.: Brookings Institution, 1978).

33 Richard J. Barber, *The Politics of Research* (Washington, D.C.: Public Affairs Press, 1966), p. 45.

34 Irving Louis Horowitz and James Everett Katz, *Social Science and Public Policy in the United States* (New York: Praeger, 1975), pp. 6–8.

35 Lyons, *The Uneasy Partnership*, p. 274.

36 U.S., National Research Council, *The Federal Investment in Knowledge of Social Problems*, Final Report, vol. 1, Study Project on Social Research and Development (Washington, D.C.: National Academy of Sciences, 1978), p. 2.

37 Paul F. Lazarsfeld and Jeffrey G. Reitz, *An Introduction to Applied Sociology* (New York: Elsevier, 1975), p. 25.

38 Carol H. Weiss, "Utilization of Evaluation: Toward Comparative Study," in *Evaluating Action Programs: Readings in Social Action and Education*, ed. Carol H. Weiss (Boston: Allyn & Bacon, 1972), pp. 318–326.

39 U.S., National Research Council, *The Behavioral Sciences and the Federal Government*, Advisory Committee on Government Programs in the Behavioral Sciences (Washington, D.C.: National Academy of Sciences, 1968); U.S., National Research Council and Social Science Research Council, *The Behavioral and Social Sciences: Outlook and Needs*, Behavioral and Social Sciences Survey Committee (Washington, D.C.: National Academy of Sciences, 1969); and U.S., National Science Foundation, *Knowledge Into Action: Improving the Nation's Use of the Social Sciences* (Washington, D.C.: Government Printing Office, 1969). For a summary of these reports, see Lazarsfeld and Reitz, *An Introduction to Applied Sociology*, pp. 15–16.

40 Stephen Toulmin, "From Form to Function: Philosophy and History of Science in the 1950s and Now," *Daedalus* 106 (Summer 1977):143–162.

41 Seymour J. Deitchman, *The Best-Laid Schemes: A Tale of Social Research and Bureaucracy* (Cambridge, Mass.: M.I.T. Press, 1976), p. 273.

42 Ibid., pp. 255–267.

43 Lyons, *the Uneasy Partnership*, pp. 289–294.

44 Deitchman, *The Best-Laid Schemes*, pp. 420–423.

45 Carol H. Weiss, "The Politicization of Evaluation Research," in *Evaluating Action Programs: Readings in Social Action and Education*, ed. Carol H. Weiss (Boston: Allyn & Bacon, 1972), p. 327.

46 Laurence E. Lynn, Jr., ed., *Knowledge and Policy: The Uncertain Connection*, Final Report, Study Project on Social Research and Development, National Research Council (Washington, D.C.: National Academy of Sciences, 1978), pp. 1–2.

47 For an interesting discussion of this use of social research, see Alice M. Rivlin, "Forensic Social Science," *Harvard Educational Review* 43 (February 1973): 61–75.

2   Toward an Explanation of the Impact of Policy Analysis

1 The "sociology of knowledge application" label stems from Burkart Holzner, "The Sociology of Applied Knowledge," *Sociological Symposium* 21 (1978):8–19. Carol H. Weiss and Michael J. Bucuvalas also suggest that research should focus on the sociology of knowledge application, in *Social Science Research and Decision-Making* (New York: Columbia University Press, 1980), p. 4. For summaries of the field, see Janice M. Beyer and Harrison M. Trice, "The Utilization Process: A

Conceptual Framework and Synthesis of Empirical Findings," *Administrative Science Quarterly* 27 (December 1982):591–622; Laura C. Leviton and Edward F. X. Hughes, "Research on the Utilization of Evaluations," *Evaluation Review* 5 (August 1981):525–548; and Edward M. Glaser, Harold H. Abelson, and Kathalee Garrison, *Putting Knowledge to Use: Facilitating the Diffusion of Knowledge and the Implementation of Planned Change* (San Francisco: Jossey-Bass, 1983). Also see Robert F. Rich, "The Pursuit of Knowledge," *Knowledge: Creation, Diffusion, Utilization* 1 (September 1979):19.

2   For discussion of conceptual and measurement issues involving utilization, see Judith K. Larsen, "Knowledge Utilization: What Is It?" *Knowledge: Creation, Diffusion, Utilization* 1 (March 1980):441–442; James A. Ciarlo, ed. *Utilizing Evaluation: Concepts and Measurement Techniques* (Beverly Hills, Calif.: Sage, 1981); and William N. Dunn, "Measuring Knowledge Use," *Knowledge: Creation, Diffusion, Utilization* 5 (September 1983):120–133; Nathan Caplan, Andrea Morrison, and R. Stambaugh, *The Use of Social Science Knowledge in Policy Decisions at the National Level* (Ann Arbor, Mich.: Institute for Social Research, 1975), p. xii; Beverly Russell and Arnold Shore, "Limitations on the Governmental Use of Social Science," *Minerva* 14 (Winter 1976):476.

3   Weiss amd Bucuvalas, *Social Science Research*, p. 10.

4   Caplan, Morrison, and Stambaugh, *The Use of Social Science Knowledge*, p. 4; Joseph R. Gusfield, "The (F)Utility of Knowledge? The Relation of Social Science to Public Policy Toward Drugs," *Annals, American Academy of Political and Social Science* 417 (January 1975):15; Robert A. Scott and Arnold R. Shore, *Why Sociology Does Not Apply: A Study of the Use of Sociology in Public Policy* (New York: Elsevier, 1979), pp. 189, 23–26.

5   Gene M. Lyons, *The Uneasy Partnership: Social Science and the Federal Government in the Twentieth Century* (New York: Russell Sage Foundation, 1969), pp. 58–61.

6   Irving Louis Horowitz and James Everett Katz, *Social Science and Public Policy in the United States* (New York: Praeger, 1975), pp. 43–46; Bruce L. R. Smith, *The Rand Corporation: Case Study of a Nonprofit Advisory Corporation* (Cambridge, Mass.: M.I.T. Press, 1966), pp. 229–237; Daniel P. Moynihan, *Maximum Feasible Misunderstanding* (New York: Free Press, 1969), pp. 170–195; Lois-ellin Datta, "The Impact of the Westinghouse/Ohio Evaluation on the Development of Project Head Start: An Examination of the Immediate and Longer-Term Effects and How They Came About," in *The Evaluation of Social Programs*, ed. Clark C. Abt (Beverly Hills, Calif.: Sage, 1976), pp. 142–144; Walter Williams, *Social Policy Research and Analysis: The Experience in the Federal Social Agencies* (New York: American Elsevier, 1971), p. 189; Russell and Shore, "Limitations on the Government Use of Social Science," p. 483.

7   Thomas D. Cook, Judith Levinson-Rose, and William E. Pollard fail to define "misutilization" but cite examples such as use to postpone action, to make programs appear as effective as possible, or purposeful generation of inaccurate findings and biased dissemination, "The Misutilization of Evaluation Research:

Some Pitfalls of Definition," *Knowledge: Creation, Diffusion, Utilization* 1 (June 1980):477–498.

8 Joel Primack and Frank von Hippel, *Advice and Dissent: Scientists in the Political Arena* (New York: Basic Books, 1974), p. 4; Ida R. Hoos, "Systems Techniques for Managing Society: A Critique," *Public Administration Review* 33 (March–April 1973):158; Henry J. Aaron, *Politics and the Professors: The Great Society in Perspective* (Washington, D.C.: Brookings Institution, 1978), p. 32 (quoted); David Mechanic, "Evaluation in Alcohol, Drug Abuse, and Mental Health Programs: Problems and Prospects," in *Program Evaluation: Alcohol, Drug Abuse, and Mental Health Services*, ed. Jack Zusman and Cecil R. Wurster (Lexington, Mass.: D.C. Heath, 1975), p. 7.

9 Michael Quinn Patton, *Utilization-Focused Evaluation* (Beverly Hills, Calif.: Sage, 1978), p. 35; Dorothy Nelkin, "Scientific Knowledge, Public Policy, and Democracy: A Review Essay," *Knowledge: Creation, Diffusion, Utilization* 1 (September 1979):118. Scientific method and logic provide little guarantee that research findings and conclusions are free from political assumptions or reflections of those who produce them. See, for example, Barry Barnes, "On the Implications of a Body of Knowledge," *Knowledge, Creation, Diffusion, Utilization* 4 (September 1982):95–110, or his earlier *Interests and the Growth of Knowledge* (London: Routledge & Kegan Paul, 1977).

10 Charles E. Lindblom and David K. Cohen, *Usable Knowledge: Social Science and Social Problem Solving* (New Haven, Conn.: Yale University Press, 1979), pp. 82–83; Scott and Shore, *Why Sociology Does Not Apply*, p. 194; Murray B. Meld, "The Politics of Evaluation of Social Programs," *Social Work* 19 (July 1974):452; Lauriston King and Philip Melanson, "Knowledge and Politics: Some Lessons from the 1960s," *Public Policy* 20 (Winter 1972):89; Weiss and Bucuvalas, *Social Science Research*, p. 165; Horowtiz and Katz, *Social Science and Public Policy*, p. 127; Russell and Shore, "Limitations on the Government Use of Social Science," pp. 479–480.

11 For relatively early discussions of the impact of analysis on belief systems, see Elisabeth T. Crawford and Albert D. Biderman, eds., *Social Scientists and International Affairs* (New York: John Wiley, 1969); and Morris Janowitz, "Sociological Models and Social Policy," in *Political Conflict: Essays in Political Sociology*, ed. Morris Janowitz (Chicago: Quadrangle, 1979). See, for example, Carol H. Weiss, "Research for Policy's Sake: The Enlightenment Function of Social Research," *Policy Analysis* 3 (Fall 1977):531–545. Weiss and Bucuvalas, *Social Science Research*, pp. 12, 172, 268, 269.

12 Scott and Shore, *Why Sociology Does Not Apply*, p 38; Lindblom and Cohen, *Usable Knowledge*, pp. 5–6; Caplan, Morrison, and Stambaugh, *The Use of Social Science Knowledge*, pp. 38–39; Bruce L. R. Smith, *The Rand Corporation: Case Study of a Nonprofit Advisory Corporation* (Cambridge, Mass.: Harvard University Press, 1966), p. 230; Aaron Wildavsky, *Speaking Truth to Power: The Art and Craft of Policy Analysis* (Boston: Little, Brown, 1979), p. 126; *Utilization-Focused Evaluation*, p. 30; Marvin C. Alkin, Richard Daillak, and Peter White,

Using Evaluations: Does Evaluation Make a Difference? (Beverly Hills, Calif.: Sage, 1979), p. 225; Datta, "The Impact of Evaluation on Head Start," p. 161; Aaron, *Politics and the Professors*, p. 16.

13 Murray Edelman, *Political Language: Words That Succeed and Policies That Fail* (New York: Academic Press, 1977), p. 144; Larry D. Spence, *The Politics of Social Knowledge* (University Park, Pa.: Pennsylvania State University Press, 1978), p. 6.

14 Herbert Blumer, "Threats from Agency-Determined Research," in *The Rise and Fall of Project Camelot: Studies in the Relationship between Social Science and Practical Politics*, rev. ed., ed. Irving Louis Horowitz (Cambridge, Mass.: M.I.T. Press, 1974), p. 168.

15 Charles E. Lindblom, *The Policy-Making Process*, 2d ed. (Englewood Cliffs, N.J.: Prentice-Hall, 1980), p. 16; Marc J. Roberts, "On the Nature and Condition of Social Science," *Daedalus* 103 (Summer 1974):49.

16 Laurence E. Lynn, Jr., "Insights and Lessons," in *Studies in the Management of Social R & D: Selected Policy Areas*, ed. Laurence E. Lynn, Jr., Final Report, vol. 3, Study Project on Social Research and Development, National Research Council (Washington, D.C.: National Academy of Sciences, 1979), p. 205.

17 Lee Rainwater and William L. Yancey, *the Moynihan Report and the Politics of Controversy* (Cambridge, Mass.: M.I.T. Press, 1967), p. xi; Ralph L. Beals, *Politics of Social Research: An Inquiry into the Ethics and Responsibilities of Social Scientists* (Chicago: Aldine, 1969), p. 3. Richard J. Barber argues that government money for university research, particularly in the physical sciences, has constricted academic freedom (*The Politics of Research* [Washington, D.C.: Public Affairs Press, 1966], p. 60). Also see Blumer, "Threats from Agency-Determined Research," pp. 155–167; Robert K. Merton, "The Role of Applied Social Science in the Formation of Policy: A Research Memorandum," *Philosophy of Science* 16 (July 1949):165–166.

18 Carol H. Weiss, "The Politicization of Evaluation Research," in *Evaluating Action Programs: Readings in Social Action and Education*, ed. Carol H. Weiss (Boston: Allyn & Bacon, 1972), p. 332; Aaron, *Politics and the Professors*, pp. 157–158, 159; Garry D. Brewer, *Politicians, Bureaucrats, and the Consultant* (New York: Basic Books, 1973), p. 163, Edelman, *Political Language*, p. 142; Howard S. Becker and Irving Louis Horowitz, "Radical Politics and Sociological Research: Observations on Methodology and Ideology," *American Journal of Sociology* 78 (July 1972):48.

19 Wildavsky, *Speaking Truth to Power*, pp. 236–237; Beals, *Politics of Social Research*, p. 14; Rainwater and Yancy, *The Moynihan Report*, p. 4; Peter H. Rossi and Katharine C. Lyall, *Reforming Public Welfare: A Critique of the Negative Income Tax Experiment* (New York: Russell Sage Foundation, 1976), pp. 161–164.

20 Wildavsky, *Speaking Truth to Power*, p. 236; Lindblom, *Policy-Making Process*, pp. 30–38; William Morrill, "What We Have Learned About Research and Policy-Making," in *Proceedings of the 1978 Conference on the Seattle and Denver Income Maintenance Experiments*, ed. Joseph G. Bell, Patricia M. Lines, and Michael Linn (Olympia, Wash.: Department of Social and Health Services, 1979),

pp. 40–41. See, for example, Burkart Holzner and Evelyn Fisher, "Knowledge in Use: Considerations in the Sociology of Knowledge Application," *Knowledge: Creation, Diffusion, Utilization* 1 (December 1979):241; and Nelkin, "Scientific Knowledge, Public Policy, and Democracy," pp. 111–113.

21 See, for example, Carol H. Weiss, "Utilization of Evaluation: Toward Comparative Study," in *Evaluating Action Programs: Readings in Social Action and Education*, ed. Carol H. Weiss (Boston: Allyn & Bacon, 1972), p. 323; and Jerome Milch, "The Politics of Technical Advice," *Administrative Science Quarterly* 22 (September 1977):530.

22 Scott and Shore, *Why Sociology Does Not Apply*, pp. 35–49.

23 Weiss, "The Politicization of Evaluation Research," p. 332.

24 See, for example, Jack Knott and Aaron Wildavsky, "If Dissemination Is the Solution, What Is the Problem?" *Knowledge: Creation, Diffusion, Utilization* 1 (June 1980):561–562.

25 See, for example, Lyons, *The Uneasy Partnership*, p. 10; Rossi and Lyall, *Reforming Public Welfare*, pp. 166–167; and Caplan, Morrison, and Stambaugh, *The Use of Social Science Knowledge*, pp. 29–30.

26 See, for example, Williams, *Social Policy Research and Analysis*, p. 104; Patton, *Utilization-Focused Evaluation*, p. 255.

27 Weiss and Bucuvalas, *Social Science Research*, p. 104; and Weiss, "Utilization of Evaluation," p. 320.

28 Weiss and Bucuvalas, *Social Science Research*, pp. 74–104, are an interesting exception in that they analyze the effect of a long list of research characteristics on decision makers' judgments of the usefulness of research.

29 Bette S. Mahoney and W. Michael Mahoney, "Policy Implications: A Skeptical View," in *Work Incentives and Income Guarantees: The New Jersey Negative Income Tax Experiment*, ed. Joseph A. Pechman and P. Michael Timpane (Washington, D.C.: Brookings Institution, 1975), p. 196; Robert Harris, "Policy Analysis and Policy Development," *Social Service Review* 47 (September 1973):366; Caplan, Morrison, and Stambaugh, *The Use of Social Science Knowledge*, p. 29; Knott and Wildavsky, "Dissemination," p. 563; Patton, *Utilization-Focused Evaluation*, pp. 252–254.

30 Weiss and Bucuvalas, *Social Science Research*, pp. 93–100; and Scott and Shore, *Why Sociology Does Not Apply*, p. 29.

31 C. P. Snow, *The Two Cultures and the Scientific Revolution* (New York: Cambridge University Press, 1959). See, for example, Jack Rothman, *Using Research in Organizations: A Guide to Successful Application* (Beverly Hills, Calif.: Sage, 1980), p. 20; Seymour J. Deitchman, *The Best-Laid Schemes: A Tale of Social Research and Bureaucracy* (Cambridge, Mass.: M.I.T. Press, 1976), p. 390; Albert Cherns, "Relations Between Research Institutes and Users of Research," *International Social Science Journal* (1970):229; and Caplan, Morrison, and Stambaugh, *The Use of Social Science Knowledge*, pp. 27–28.

32 Patton, *Utilization-Focused Evaluation*, pp. 42–43; Gunnar Myrdal, "The Social Sciences and Their Impact on Society," in *Social Theory and Social Intervention*, ed. Herman D. Stein (Cleveland, Ohio: Case Western Reserve University Press,

1968), p. 156; Morrill, "What We Have Learned About Research and Policy-Making," pp. 39–40; Edward A. Suchman, *Evaluative Research: Principles and Practice in Public Service and Social Action Programs* (New York: Russell Sage Foundation, 1967), p. 146; Robert K. Merton, *The Sociology of Science: Theoretical and Empirical Investigations* (Chicago: University of Chicago Press, 1973), p. 9.

33 William N. Dunn, "The Two-Communities Metaphor and Models of Knowledge Use: An Exploratory Case Study," *Knowledge: Creation, Diffusion, Utilization* 1 (June 1980):515–536; Kathleen Archibald, "Alternative Orientations to Social Science Utilization," *Social Science Information* 9 (April 1970):30.

34 See, for example, Milch, "Politics of Technical Advice," p. 531; Robert S. Friedman, *Professionalism: Expertise and Policy Making* (New York: General Learning Press, 1971), p. 6; Merton, *The Sociology of Science*, p. 264; Richard A. Berk and Peter H. Rossi, "Doing Good or Worse: Evaluation Research Politically Reexamined," *Social Problems* 23 (February 1976):342.

35 Irving Louis Horowitz, "Social Science and Public Policy: Implications for Modern Research," in *The Rise and Fall of Project Camelot: Studies in the Relationship Between Social Science and Practical Politics*, rev. ed., ed. Irving Louis Horowitz (Cambridge, Mass.: M.I.T. Press, 1974), p. 340.

36 See, for example, Moynihan's discussion of the new social science professionals, in *Maximum Feasible Misunderstanding*, pp. 19–24.

37 Weiss and Bucuvalas, *Social Science Research*, p. 249.

38 Lyons, *The Uneasy Partnership*, pp. 15–16; Aaron, *Politics and the Professors*, pp. 151–152; Moynihan, *Maximum Feasible Misunderstanding*, pp. 25–32.

39 The list includes (1) preexisting evaluation bounds, (2) orientation of the users, (3) evaluator's approach, (4) evaluator credibility, (5) organizational factors, (6) extraorganizational factors, (7) information content and reporting, and (8) administrator's style (Alkin, Daillak, and White, *Using Evaluations*, pp. 235–259). The president's use of social research may be influenced by (1) perception of a crisis, (2) utilization of research by previous presidents, (3) ideological factors, (4) distrust of experts, (5) vague images of planning, (6) elections, (7) political feasibility, (8) the stage of the policy process, and (9) the age of the agency (Scott and Shore, *Why Sociology Does Not Apply*, pp. 168–184). It is suggested that any typology would need to consider "(1) participants in the utilization process, (2) the purpose of the potential utilization, (3) beneficiaries of the potential utilization, (4) internal and external factors influencing utilization, (5) the intended nature of the utilization, and (6) an indication of the time frame" (Judith K. Larsen, "Knowledge Utilization: What Is It?" *Knowledge: Creation, Diffusion, Utilization* 1 [March 1980]:433).

40 See, for example, Cherns, "Research Institutes and Users of Research," pp. 232–233; and U.S. National Research Council, *The Federal Investment in Knowledge of Social Problems*, Final Report, vol. 1, Study Project on Social Research and Development (Washington, D.C.: National Academy of Sciences, 1978), pp. 40–41; Merton, "The Role of Applied Social Science," p. 167; "Dunn, The Two-Communities Metaphor and Knowledge Use," pp. 526, 527.

41   See, for example, Scott and Shore, *Why Sociology Does Not Apply*, p. 188; Wildavsky, *Speaking Truth to Power*, p. 37; Weiss, "Utilization of Evaluation," p. 319; and Primack and von Hippel, *Advice and Dissent*, p. 4.

42   See, for example, Nelkin, "Scientific Knowledge, Public Policy, and Democracy," p. 106; Rich, "The Pursuit of Knowledge," p. 24; Datta, "The Impact of Evaluation on Head Start," pp. 151–152; Walter Williams, *The Struggle for a Negative Income Tax: A Case Study, 1965–1970* (Seattle: Institute of Government Research, 1972), p. 37; Horowitz and Katz, *Social Science and Public Policy*, p. 48; Brewer, *Politicians, Bureaucrats, and the Consultant*, p. 212.

43   See, for example, Wildavsky, *Speaking Truth to Power*; Lindblom and Cohen, *Usable Knowledge*.

44   See, for example, Becker and Horowitz, "Radical Politics and Sociological Research"; Edelman, *Political Language*; and Alvin W. Gouldner, *The Dialectic of Ideology and Technology: The Origins of Grammar and Future of Ideology* (New York: Seabury Press, 1976).

45   Theodore J. Lowi, "American Business, Public Policy, Case-Studies, and Political Theory," *World Politics* 56 (July 1964):689–703; George D. Greenberg, Jeffrey A. Miller, Lawrence B. Mohr, and Bruce C. Vladek, "Developing Public Policy Theory: Perspectives from Empirical Research," *American Political Science Review* 71 (December 1977):1534–1535.

46   Horowitz and Katz, *Social Science and Public Policy*, p. 139; Wildavsky, *Speaking Truth to Power*, 234; Lindblom, *Policy-Making Process*, p. 31.

47   Smith, *The Rand Corporation*, pp. 216–218; Barber, *Politics of Research*, pp. 91–103; Roberts, "On Social Science," pp. 59–60; Rossi and Lyall, *Reforming Public Welfare*, p. 167; Deitchman, *The Best-Laid Schemes*, p. 392; Knott and Wildavsky, "Dissemination," pp. 537–538; Patton, *Utilization-Focused Evaluation*, p. 69; Weiss, "Utilization of Evaluation," p. 324; Weiss and Bucuvalas, *Social Science Research*, pp. 244–245.

48   Weiss and Bucuvalas, *Social Science Research*, pp. 17–23.

49   Brewer, *Politicians, Bureaucrats, and the Consultant*, pp. 92–95; Robert F. Rich, *Social Science Information and Public Policy Making* (San Francisco: Jossey-Bass, 1981); Gouldner, *The Dialectic of Ideology and Technology*, p. 213; Caplan, Morrison, and Stambaugh, *The Use of Social Science Knowledge*, pp. 27–28; Weiss and Bucuvalas, *Social Science Research*, pp. 137–138.

50   See, for example, Patton, *Utilization-Focused Evaluation*; and Rothman, *Using Research in Organizations*.

3   Development of Explanations

1   While I define "explanation" below as having the same meaning as "theory" in some of its usages, the label "theory" is used and defined in such a wide manner that the analytic construct is here referred to as "explanation" in the hope of reducing misunderstanding.

2   This conceptualization of explanation owes much to that presented by Eugene J. Meehan, *The Foundations of Political Analysis: Empirical and Normative*

(Homewood, Ill.: Dorsey Press, 1971). For a more recent statement, see Eugene J. Meehan, *Reasoned Argument in Social Science: Linking Research to Policy* (Westport, Conn.: Greenwood Press, 1981).

3　See, for example, George J. Graham, *Methodological Foundations of Political Analysis* (Waltham, Mass.: Xerox College Publishing, 1971), pp. 138–158; E. Terrence Jones, *Conducting Political Research* (New York: Harper & Row, 1971), pp. 5–6; or W. Phillips Shively, *The Craft of Political Research: A Primer* (Englewood Cliffs, N.J.: Prentice-Hall, 1974), pp. 164–167.

4　For a detailed description of retroduction, see Charles Sanders Peirce, *Philosophical Writings of Peirce*, ed. Justus Buchler (New York: Dover, 1955), pp. 150–156.

5　My thinking on this matter has benefited considerably from Harry Eckstein, "Case Study and Theory in Political Science," in *Handbook of Political Science*, vol. 7: *Strategies of Inquiry*, ed. Fred I. Greenstein and Nelson W. Polsby (Reading, Mass.: Addison-Wesley, 1975), pp. 79–137. For a parallel treatment of case study method linked to the field of knowledge utilization, see Robert K. Yin, "The Case Study as a Serious Research Strategy," *Knowledge: Creation, Diffusion, Utilization* 3 (September 1981):97–114.

6　Eckstein, "Case Study and Theory in Political Science," pp. 104–108.

7　Ibid.

8　For a detailed description of the program for better jobs and income, see U.S., Congress, House, Welfare Reform Subcommittee of the Committee on Agriculture, Committee on Education and Labor, and the Committee on Ways and Means, *Explanatory Materials to Accompany H.R. 10950, The Better Jobs and Income Act*, 95th Cong., 2d sess., March 24, 1978.

9　For early statements by those who advocated a negative income tax, see Milton Friedman, "The Case for the Negative Income Tax," *Republican Papers*, ed. Melvin R. Laird (New York: Frederick A. Praeger, 1968), pp. 202–220; and James Tobin, "The Case for an Income guarantee," *Public Interest* 4 (Summer 1966):31–41. An early and insightful analysis of the negative income tax was conducted by Christopher Green, *Negative Taxes and the Poverty Problem* (Washington, D.C.: Brookings Institution, 1967).

10　For a report on the New Jersey–Pennsylvania experiment which includes a justification for the experimental approach and discussion of the findings, see Joseph A. Pechman and P. Michael Timpane, eds., *Work Incentives and Income Guarantees* (Washington, D.C.: Brookings Institution, 1975).

11　These include experiments with health insurance sponsored by HEW and experiments with housing allowances funded by the Department of Housing and Urban Development.

12　See, for example, Alice M. Rivlin, *Systematic Thinking for Social Action* (Washington, D.C.: Brookings Institution, 1971); and Carol H. Weiss, *Evaluation Research: Methods for Assessing Program Effectiveness* (Englewood Cliffs, N.J.: Prentice-Hall, 1972).

13　A comprehensive summary and assessment of contemporary research is found in U.S., National Research Council, *Evaluating Federal Support for Poverty*

Research, Final Report, Committee on Evaluation of Poverty Research, Assembly of Behavioral Sciences (Washington, D.C.: National Academy of Sciences, 1979).

14   Most investigators of welfare policy and reform acknowledge the highly conflictual nature of the policy area. See, for example, Williams, *The Struggle for a Negative Income Tax,* p. 6; James Lyday, "An Advocate's Process Outline for Policy Analysis," *Urban Affairs Quarterly* 7 (June 1972):390; and Bill Cavala and Aaron Wildavsky, "The Political Feasibility of Income by Right," *Public Policy* 18 (1970):321–350.

15   Lee Rainwater and William L. Yancy, in *The Moynihan Report and the Politics of Controversy* (Cambridge, Mass.: M.I.T. Press, 1967), p. viii, suggest that the interview process itself and the interaction between interviewer and respondent provide data which are often as illuminating as straightforward responses and which can be cross-checked.

4   An Explanation of the Impact of Policy Analysis

1   This work manifests the basic approach of the sociology of knowledge and science. For an update on developments in these fields, see Michael J. Mulkay, *Science and the Sociology of Knowledge* (London: Allen & Unwin, 1979), and "Sociology of the Scientific Research Community," in *Science, Technology, and Society: A Cross-Disciplinary Perspective,* ed. Ina Spiegal-Rosing and Derek de Solla Price (London: Sage, 1977); Stephen D. Nelson, "Knowledge Creation: An Overview," *Knowledge: Creation, Diffusion, Utilization* 1 (September 1979):123–149; and Edward Shils, "Knowledge and the Sociology of Knowledge," *Knowledge: Creation, Diffusion, Utilization* 4 (September 1982):7–32.

2   See, for example, Paul Feyerabend, *Science in a Free Society* (London: NLB, 1978); and Alvin W. Gouldner, *The Dialectic of Ideology and Technology: The Origins of Grammar and Future of Ideology* (New York: Seabury Press, 1976).

3   See Robert S. Friedman, *Professionalism: Expertise and Policy Making* (New York: General Learning Press, 1971); Guy Benveniste, *The Politics of Expertise* (San Francisco: Boyd & Fraser/Glendessary, 1972), and Burkart Holzner and John Marx, *Knowledge Application: The Knowledge System in Society* (Boston: Allyn & Bacon, 1979).

4   Since the 1960s many national executive departments and agencies in the United States have established research, planning, and evaluation units. In 1974 the Congress established its own analytic office to assist it in performing its budget function, the Congressional Budget Office. In addition, the General Accounting Office has expanded beyond its traditional accounting responsibilities to include program research and evaluation and has added professional staff to work in these areas.

5   Robert S. Friedman, *Professionalism: Expertise and Policy Making,* p. 6.

6   See, for example, Don K. Price, *The Scientific Estate* (Cambridge, Mass.: Harvard University Press, 1965); Daniel S. Greenberg, *The Politics of Pure Science* (New York: New American Library, 1967); James L. Penick, Carroll W. Pursell, Jr.,

174

Morgan B. Sherwood, and Donald C. Swain, eds., *The Politics of American Science, 1939 to Present*, rev. ed. (Cambridge, Mass.: M.I.T. Press, 1972); and Robert K. Merton, *The Sociology of Science: Theoretical and Empirical Investigations* (Chicago: University of Chicago Press, 1973); and Mulkay, "Sociology of the Scientific Research Community."

7 See U.S., National Research Council, *The Behavioral Sciences and the Federal Government*, Advisory Committee on Government Programs in the Behavioral Sciences (Washington, D.C.: National Academy of Sciences, 1968); Gene M. Lyons, *The Uneasy Partnership: Social Science and the Federal Government in the Twentieth Century* (New York: Russell Sage Foundation, 1969); and James B. Rule, *Insight and Social Betterment: A Preface to Applied Social Science* (New York: Oxford University Press, 1978).

8 See, for example, Larry D. Spence, *The Politics of Social Knowledge* (University Park, Pa.: Pennsylvania State University Press, 1978).

9 See, for example, Lyons, *The Uneasy Partnership*.

10 Although power has proven to be a difficult concept to work with, it is crucial to many broad-gauged social theories. A common definition of power is adequate for the purposes of this research: "A has power over B to the extent that he can get B to do something that B would not otherwise do" (Robert A. Dahl, "The Concept of Power," *Behavioral Science* 2 [1957]:203).

11 See, for example, Paul A. Baran and Paul M. Sweezy, *Monopoly Capital: An Essay on the American Economic and Social Order* (New York: Modern Reader Paperbacks, 1966), or Nicos Poulantzas, *Classes in Contemporary Capitalism* (London: Verso, 1978).

12 See, for example, Charles E. Lindblom, *Politics and Markets: The World's Political-Economic Systems* (New York: Basic Books, 1977), or Robert A. Dahl, *Dilemmas of Pluralist Democracy: Autonomy versus Control* (New Haven: Yale University Press, 1982).

13 For an interesting example, see Donald C. Hodges, *The Bureaucratization of Socialism* (Amherst: University of Massachusetts Press, 1981).

14 Frances Fox Piven and Richard A. Cloward, *Poor People's Movements: Why They Succeed, How They Fail* (New York: Vintage Books, 1979).

15 The discussion of the scope and contagion of conflict is indebted to E. E. Schattschneider, *The Semi-Sovereign People: A Realist's View of Democracy in America* (New York: Holt, Rinehart & Winston, 1960).

16 Robert Axelrod, ed., *Structure of Decision: The Cognitive Maps of Political Elites* (Princeton, N.J.: Princeton University Press, 1976), p. 239.

17 Jean Piaget, *The Psychology of Intelligence* (1950; repr., Totowa, N.J.: Littlefield, Adams, 1960).

18 Milton Rokeach, *The Open and Closed Mind* (New York: Basic Books, 1960), pp. 57–69.

19 For an extended discussion of the politics of policy analysis, see chapter 2.

20 Conflict over social policy analysis has become quite newsworthy. Articles reporting disputes involving research reports are common in major newspapers. See, for example, "Points of Controversy Emerge Swiftly as Clean Air Act Hearing

Opens," *New York Times*, 3 March 1981; "Linguist Whose Work Bush Derided Defends His Research in Philadelphia," *New York Times*, 30 March 1981; and "New Coleman Study is Defended and Criticized by Five Hundred Educators," *New York Times*, 8 April 1981.

21 The discussion of symbolic politics relies heavily on Murray Edelman, *The Symbolic Uses of Politics* (Urbana: University of Illinois Press, 1964); and Murray Edelman, *Political Language: Words That Succeed and Policies That Fail* (New York: Academic Press, 1977).

22 For insight on the importance of visibility to political decision making, see James Eisenstein, *Politics and the Legal Process* (New York: Harper & Row, 1973), pp. 317–321.

23 My own beliefs regarding belief systems have been influenced by the following works to such an extent that it is difficult to separate the contribution of one from that of another: John D. Steinbruner, *The Cybernetic Theory of Decision: New Dimensions of Political Analysis* (Princeton, N.J.: Princeton University Press, 1974); Robert E. Lane, "Patterns of Political Belief," in *Handbook of Political Psychology*, ed. Jeanne Knutson (San Francisco: Jossey-Bass, 1973), pp. 83–116; and Edelman, *Political Language*.

5 The Negative Income Tax: Experiments and Proposals

1 This quoted phase is Gilbert Y. Steiner's. See *The State of Welfare* (Washington, D.C.: Brookings Institution, 1971), pp. 31–74.

2 For descriptions of the family assistance plan policy process, see Vincent J. Burke and Vee Burke, *Nixon's Good Deed* (New York: Columbia University Press, 1974); and Daniel P. Moynihan, *The Politics of a Guaranteed Income: The Nixon Administration and the Family Assistance Plan* (New York: Random House, 1973). A history of the 1974 income supplement plan appears in Cynthia Horan, "Casper Weinberger and Welfare Reform," in *Designing Public Policy*, ed. Laurence E. Lynn, Jr. (Santa Monica, Calif.: Goodyear, 1980), pp. 82–103. On the Carter administration's proposals and others that surfaced at this time, see Gordon L. Weil, *The Welfare Debate of 1978* (White Plains, N.Y.: Institute for Socioeconomic Studies, 1978); and David Whitman and Laurence E. Lynn, Jr., *The Carter Administration and Welfare Reform A, B, C, D, and Sequel* (Cambridge, Mass.: Kennedy School of Government, Harvard University, 1979).

3 For an excellent analysis of the negative income tax and a discussion of its history, see Christopher Green, *Negative Taxes and the Poverty Problem* (Washington D.C.: Brookings Institution, 1967).

4 For discussion of the experiments and findings in New Jersey and Pennsylvania, see David Kershaw and J. Fair, *The New Jersey Income-Maintenance Experiment: Operations, Surveys, and Administration* (New York: Academic Press, 1976); Joseph A. Pechman and P. Michael Timpane, eds., *Work Incentives and Income Guarantees: The New Jersey Negative Income Tax Experiment* (Washington, D.C.: Brookings Institution, 1975); U.S., Department of Health, Education, and Welfare, Office of the Assistant Secretary for Planning and Evaluation,

New Jersey Graduated Work Incentive Experiment, Summary Report (Washington, D.C., 1973); Harold W. Watts and Albert Rees, *The New Jersey Income-Maintenance Experiments: Labor Supply Responses* (New York: Academic Press, 1977); and Harold W. Watts and Albert Rees, *The New Jersey Income-Maintenance Experiment: Expenditures, Health and Social Behavior, and the Quality of Evidence* (New York: Academic Press, 1977). On the rural experiment, see John L. Palmer and Joseph A. Pechman, eds., *Welfare in Rural Areas: The North Carolina–Iowa Income Maintenance Experiments* (Washington, D.C.: Brookings Institution, 1978); and U.S., Department of Health, Education, and Welfare, Office of the Assistant Secretary for Planning and Evaluation, *The Rural Income Maintenance Experiment, Summary Report,* November 1976. On the Gary experiment, see Kenneth C. Kehrer, *The Gary Income Maintenance Experiment: Summary of Initial Findings* (Princeton, N.J.: Mathematica Policy Research, 1977). On the Seattle and Denver experiments, see Joseph G. Bell, Patricia M. Lines, and Michael Linn, eds., *Proceedings of the 1978 Conference on the Seattle and Denver Income Maintenance Experiments* (Olympia, Wash.: Department of Social and Health Services, 1979); U.S., Department of Health, Education, and Welfare, Office of the Assistant Secretary for Planning and Evaluation, *Seattle-Denver Income Maintenance Experiment: Mid-Experimental Labor Supply Results and a Generalization to the National Population* (Washington, D.C. 1978).

5 See Milton Friedman, *Capitalism and Freedom* (Chicago: University of Chicago Press, 1962); and Robert Theobald, *Free Men and Free Markets* (New York: Clarkson N. Potter, 1963).

6 Milton Friedman, "The Case for the Negative Income Tax," in *Republican Papers,* ed. Melvin R. Laird (New York: Frederick A. Praeger, 1968), p. 207.

7 See Gilbert Y. Steiner, *The State of Welfare* (Washington, D.C.: Brookings Institution, 1971), pp. 6–11.

8 Milton Friedman, "The Case for the Negative Income Tax," pp. 210–213.

9 Steiner, *The State of Welfare,* pp. 95–96.

10 See, for example, Walter Williams, *The Struggle for a Negative Income Tax: A Case Study, 1965–1970* (Seattle: Institute of Governmental Research, 1972), pp. 2–9; and James Lyday, "An Advocate's Process Outline for Policy Analysis," *Urban Affairs Quarterly* 7 (June 1972):389–400.

11 U.S., National Research Council, *Evaluating Federal Support for Poverty Research,* Final Report, Committee on Evaluation of Poverty Research, Assembly of Behavioral and Social Sciences (Washington, D.C.: National Academy of Sciences, 1979), p. 31.

12 Williams, *The Struggle for a Negative Income Tax,* pp. 10–12.

13 See, for example, Alice M. Rivlin, *Systematic Thinking for Social Action* (Washington, D.C.: Brookings Institution, 1971), pp. 22–23; Franklin D. Raines, *Family Assistance Program, Parts A & B* (Cambridge, Mass.: Kennedy School of Government, Harvard University, 1977), Part A, pp. 20–24, Part B, pp. 9–14.

14 James C. Vadakin, "A Critique of the Guaranteed Annual Income," *Public Interest* 11 (Spring 1968):53–66.

15 Alvin L. Schorr, "Against a Negative Income Tax," *Public Interest* 5 (Fall 1966):112.

16 Green, *Negative Taxes and the Poverty Problem*, pp. 10–13.

17 Williams, *The Struggle for a Negative Income Tax*, p. 5.

18 See, for example, Edward F. Lawlor, "Income Security," in *Studies in the Management of Social R & D: Selected Policy Areas*, ed. Laurence E. Lynn, Jr., Final Report, vol. 3, Study Project on Social Research and Development, National Research Council (Washington, D.C.: National Academy of Sciences, 1979), pp. 18–19; and Williams, *The Struggle for a Negative Income Tax*, pp. 12–13.

19 Steiner, *The State of Welfare*, p. 96.

20 Williams, *The Struggle for a Negative Income Tax*, p. 11.

21 U.S., Congress, Senate, Committee on Finance, *President's Statement on Principles of Welfare Reform: Hearings Before the Subcommittee on Public Assistance*, 95th Cong., 1st sess., May 5 and 12, 1977, p 35.

22 Walter Williams, *Social Policy Research and Analysis: The Experience in the Federal Agencies* (New York: American Elsevier, 1971), p. 157.

23 Pechman and Timpane, *Work Incentives and Income Guarantees*, pp. 95–101.

24 Irving Louis Horowitz and James Everett Katz, *Social Science and Public Policy in the United States* (New York: Praeger, 1975), p. 140.

25 U.S. Congress, Senate, *President's Statement on Principles of Welfare Reform*, p. 35.

26 Larry L. Orr, "Introduction: Strategy for a Broad Program of Experimentation in Income Maintenance," in *Income Maintenance: Interdisciplinary Approaches to Research*, Larry L. Orr, Robin G. Hollister, and Myron J. Lefcowitz (Chicago: Markham, 1971), pp. 69–70.

27 See, for example, Lyday, "Policy Analysis," p. 394; Williams, *The Struggle for a Negative Income Tax*, pp. 1–9; and Bette S. Mahoney and W. Michael Mahoney, "Policy Implications: A Skeptical View," in *Work Incentives and Income Guarantees: The New Jersey Negative Income Tax Experiment*, ed. Joseph A. Pechman and P. Michael Timpane (Washington, D.C.: Brookings Institution, 1975), pp. 193–194.

28 Williams, *Social Policy Research and Analysis*, p. 173.

29 U.S., National Research Council, *Evaluating Federal Support for Poverty Research*, pp. 60–63.

30 Martin Rein and Lisa Peattie, "Problem Frames in Poverty Research," in *Poverty and Public Policy: An Evaluation of Social Science Research*, ed. Vincent T. Covello (Cambridge, Mass.: Schenkman, 1980), pp. 243–244.

31 See, for example, Rivlin, *Systematic Thinking for Social Action*, pp. 31–32; Moynihan, *The Politics of a Guaranteed Income*, pp. 184–197; Robert Harris, "Policy Analysis and Policy Development," *Social Service Review* 47 (September 1973):365–369; Margaret E. Boeckmann, "Policy Impacts of the New Jersey Income Maintenance Experiment," *Policy Sciences* 7 (1976):57–58; and James R. Storey, "Systems Analysis and Welfare Reform: A Case Study of the Family Assistance Plan," *Policy Sciences* 4 (March 1973):4–6.

32 For references to further discussion of these proposals see note 2.

33 Raines, *Family Assistance Program, Part A*, pp. 26–28.

34 U.S., Congress, Senate, Committee on Finance, *Welfare Research and Experimentation: Hearings Before the Subcommittee on Public Assistance*, 95th Cong., 2d sess., 1978, p. 3.

35 Raines, *Part A*, pp. 30–34.

34 Williams, *The Struggle for a Negative Income Tax*, p. 22.

37 Moynihan, *The Politics of a Guaranteed Income*, pp. 136–143.

38 Ibid., pp. 399–438.

39 Ibid., pp. 453–531.

40 Boeckmann, "Policy Impacts of the New Jersey Income Maintenance Experiment," p. 61.

41 Congressional Quarterly, *Urban America: Policies and Problems* (Washington, D.C.: Congressional Quarterly, 1978), p. 84.

42 Horan, "Casper Weinberger and Welfare Reform," pp. 88–97.

6 Income Maintenance Experimentation and Policy Decisions

1 Respondents were granted anonymity. Where their organizational affiliation can be given without jeopardizing anonymity, I have done so, but in some instances I could not.

2 Thorstein Veblen, *The Place of Science in Modern Civilization* (New York: Russell & Russell, 1961), pp. 50–55.

3 Paul Feyerabend, *Science in a Free Society* (London: NLB, 1978), p. 74. For a similar argument, see Alvin W. Gouldner, *The Dialectic of Ideology and Technology: The Origins of Grammar and the Future of Ideology* (New York: Seabury Press, 1976), pp. 14–45.

4 Fritz Machlup, *The Production and Distribution of Knowledge in the United States* (Princeton, N.J.: Princeton University Press, 1962), p. 370; Gene M. Lyons, *The Uneasy Partnership: Social Science and the Federal Government in the Twentieth Century* (New York: Russell Sage Foundation, 1969), p. 274.

5 George H. Gallup, *The Gallup Poll, Public Opinion, 1972–1977*, vol. 1 (Wilmington, Del.: Scholarly Resources, 1978), pp. 216, 255.

6 Richard A. Musgrave and Peggy B. Musgrave, *Public Finance in Theory and Practice*, 2d ed. (New York: McGraw-Hill, 1976), p. 133.

7 U.S., Advisory Commission on Intergovernmental Relations, *Significant Features of Fiscal Federalism, 1980–1981* (Washington, D.C.: Government Printing Office, 1981), p. 10.

8 U.S., Executive Office of the President, Office of Management and Budget, *Special Analyses, Budget of the United States Government, Fiscal Year 1987* (Washington, D.C.: Government Printing Office, 1987), pp. I–10, H-20.

9 George C. Berkley, *The Craft of Public Administration*, 3d ed. (Boston: Allyn & Bacon, 1981), p. 477.

10 Robert K. Merton, *The Sociology of Science: Theoretical and Empirical Investigations* (Chicago: University of Chicago Press, 1973), pp. 269, 270–276.

11 Daniel S. Greenberg, The Politics of Pure Science (New York: New American Library, 1967), p. 5; Merton, The Sociology of Science, p. 260.

12 Daniel S. Greenberg, The Politics of Pure Science, pp. 151–152.

13 U.S., Executive Office of the President, Special Analyses, Budget 1987, p. K-29; U.S., Executive Office of the President, Office of Management and Budget, Special Analyses, Budget of the United States Government, Fiscal Year 1979 (Washington, D.C.: Government Printing Office, 1979), pp. 329, 310.

14 U.S., General Service Administration, National Archives and Records Service, Office of the Federal Register, 1977/78 United States Government Manual (Washington, D.C.: Government Printing Office, 1977).

15 See, for example, U.S., National Research Council, The Federal Investment in Knowledge of Social Problems, Final Report, vol. 1, Study Project on Social Research and Development (Washington, D.C.: National Academy of Sciences, 1978), pp. 44–46; Lyons, The Uneasy Partnership, pp. 220–240; and James L. Sundquist, "Research Brokerage: The Weak Link," in Knowledge and Policy: the Uncertain Connection, ed. Laurence E. Lynn, Jr., Final Report, vol. 5, Study Project on Social Research and Development, National Research Council (Washington, D.C.: National Academy of Science, 1978), pp. 130–142.

16 See, for example, Raymond G. Hunt, "The University Social Research Center: Its Role in the Knowledge-Making Process," Knowledge: Creation, Diffusion, Utilization 2 (September 1980):83–85; Bruce L. R. Smith, The Rand Corporation: Case Study of a Nonprofit Advisory Corporation (Cambridge, Mass.: Harvard University Press, 1966); Albert Cherns, "Relations Between Research Institutes and Users of Research," International Social Science Journal 22 (1970):226–227; and Ralph L. Beals, Politics of Social Research: An Inquiry into the Ethics and Responsibilities of Social Scientists (Chicago: Aldine, 1969), pp. 142–144.

17 For a stimulating exchange on the relation of social science research to social action, see William N. Dunn, "Reforms as Experiments," Knowledge: Creation, Diffusion, Utilization 3 (March 1982):293–326, and Donald T. Campbell, "Experiments as Arguments," Knowledge: Creation, Diffusion, Utilization 3 (March 1982):327–337.

18 U.S., Bureau of the Census, Statistical Abstract of the United States 1986, 106th ed. (Washington, D.C., 1985), p. 452; U.S., Bureau of the Census, Historical Statistics of the United States, Colonial Times to 1970, Bicentennial Edition, pt. 1 (Washington, D.C., 1975), p. 293.

19 U.S., Bureau of the Census, Statistical Abstract of the United States, 1986, pp. 465, 464.

20 Ira Katznelson and Mark Kesselman, The Politics of Power: A Critical Introduction to American Government, 2d ed. (New York: Harcourt Brace Jovanovich, 1979), p. 78; J. D. Smith and S. D. Franklin, "The Concentration of Personal Wealth, 1922–1969," American Economic Review 64 (May 1974):166; Musgrave and Musgrave, Public Finance in Theory and Practice, p. 348.

21 Edward S. Greenberg, Understanding Modern Government: The Rise and Decline of the American Political Economy (New York: John Wiley, 1979), p. 95; Katznelson and Kesselman, the Politics of Power, p. 76.

22 For one recent round in this skirmish, see John Manley, "Neopluralism: A Class Analysis of Pluralism I and Pluralism II," *American Political Science Review* 77 (1983):368–383, and the comments by Charles E. Lindblom and Robert Dahl that follow, pp, 384–389. Also see Charles E. Lindblom, *Politics and Markets: The World's Political-Economic Systems* (New York: Basic Books, 1977), p. 172; Robert A. Dahl, *Dilemmas of Pluralist Democracy: Autonomy versus Control* (New Haven: Yale University Press, 1982), p. 12.

23 See, for example, Edwin M. Epstein, *The Corporation in American Politics* (Englewood Cliffs, N.J.: Prentice-Hall, 1969); Lindblom, *Politics and Markets*, p. 194; Thomas Byrne Edsall, *The New Politics of Inequality* (New York: W. W. Norton, 1984) provides careful analysis of business policy success during the first term of the Reagan administration.

24 See, for example, Theodore J. Lowi, *The End of Liberalism: The Second Republic of the United States*, 2d ed. (New York: W. W. Norton, 1979); Grant McConnell, *Private Power and American Democracy* (New York: Vantage Books, 1966); and Michael Parenti, "Power and Pluralism: A View from the Bottom," *Journal of Politics* 32 (1970):501–530.

25 The constructivist approach within the sociology of science also considers knowledge to be in part a product of the social context within which it is produced rather than simply reflections of reality. See Karin D. Knorr-Cetina, *The Manufacture of Knowledge: An Essay on the Constructivist and Contextual Nature of Science* (Oxford: Pergamon Press, 1981), and Karin D. Knorr-Cetina, "The Ethnographic Study of Scientific Work: Towards a Constructivist Interpretation of Science," in *Science Observed: Perspectives on the Social Study of Science*, ed. Karin D. Knorr-Cetina and Michael Mulkay (London: Sage, 1983); Bruno Latour and Steve Woolgar, *Laboratory Life: the Social Construction of Scientific Facts* (London: Sage, 1979).

26 U.S., National Research Council, *The Federal Investment in Knowledge of Social Problems*, p. 23; Martin Rein and Lisa Peattie, "Problem Frames in Poverty Research," in *Poverty and Public Policy: An Evaluation of Social Science Research*, ed. Vincent T. Covello (Cambridge, Mass.: Schenkman, 1980), pp. 235–237.

27 For early participants' discussion of expected benefits of a negative income tax, see Christopher Green, *Negative Taxes and the Poverty Problem* (Washington, D.C.: Brookings Institution, 1967), pp. 159–162. For a presentation of the advantages of a negative income tax by an early advocate, see Milton Friedman, "The Case for a Negative Income Tax," in *Republican Papers*, ed. Melvin R. Laird (New York: Frederick A. Praeger, 1968), pp. 210–213.

28 Some economists argue that in-kind transfer programs are paternalistic in that they prescribe goods or services for people in need rather than giving such people cash and letting them purchase what they think they need the most. As in-kind transfer programs interfere with individual choices, there are losses in allocative efficiency. See, for example, Musgrave and Musgrave, *Public Finance in Theory and Practice*, pp. 65–66.

29 Henry J. Aaron notes that marginal tax rates range from 67 percent to 80 percent with the AFDC program, depending on whether or not the recipients are eligible

for food stamps and Medicaid. He also illustrates the "notch effect," where, at certain points on the income scale, marginal tax rates exceed 100 percent. A family of four with an income of $8,390, for example, stands to lose $1,288 in Medicaid and food stamp benefits if it earns any additional income. (*Why Is Welfare So Hard to Reform?* [Washington, D.C.: Brookings Institution, 1973], pp. 33–34). For a theoretical discussion of the ways in which income taxation, especially with high marginal tax rates, interferes with economic efficiency by altering work and leisure decisions, see Musgrave and Musgrave, *Public Finance in Theory and Practice*, pp. 94–96, 467–468.

30   See, for example, Milton Friedman, "The Case for a Negative Income Tax," pp. 210–213. Also see Edgar K. Browning and Jacquelene M. Browning, *Public Finance and the Price System* (New York: Macmillan, 1979), pp. 107–109.

31   See, for example, Musgrave and Musgrave, *Public Finance in Theory and Practice*, pp. 673–675. See, for example, Green, *Negative Taxes and the Poverty Problem*, p. 161.

32   The experiments varied considerably in cost: New Jersey–Pennsylvania, $7.8 million; Iowa–North Carolina, $6 million; Gary, $20 million; and Seattle–Denver, $75 million (estimated) (U.S., Congress, Senate, Committee on Finance, *President's Statement on Principles of Welfare Reform: Hearings Before the Subcommittee on Public Assistance*, 95th Cong., 1st sess., May 5 and 12, 1977, p. 13).

33   David H. Greenberg and Philip K. Robins, "The Changing Role of Social Experiments in Policy Analysis," *Journal of Policy Analysis and Management* 5 (Winter 1986):340–362.

34   See, for example, Aaron, *Why Is Welfare So Hard to Reform?* p. 1; Robert H. Bork, *Welfare Reform: Why?* (Washington, D.C.: American Enterprise Institute, 1976), p. 13; Bill Cavala and Aaron Wildavsky, "The Political Feasibility of Income by Right," *Public Policy* 18 (1970):321–350; and Gordon L. Weil, *The Welfare Debate of 1978* (White Plains, N.Y.: Institute for Socioeconomic Studies, 1978), p. 9.

35   George H. Gallup, *The Gallup Poll: Public Opinion, 1935–1971*, vol. 3 (New York: Random House, 1972), p. 1919. George H. Gallup, *The Gallup Poll: Public Opinion, 1972–1977*, vol. 2 (Wilmington, Del.: Scholarly Resources, 1978), p. 1116; George H. Gallup, *The Gallup Poll: Public Opinion, 1979* (Wilmington, Del.: Scholarly Resources, 1980), p. 66.

36   Gallup, *the Gallup Poll, 1935–1971*, p. 1920; Gallup, *The Gallup Poll, 1979*, pp. 67–69.

37   Gallup, *The Gallup Poll, 1935–1971*, pp. 1965, 2133, 2177–2178, 2133, 2177.

38   Gallup, *The Gallup Poll, 1972–1977*, vol. 1, p. 374.

39   Nick Kotz describes the difficulty the administration had when it dealt with program issues while goals were left unspecified. The struggle over the basic issue of jobs versus income was compounded by the open question of cost: how much to spend? ("The Politics of Welfare Reform," *New Republic* 1976 [May 14, 1977]:16–19).

40   These requests from Packer at the DOL infuriated the staff at HEW (David Whitman and Laurence E. Lynn, Jr., *The Carter Administration and Welfare Reform, Part A* (Cambridge, Mass.: Kennedy School of Government, Harvard University,

1979), p. 17; U.S., Department of Health, Education, and Welfare, *Seattle-Denver Income Maintenance Experiment: Mid-Experimental Labor Supply Results*, pp. xi, vii.

41 Weil, *The Welfare Reform Debate of 1978*, pp. 87–91; U.S., Congress, Senate, Committee on Finance, *How to Think About Welfare Reform for the 1980s: Hearings Before the Subcommittee on Public Assistance*, 96th Cong., 2d sess., February 6 and 7, 1980, pp. 15–87.

42 U.S., Department of Health, Education, and Welfare, *Seattle-Denver Income Maintenance Experiment*, p. 18; U.S., General Accounting Office, *Income Maintenance Experiments: Need to Summarize the Results and Communicate the Lessons Learned*, 1981.

43 Whitman and Lynn, *The Carter Administration and Welfare Reform, Part A*, p. 48. Bertram Carp of the Domestic Policy Staff at the White House suggests that the president was using the zero-cost formula as a "disciplinary tool" to keep the departments in line during the formulation process. (Linda Demkovich, "Welfare Reform—Can Carter Succeed Where Nixon Failed?" *National Journal*, August 27, 1977, p. 1334).

44 See, for example, Weil, *The Welfare Reform Debate of 1978*, pp. 21, 65–67, 41–43, 81–86.

45 Whitman and Lynn, *The Carter Administration and Welfare Reform, Part A*, pp. 28–42.

46 The range of figures presented demonstrates the way statisticians can manipulate numbers to get desired results. The low-end estimate comes from the testimony of Robert Spiegelman (SRI) before a Finance Committee subcommittee and represents the response rate of black and white employed husbands, not of all husbands. The higher figure comes from the testimony of Jodie Allen (DOL) before the Finance Committee, includes more participants, and takes into consideration those who participated in a five-year program as well as a three-year program. Inclusion of the five-year program results in a higher negative response (U.S., Congress, Senate, Committee on Finance, Subcommittee on Public Assistance, *Materials Related to Welfare Research and Experimentation*, 95th Cong., 2d sess., November 1978, p. 114–117; and U.S., Congress, Senate, Committee on Finance, *Welfare Research and Experimentation: Hearings Before the Subcommittee on Public Assistance*, 95th Cong., 2d sess., 1978, pp. 9–11). Also see U.S., Congress, Senate, Committee on Finance, *Welfare Research and Experimentation: Hearings Before the Subcommittee on Public Assistance*, 95th Cong., 2d sess., 1978, pp. 9–11; Michael T. Hannan, Nancy Brandon Tuma, and Lyle P. Groeneveld, *A Model of the Effect of Income Maintenance on Rates of Marital Dissolution: Evidence from the Seattle and Denver Income Maintenance Experiments* (Menlo Park, Calif.: SRI International, 1977), p. 2.

47 Linda Demkovich, "The Numbers Are the Issue in the Debate Over Welfare Reform," *National Journal*, April 22, 1978, p. 633.

48 The twelve principles are (1) no higher initial cost, (2) access to a job for every family with children, (3) incentives for private sector employment, (4) public training and employment programs as a supplement to private sector efforts,

(5) more income if the family works than otherwise, (6) incentives for family stability, (7) expansion of the earned income tax credit, (8) decent cash benefits and a consolidated program, (9) a simpler program, (10) incentives to be honest, (11) reduced state and local financial burdens, (12) and local administration of jobs programs (Whitman and Lynn, *The Carter Administration and Welfare Reform, Part B* (Cambridge, Mass.: Kennedy School of Government, Harvard University, 1979), p. 46. Also see Henry Aaron and John Todd, "The Use of Income Maintenance Experiment Findings in Public Policy 1977–1978," Department of Health, Education, and Welfare, 1978, pp. 13–20.

49 U.S., Senate, Committee on Finance, *Materials Related to Welfare Research and Experimentation,* p. 1 (quoted); Margaret E. Boeckmann, "Policy Impacts of the New Jersey Income Maintenance Experiment," *Policy Sciences* 7 (1976):58.

50 U.S., Department of Health, Education, and Welfare, *Seattle-Denver Income Maintenance Experiment,* p. 4. U.S., Congress, Congressional Budget Office, *The Administration's Welfare Reform Proposal: An Analysis of the Program for Better Jobs and Income* (Washington, D.C., 1978); U.S., Department of Health, Education, and Welfare, *Seattle-Denver Income Maintenance Experiment,* p. xi.

8 Postscript

1 Congressional Quarterly, Inc., *Urban America: Policies and Problems* (Washington, D.C.: Congressional Quarterly, 1978), p. 90.

2 Ibid., p. 91.

3 Ibid.

Bibliography

General References

Aaron, Henry J. *Politics and the Professors: The Great Society in Perspective.* Washington, D.C.: Brookings Institution, 1978.

Abramson, Mark A. *The Funding of Social Knowledge Production and Application: A Survey of Federal Agencies.* Vol. 2. Study Project on Social Research and Development. National Research Council. Washington, D.C.: National Academy of Sciences, 1978.

Alkin, Marvin C., Daillak, Richard, and White, Peter. *Using Evaluations: Does Evaluation Make a Difference?* Beverly Hills, Calif.: Sage, 1979.

Archibald, Kathleen. "Alternative Orientations to Social Science Utilization." *Social Science Information* 9 (April 1970):7–34.

Axelrod, Robert, ed. *Structure of Decision: The Cognitive Maps of Political Elites.* Princeton, N.J.: Princeton University Press, 1976.

Baran, Paul A., and Sweezy, Paul M. *Monopoly Capital: An Essay on the American Economic and Social Order.* New York: Modern Reader Paperbacks, 1966.

Barber, Richard J. *The Politics of Research.* Washington, D.C.: Public Affairs Press, 1966.

Barnes, Barry. *Interests and the Growth of Knowledge.* London: Routledge & Kegan Paul, 1977.

———. "On the Implications of a Body of Knowledge." *Knowledge: Creation, Diffusion, Utilization* 4 (September 1982):95–110.

Barnes, J. A. *Who Should Know What? Social Science, Privacy, and Ethics.* New York: Cambridge University Press, 1979.

Beals, Ralph L. *Politics of Social Research: An Inquiry into the Ethics and Responsibilities of Social Scientists.* Chicago: Aldine, 1969.

Becker, Howard S., and Horowitz, Irving Louis. "Radical Politics and Sociological Research: Observations on Methodology and Ideology." *American Journal of Sociology* 78 (July 1972):48–67.

185

Benveniste, Guy. *The Politics of Expertise.* San Francisco: Boyd & Fraser/Glendessary, 1972.

Berk, Richard A., and Rossi, Peter H. "Doing Good or Worse: Evaluation Research Politically Reexamined." *Social Problems* 23 (February 1976):337–349.

Berkley, George E. *The Craft of Public Administration.* 3d ed. Boston: Allyn & Bacon, 1981.

Beyer, Janice M., and Trice, Harrison M. "The Utilization Process: A Conceptual Framework and Synthesis of Empirical Findings." *Administrative Science Quarterly* 27 (December 1982):591–622.

Blumer, Herbert. "Threats from Agency-Determined Research." In *The Rise and Fall of Project Camelot: Studies in the Relationship Between Social Science and Practical Politics,* rev. ed., edited by Irving Louis Horowitz. Cambridge, Mass.: M.I.T. Press, 1974.

Brewer, Garry D. *Politicians, Bureaucrats, and the Consultant.* New York: Basic Books, 1973.

Campbell, Donald T. "Experiments as Arguments." *Knowledge: Creation, Diffusion, Utilization* 3 (March 1982):327–337.

——. "A Tribal Model of the Social System Vehicle Carrying Scientific Knowledge." *Knowledge: Creation, Diffusion, Utilization* 1 (December 1979):181–201.

Caplan, Nathan, Morrison, Andrea, and Stambaugh, R. *The Use of Social Science Knowledge in Policy Decisions at the National Level.* Ann Arbor, Mich.: Institute for Social Research, 1975.

Cherns, Albert. "Relations Between Research Institutes and Users of Research." *International Social Science Journal* 22 (1970):226–242.

Ciarlo, James A. *Utilizing Evaluation: Concepts and Measurement Techniques.* Beverly Hills, Calif.: Sage, 1981.

Coleman, James S. "The Structure of Society and the Nature of Social Research." *Knowledge: Creation, Diffusion, Utilization* 1 (March 1980):333–350.

Cook, Thomas D., Levinson-Rose, Judith, and Pollard, William E. "The Misutilization of Evaluation Research: Some Pitfalls of Definition." *Knowledge: Creation, Diffusion, Utilization* 1 (June 1980):477–498.

Crawford, Elisabeth T., and Biderman, Albert D., eds. *Social Scientists and International Affairs.* New York: John Wiley, 1969.

Dahl, Robert A. "The Concept of Power." *Behavioral Science* 2 (1957):201–215.

——. *Dilemmas of Pluralist Democracy: Autonomy verus Control.* New Haven, Conn.: Yale University Press, 1982.

Datta, Lois-ellin. "The Impact of the Westinghouse/Ohio Evaluation on the Development of Project Head Start: An Examination of the Immediate and Longer-Term Effects and How They Came About." In *The Evaluation of Social Programs,* edited by Clark C. Abt. Beverly Hills, Calif.: Sage, 1976.

Davis, Abraham. *The United States Supreme Court and the Uses of Social Science Data.* New York: MSS Information, 1973.

Deitchman, Seymour J. *The Best-Laid Schemes: A Tale of Social Research and Bureaucracy.* Cambridge, Mass.: M.I.T. Press, 1976.

Dewey, John. *The Public and Its Problems.* 1927. Reprint. Denver: Allen Swallow, 1954.

Dror, Yehezkel. "Policy Analysts: A New Professional Role in Government Service." *Public Administration Review* 27 (December 1967):197–203.

Dunn, William N. "Measuring Knowledge Use." *Knowledge: Creation, Diffusion, Utilization* 5 (September 1983):120–133.

———. "Reforms as Experiments." *Knowledge: Creation, Diffusion, Utilization* 3 (March 1982):293–326.

———. "The Two-Communities Metaphor and Models of Knowledge Use: An Exploratory Case Survey." *Knowledge: Creation, Diffusion, Utilization* 1 (June 1980):515–536.

Eckstein, Harry. "Case Study and Theory in Political Science." In *Handbook of Political Science,* vol. 7: *Strategies of Inquiry,* edited by Fred I. Greenstein and Nelson W. Polsby. Reading, Mass.: Addison-Wesley, 1975.

Edelman, Murray. *Political Language: Words That Succeed and Policies That Fail.* New York: Academic Press, 1977.

———. *The Symbolic Uses of Politics.* Urbana: University of Illinois Press, 1964.

Edsall, Thomas Byrne. *The New Politics of Inequality.* New York: W. W. Norton, 1984.

Eisenstein, James. *Politics and the Legal Process.* New York: Harper & Row, 1973.

Epstein, Edwin M. *The Corporation in American Politics.* Englewood Cliffs, N.J.: Prentice-Hall, 1969.

Feyerabend, Paul. *Science in a Free Society.* London: NLB, 1978.

Friedman, Robert S. *Professionalism: Expertise and Policy Making.* New York: General Learning Press, 1971.

Furner, Mary O. *Advocacy and Objectivity: A Crisis in the Professionalization of American Social Science, 1865–1905.* Lexington: University of Kentucky Press, 1975.

Galbraith, John K. *The Affluent Society.* New York: New American Library, 1958.

Gallup, George H. *The Gallup Poll: Public Opinion, 1935–1971.* Vol. 3. New York: Random House, 1972.

———. *The Gallup Poll: Public Opinion, 1972–1977.* Vols. 1 and 2. Wilmington, Del.: Scholarly Resources, 1978.

———. *The Gallup Poll: Public Opinion 1979.* Wilmington, Del.: Scholarly Resources, 1980.

Glaser, Edward M., Abelson, Harold H., and Garrison, Kathalee. *Putting Knowledge to Use: Facilitating the Diffusion of Knowledge and the Implementation of Planned Change.* San Francisco: Jossey-Bass, 1983.

Graham, George J. *Methodological Foundations of Political Analysis.* Waltham, Mass.: Xerox College, 1971.

Greenberg, Daniel S. *The Politics of Pure Science.* New York: New American Library, 1967.

Greenberg, David H., and Robins, Philip K. "The Changing Role of Social Experiments in Policy Analysis." *Journal of Policy Analysis and Management* 5 (Winter 1986):340–362.

Greenberg, Edward S. *Understanding Modern Government: The Rise and Decline of the American Political Economy.* New York: John Wiley, 1979.

Greenberg, George D., Miller, Jeffrey A., Mohr, Lawrence B., and Vladek, Bruce C. "Developing Public Policy Theory: Perspectives from Empirical Research." *American Political Science Review* 71 (December 1977):1532–1543.

Gouldner, Alvin W. *The Dialectic of Ideology and Technology: The Origins of Grammar and Future of Ideology.* New York: Seabury Press, 1976.

Gusfield, Joseph R. "The (F)Utility of Knowledge? The Relation of Social Science to Public Policy Towards Drugs." *American Academy for Political and Social Science* 417 (January 1975):1–15.

Hodges, Donald C. *The Bureaucratization of Socialism.* Amherst: University of Massachusetts Press, 1981.

Holzner, Burkart. "The Sociology of Applied Knowledge." *Sociological Symposium* 21 (1978):8–19.

Holzner, Burkart, and Fisher, Evelyn. "Knowledge in Use: Considerations in the Sociology of Knowledge Application." *Knowledge: Creation, Diffusion, Utilization* 1 (December 1979):219–244.

Holzner, Burkart, and Marx, John. *Knowledge Application: The Knowledge System in Society.* Boston: Allyn & Bacon, 1979.

Hoos, Ida R. "Systems Techniques for Managing Society: A Critique." *Public Administration Review* 33 (March–April 1973):157–164.

Horowitz, Irving Louis. "Social Science and Public Policy: Implications of Modern Research." In *The Rise and Fall of Project Camelot: Studies in the Relationship Between Social Science and Practical Politics,* rev. ed., edited by Irving Louis Horowitz. Cambridge, Mass.: M.I.T. Press, 1974.

Horowitz, Irving Louis, and Katz, James Everett. *Social Science and Public Policy in the United States.* New York: Praeger, 1975.

Hunt, Raymond G. "The University Social Research Center: Its Role in the Knowledge-Making Process." *Knowledge, Creation, Diffusion, Utilization* 2 (September 1980):77–92.

Janowitz, Morris. "Sociological Models and Social Policy." In *Political Conflict: Essays in Political Sociology,* edited by Morris Janowitz. Chicago: Quadrangle, 1970.

Jones, E. Terrence. *Conducting Political Research.* New York: Harper & Row, 1971.

Katznelson, Ira, and Kesselman, Mark. *The Politics of Power: A Critical Introduction to American Government.* 2d ed. New York: Harcourt Brace Jovanovich, 1979.

King, Lauriston, and Melanson, Philip. "Knowledge and Politics: Some Lessons from the 60s." *Public Policy* 20 (Winter 1972):83–101.

Knorr-Cetina, Karin D. "The Ethnographic Study of Scientific Work: Towards a Constructivist Interpretation of Science." In *Science Observed: Perspectives on the Social Study of Science,* edited by Karin D. Knorr-Cetina and Michael Mulkay. London: Sage, 1983.

———. *The Manufacture of Knowledge: An Essay on the Constructivist and Contextual Nature of Science.* Oxford: Pergamon Press, 1981.

Knorr-Cetina, Karin D., and Mulkay, Michael, ed. *Science Observed: Perspectives on the Social Study of Science.* London: Sage, 1983.

Knott, Jack, and Wildavsky, Aaron. "If Dissemination Is the Solution, What Is the Problem?" *Knowledge: Creation, Diffusion, Utilization* 1 (June 1980):537–578.

Lakoff, Sanford A. "The Third Culture: Science in Social Thought." In *Knowledge and Power: Essays on Science and Government*, edited by Sanford A. Lakoff. New York: Free Press, 1966.

Lane, Robert E. "Patterns of Political Belief." In *Hanbook of Political Psychology*, edited by Jeanne Knutson. San Francisco: Jossey-Bass, 1973.

Larsen, Judith K. "Knowledge Utilization: What Is It?" *Knowledge: Creation, Diffusion, Utilization* 1 (March 1980):421–442.

Latour, Bruno, and Woolgar, Steve. *Laboratory Life: The Social Construction of Scientific Facts.* London: Sage, 1979.

Lazarsfeld, Paul F., and Reitz, Jeffrey G. *An Introduction to Applied Sociology.* New York: Elsevier, 1975.

Leviton, Laura C., and Hughes, Edward F. X. "Research on the Utilization of Evaluation." *Evaluation Review* 5 (August 1981):525–548.

Lindblom, Charles E. *The Policy-Making Process.* 2d ed. Englewood Cliffs, N.J.: Prentice-Hall, 1980.

―――. *Politics and Markets: The World's Political-Economic Systems.* New York: Basic Books, 1977.

Lindblom, Charles E., and Cohen, David K. *Usable Knowledge: Social Science and Social Problem Solving.* New Haven: Yale University Press, 1979.

"Linguist Whose Work Bush Derided Defends His Research in Philadelphia." *New York Times,* 30 March 1981.

Long, Norton E. *The Polity.* Edited by Charles Press. Chicago: Rand McNally, 1962.

Lowi, Theodore J. "American Business, Public Policy, Case-Studies, and Political Theory." *World Politics* 56 (July 1964):677–715.

―――. *The End of Liberalism: The Second Republic of the United States.* 2d ed. New York: W. W. Norton, 1979.

―――. "Four Systems of Policy, Politics, and Choice." *Public Administration Review* 32 (July–August 1972):298–310.

Lynd, Robert S. *Knowledge for What?* Princeton, N.J.: Princeton University Press, 1939.

Lynn, Laurence E., Jr. "Insights and Lessons." In *Studies in the Management of Social R & D: Selected Policy Areas,* edited by Laurence E. Lynn, Jr. Final Report. Vol. 3. Study Project on Social Research and Development. National Research Council. Washington, D.C.: National Academy of Sciences, 1979.

―――. ed. *Knowledge and Policy: The Uncertain Connection.* Final Report. Vol. 5. Study Project on Social Research and Development. National Research Council. Washington, D.C.: National Academy of Sciences, 1978.

Lyons, Gene M. *The Uneasy Partnership: Social Science and the Federal Government in the Twentieth Century.* New York: Russell Sage Foundation, 1969.

Machlup, Fritz. *The Production and Distribution of Knowledge in the United States.* Princeton, N.J.: Princeton University Press, 1962.

Manley, John. "Neopluralism: A Class Analysis of Pluralism I and Pluralism II." *American Political Science Review* 77 (June 1983):368–383.

McConnell, Grant. *Private Power and American Democracy.* New York: Vantage Books, 1966.

Mechanic, David. "Evaluation in Alcohol, Drug Abuse, and Mental Health Programs: Problems and Prospects." In *Program Evaluation: Alcohol, Drug Abuse, and Mental Health Services,* edited by Jack Zusman and Cecil R. Wurster. Lexington, Mass.: D.C. Heath, 1975.

Meehan, Eugene J. *The Foundations of Political Analysis: Empirical and Normative.* Homewood, Ill.: Dorsey Press, 1971.

_____. "Science, Values, and Politics." *American Behavioral Scientist* 17 (September–October 1973):53–100.

_____. *Reasoned Argument in Social Science: Linking Research to Policy.* Westport, Conn.: Greenwood Press, 1981.

Meld, Murray B. "The Politics of Evaluation of Social Programs." *Social Work* 19 (July 1974):448–455.

Meltsner, Arnold J. *Policy Analysts in the Bureaucracy.* Berkeley, Calif.: University of California Press, 1976.

Merton, Robert K. "The Role of Applied Social Science in the Formation of Policy: A Research Memorandum." *Philosophy of Science* 16 (July 1949):161–181.

_____. *The Sociology of Science: Theoretical and Empirical Investigations.* Chicago: University of Chicago Press, 1973.

Milch, Jerome. "The Politics of Technical Advice." *Administrative Science Quarterly* 22 (1977):526–536.

Mulkay, Michael. *Science and the Sociology of Knowledge.* London: Allen & Unwin, 1979.

_____. "Sociology of the Scientific Research Community." In *Science, Technology, and Society: A Cross-Disciplinary Perspective,* edited by Ina Spiegal-Rosing and Derek de Solla Price. London: Sage, 1977.

Myrdal, Gunnar. *The Political Element in the Development of Economic Theory.* Translated by Paul Streeten. Cambridge, Mass.: Harvard University Press, 1954.

_____. "The Social Sciences and Their Impact on Society." In *Social Theory and Social Invention,* edited by Herman D. Stein. Cleveland: Case Western Reserve University Press, 1968.

Nelkin, Dorothy. "The Political Impact of Technical Expertise." *Social Studies of Science* 5 (February 1975):35–54.

_____. "Scientific Knowledge, Public Policy, and Democracy: A Review Essay." *Knowledge: Creation, Diffusion, Utilization* 1 (September 1979):106–122.

Nelson, Stephen D. "Knowledge Creation: An Overview." *Knowledge: Creation, Diffusion, Utilization* 1 (September 1979):123–149.

"New Coleman Study Is Defended and Criticized by 500 Educators." *New York Times,* 8 April 1981.

Orlans, Harold. "Making Social Research More Useful to Government." *Social Science Information* 7 (December 1968):151–158.

_____. *The Nonprofit Research Institute: Its Origin, Operation, Problems, and Prospects.* New York: McGraw-Hill, 1972.

Parenti, Michael. "Power and Pluralism: A View from the Bottom." *Journal of Politics* 32 (August 1970):501–530.

Patton, Michael Quinn. *Utilization-Focused Evaluation*. Beverly Hills, Calif.: Sage, 1978.

Peirce, Charles Sanders. *Philosophical Writings of Peirce*. Edited by Justus Buchler. New York, Dover, 1955.

Penick, James L., Jr., Pursell, Carroll W., Jr., Sherwood, Morgan B., and Swain, Donald C., eds. *The Politics of American Science, 1939 to the Present*. Rev. ed. Cambridge, Mass.: M.I.T. Press, 1972.

Piaget, Jean. *The Psychology of Intelligence*. 1950. Reprint ed. Totowa, N.J.: Littlefield, Adams, 1960.

"Points of Controversy Emerge Swiftly as Clean Air Act Hearings Opens." *New York Times*, 3 March 1981.

Polanyi, Michael. *The Study of Man*. Chicago: University of Chicago Press, 1959.

Poulantzas, Nicos. *Classes in Contemporary Capitalism*. London: Verso, 1978.

Price, Don K. *The Scientific Estate*. Cambridge, Mass.: Harvard University Press, 1965.

Primack, Joel, and von Hippel, Frank. *Advice and Dissent: Scientists in the Political Arena*. New York: Basic Books, 1974.

Quade, E. S. *Analysis for Public Decisions*. New York: Elsevier, 1975.

Ricci, David M. *The Tragedy of Political Science: Politics, Scholarship, and Democracy*. New Haven: Yale University Press, 1984.

Rich, Robert F. "The Pursuit of Knowledge." *Knowledge: Creation, Diffusion, Utilization* 1 (September 1979):6–30.

_____. *Social Science Information and Public Policy Making*. San Francisco: Jossey-Bass, 1981.

Rivlin, Alice M. "Forensic Social Science." *Harvard Educational Review* 43 (February 1973):61–75.

_____. *Systematic Thinking for Social Action*. Washington, D.C.: Brookings Institution, 1971.

Roberts, Marc J. "On the Nature and Condition of Social Science." *Daedalus* 103 (Summer 1974):47–64.

Rokeach, Milton. *The Open and Closed Mind*. New York: Basic Books, 1969.

Rothman, Jack. *Using Research in Organizations: A Guide to Successful Applications*. Beverly Hills, Calif.: Sage, 1980.

Rule, James B. *Insight and Social Betterment: A Preface to Applied Social Science*. New York: Oxford University Press, 1978.

Russell, Beverly, and Shore, Arnold. "Limitations on the Governmental Use of Social Science." *Minerva* 14 (Winter 1976):475–495.

Salisbury, Robert H. "The Analysis of Public Policy: A Search for Theories and Roles." In *Political Science and Public Policy*, edited by Austin Ranney. Chicago: Markham, 1968.

Schattschneider, E. E. *The Semisovereign People: A Realist's View of Democracy in America*. New York: Holt, Rinehart & Winston, 1960.

Scott, Robert A., and Shore, Arnold R. *Why Sociology Does Not Apply: A Study of the Use of Sociology in Public Policy.* New York: Elsevier, 1979.

Shils, Edward. "Knowledge and the Sociology of Knowledge." *Knowledge: Creation, Diffusion, Utilization* 4 (September 1982):7–32.

Shively, W. Phillips. *The Craft of Political Research: A Primer.* Englewood, Cliffs, N.J.: Prentice-Hall, 1974.

Smith, Bruce L. R. *The Rand Corporation: Case Study of a Nonprofit Advisory Corporation.* Cambridge, Mass: Harvard University Press, 1966.

Smith, J. D., and Franklin, S. D. "The Concentration of Personal Wealth, 1922–1969." *American Economic Review* 64 (May 1974):162–167.

Snow, C. P. *The Two Cultures and the Scientific Revolution.* New York: Cambridge University Press, 1959.

Somit, Albert, and Tanenhaus, Joseph. *The Development of American Political Science: From Burgess to Behavioralism.* Boston: Allyn & Bacon, 1967.

Spence, Larry D. *The Politics of Social Knowledge.* University Park: Pennsylvania State University Press, 1978.

Spiegal-Rosing, Ina, and de Solla Price, Derek, eds. *Science, Technology, and Society: A Cross-Disciplinary Perspective.* London: Sage, 1977.

Steinbruner, John D. *The Cybernetic Theory of Decision: New Dimensions of Political Analysis.* Princeton, N.J.: Princeton University Press, 1974.

Suchman, Edward A. *Evaluative Research: Principles and Practice in Public Service and Social Action Programs.* New York: Russell Sage Foundation, 1967.

Sundquist, James L. "Research Brokerage: The Weak Link." In *Knowledge and Policy: The Uncertain Connection,* edited by Laurence E. Lynn, Jr. Study Project on Social Research and Development. National Research Council. Washington, D.C.: National Academy of Sciences, 1978.

Thurrow, Lester C. "Economics 1977." *Daedalus* 106 (Fall 1977):79–94.

Toulmin, Stephen. "From Form to Function: Philosophy and History of Science in the 1950s and Now." *Daedalus* 106 (Summer 1977):143–162.

U.S. Advisory Commission on Intergovernmental Relations. *Significant Features of Fiscal Federalism.* 1980–1981 ed. Washington, D.C.: Government Printing Office, 1981.

U.S. Bureau of the Census. *Historical Statistics of the United States, Colonial Times to 1970, Bicentennial Edition.* Pt. 1. Washington, D.C.: Government Printing Office, 1975.

U.S. Bureau of the Census. *Statistical Abstract of the United States 1986.* 106th ed. Washington, D.C., 1985.

U.S. Executive Office of the President. Office of Management and Budget. *Special Analyses, Budget of the United States Government, Fiscal Year 1979.* Washington, D.C.: Government Printing Office, 1978.

U.S. Executive Office of the President. Office of Management and Budget. *Special Analyses, Budget of the United States Government, Fiscal Year 1987.* Washington, D.C.: Government Printing Office, 1986.

U.S. General Services Administration. National Archives and Records Service. Office of the Federal Register. *1977/78 United States Government Manual.* Washington, D.C.: Government Printing Office, 1977.

U.S. National Research Council. *The Behavioral Sciences and the Federal Government.* Advisory Committee on Government Programs in the Behavioral Sciences. Washington, D.C.: National Academy of Science, 1968.

U.S. National Research Council. *The Federal Investment in Knowledge of Social Problems.* Final Report. Vol. 1. Study Project on Social Research and Development. Washington, D.C.: National Academy of Sciences, 1978.

U.S. National Research Council and Social Science Research Council. *The Behavioral and Social Sciences: Outlook and Needs.* Behavioral and Social Sciences Survey Committee. Washington, D.C.: National Academy of Sciences, 1969.

U.S. National Science Foundation. *Knowledge into Action: Improving the Nation's Use of the Social Sciences.* Washington, D.C.: Government Printing Office, 1969.

Veblen, Thorstein. *The Place of Science in Modern Civilization.* New York: Russell & Russell, 1961.

Weiss, Carol H. *Evaluation Research: Methods for Assessing Program Effectiveness.* Englewood Cliffs, N.J.: Prentice-Hall, 1972.

———. "Improving the Linkage Between Social Research and Public Policy." In *Knowledge and Policy: The Uncertain Connection,* edited by Laurence E. Lynn, Jr. Study Project on Social Research and Development. National Research Council. Washington, D.C.: National Academy of Sciences, 1978.

———. "The Politicization of Evaluation Research." In *Evaluating Action Programs: Readings in Social Action and Education,* edited by Carol H. Weiss. Boston: Allyn & Bacon, 1972.

———. "Research for Policy's Sake: The Enlightenment Function of Social Research." *Policy Analysis* 3 (Fall 1977):531–545.

———. "Utilization of Evaluation: Toward Comparative Study." In *Evaluating Action Programs: Readings in Social Action and Education,* edited by Carol H. Weiss. Boston: Allyn & Bacon, 1972.

Weiss, Carol H., and Bucuvalas, Michael J. *Social Science Research and Decision-Making.* New York: Columbia University Press, 1980.

Wildavsky, Aaron. *Speaking Truth to Power: The Art and Craft of Policy Analysis.* Boston: Little, Brown, 1979.

Yin, Robert K. "The Case Study as a Serious Research Strategy." *Knowledge: Creation, Diffusion, Utilization* 3 (September 1981):97–114.

Welfare Policy, Research, and Analysis

Aaron, Henry J. *Why Is Welfare So Hard to Reform?* Washington, D.C.: Brookings Institution, 1973.

Aaron, Henry J., and Todd, John. "The Use of Income Maintenance Experiment Findings in Public Policy 1977–78." Department of Health, Education, and Welfare, 1978.

Allen, Jodie. "An Introduction to the Seattle/Denver Income Maintenance Experiment: Origins, Limitations, and Policy Relevance." In *Proceedings of the 1978 Conference on the Seattle and Denver Income Maintenance Experiments*, edited by Joseph G. Bell, Patricia M. Lines, and Michael Linn. Olympia, Wash.: Department of Social and Health Services, 1979.

Barth, Michael, Orr, Larry, and Palmer, John L. "Policy Implications: A Positive View." In *Work Incentives and Income Guarantees: The New Jersey Negative Income Tax Experiment*, edited by Joseph A. Pechman and P. Michael Timpane. Washington, D.C.: Brookings Institution, 1975.

Bell, Joseph G., Lines, Patricia M., and Linn, Michael, eds. *Proceedings of the 1978 Conference on the Seattle and Denver Income Maintenance Experiments*. Olympia, Wash.: Department of Social and Health Services, 1979.

Boeckmann, Margaret E. "Policy Impacts of the New Jersey Income Maintenance Experiment." *Policy Sciences* 7 (1976):53–76.

Bork, Robert H. *Welfare Reform: Why?* Washington, D.C.: American Enterprise Institute, 1976.

Browning, Edgar K., and Browning, Jacquelene M. *Public Finance and the Price System*. New York: Macmillan, 1979.

Burke, Vincent J., and Burke, Vee. *Nixon's Good Deed*. New York: Columbia University Press, 1974.

Cavala, Bill, and Wildavsky, Aaron. "The Political Feasibility of Income by Right." *Public Policy* 18 (1970):321–354.

Congressional Quarterly, Inc. *Urban America: Policies and Problems*. Washington, D.C.: Congressional Quarterly, 1978.

Covello, Vincent T., ed. *Poverty and Public Policy: An Evaluation of Social Science Research*. Cambridge, Mass.: Schenkman, 1980.

Demkovich, Linda E. "Another Chance for Welfare Reform." *National Journal*, 10 March 1979, p. 404.

———. "Good News and Bad News for Welfare Reform." *National Journal*, 30 December 1978, pp. 2061–63.

———. "The Numbers Are the Issue in the Debate Over Welfare Reform." *National Journal*, 22 April 1978, pp. 663–37.

———. "State and Local Officials Rescue Welfare Reform—Too Late." *National Journal*, 24 June 1978, pp. 1007–09.

———. "Welfare Reform—Can Carter Succeed Where Nixon Failed?" *National Journal*, 27 August 1977, pp. 1328–34.

Friedman, Milton. *Capitalism and Freedom*. Chicago: University of Chicago Press, 1962.

———. "The Case for a Negative Income Tax." In *Republican Papers*, edited by Melvin R. Laird. New York: Frederick A. Praeger, 1968.

Gramlich, Edward M. "Future Research on Poverty and Income Maintenance." In *Poverty and Public Policy: An Evaluation of Social Science Research*, edited by Vincent T. Covello. Cambridge, Mass.: Schenkman, 1979.

Green, Christopher. *Negative Taxes and the Poverty Problem*. Washington, D.C.: Brookings Institution, 1967.

Hannan, Michael T., Tuma, Nancy Brandon, and Groeneveld, Lyle P. "Income and

Marital Events: Evidence from an Income-Maintenance Experiment." *American Journal of Sociology* 82 (May 1977):1186–1211.

———. *A Model of the Effect of Income Maintenance on Rates of Marital Dissolution: Evidence from the Seattle and Denver Income Maintenance Experiments.* Menlo Park, Calif.: SRI International, 1977.

Harris, Robert. "Policy Analysis and Policy Development." *Social Service Review* 47 (September 1973):360–372.

Hershey, Alan M., Morris, J. Jeffrey, and Williams, Robert G. *Colorado Monthly Reporting Experiment and Pre-Test: Preliminary Research Results.* Denver: Mathematica Policy Research, 1977.

Horan, Cynthia. "Casper Weinberger and Welfare Reform." In *Designing Public Policy,* edited by Laurence E. Lynn, Jr. Santa Monica, Calif.: Goodyear, 1980.

Kehrer, Kenneth C. "Designing Income Maintenance Programs: Evidence, Problems, and Suggestions for Further Research." In *Proceedings of the 1978 Conference on the Seattle and Denver Income Maintenance Experiments,* edited by Joseph G. Bell, Patricia M. Lines, and Michael Linn. Olympia, Wash.: Department of Social and Health Services, 1979.

———. *The Gary Income Maintenance Experiment: Summary of Initial Findings.* Princeton, N.J.: Mathematica Policy Research, 1977.

Kershaw, David, and Fair, J. *The New Jersey Income-Maintenance Experiment: Operations, Surveys and Administration.* New York: Academic Press, 1976.

Kotz, Nick. "The Politics of Welfare Reform." *New Republic* 176 (14 May 1977):16–21.

Lawlor, Edward F. "Income Security." In *Studies in the Management of Social R & D: Selected Policy Areas,* edited by Laurence E. Lynn, Jr. Final Report. Vol. 3. Study Project on Social Research and Development. National Research Council. Washington, D.C.: National Academy of Sciences, 1979.

Lerman, Robert I. *Welfare Reform Alternatives: Employment Subsidy Proposals Versus the Negative Income Tax.* Madison, Wis.: Institute for Research on Poverty, 1977.

Levine, Robert A. "How and Why the Experiment Came About." In *Work Incentives and Income Guarantees: The New Jersey Negative Income Tax Experiment,* edited by Joseph A. Pechman and P. Michael Timpane. Washington, D.C.: Brookings Institution, 1975.

Lyday, James. "An Advocate's Process Outline for Policy Analysis." *Urban Affairs Quarterly* 7 (June 1972):385–402.

Lynn, Lawrence E., Jr. "A Decade of Policy Developments in the Income-Maintenance System." In *A Decade of Federal Antipoverty Programs: Achievements, Failures, and Lessons,* edited by Robert H. Haveman. New York: Academic Press, 1977.

Mahoney, Bette S., and Mahoney, W. Michael. "Policy Implications: A Skeptical View." In *Work Incentives and Income Guarantees: The New Jersey Negative Income Tax Experiment,* edited by Joseph A. Pechman and P. Michael Timpane. Washington, D.C.: Brookings Institution, 1975.

Metcalf, Charles E., and Kershaw, David N. "What We Have Learned from the Experiments." In *Proceedings of the 1978 Conference on the Seattle and Denver Income Maintenance Experiments,* edited by Joseph G. Bell, Patricia M. Lines, and Michael Linn. Olympia, Wash.: Department of Social and Health Services, 1979.

Morrill, William. "What We Have Learned About Research and Policy-Making." In *Proceedings of the 1978 Conference on the Seattle and Denver Income Maintenance Experiments*, edited by Joseph G. Bell, Patricia M. Lines, and Michael Linn. Olympia, Wash.: Department of Social and Health Services, 1979.

Moynihan, Daniel P. *Maximum Feasible Misunderstanding*. New York: Free Press, 1969.

———. *The Politics of a Guaranteed Income: The Nixon Administration and the Family Assistance Plan*. New York: Random House, 1973.

Musgrave, Richard A., and Musgrave, Peggy B. *Public Finance in Theory and Practice*. 2d ed. New York: McGraw-Hill, 1976.

Orr, Larry L. "Introduction: Strategy for a Broad Program of Experimentation in Income Maintenance." In *Income Maintenance: Interdisciplinary Approaches to Research*, edited by Larry L. Orr, Robinson G. Hollister, and Myron J. Lefcowitz. Chicago: Markham, 1971.

———. "An Overview." In *Welfare in Rural Areas: The North Carolina–Iowa Income Maintenance Experiment*, edited by John L. Palmer and Joseph A. Pechman. Washington, D.C.: Brookings Institution, 1978.

Packer, Arnold. "The Administration's Approach: The Premise of the Better Jobs and Income Proposal." In *Proceedings of the 1978 Conference on the Seattle and Denver Income Maintenance Experiments*, edited by Joseph G. Bell, Patricia M. Lines, and Michael Linn. Olympia, Wash.: Department of Social and Health Services, 1979.

Palmer, John L., and Pechman, Joseph A., eds. *Welfare in Rural Areas: The North Carolina–Iowa Income Maintenance Experiment*. Washington, D.C.: Brookings Institution, 1978.

Pechman, Joseph A., and Timpane, P. Michael, eds. *Work Incentives and Income Guarantees: The New Jersey Negative Income Tax Experiment*. Washington, D.C.: Brookings Institution, 1975.

Piven, Frances Fox, and Cloward, Richard A. *Poor People's Movements: Why They Succeed, How They Fail*. New York: Vintage Books, 1979.

———. *Regulating the Poor: The Functions of Public Welfare*. New York: Vintage Books, 1971.

Raines, Franklin D. *Family Assistance Programs, Parts A & B*. Cambridge, Mass.: Kennedy School of Government, Harvard University, 1977.

Rainwater, Lee, and Yancey, William L. *The Moynihan Report and the Politics of Controversy*. Cambridge, Mass.: M.I.T. Press, 1967.

Rein, Martin, and Peattie, Lisa. "Problem Frames in Poverty Research." In *Poverty and Public Policy: An Evaluation of Social Science Research*, edited by Vincent T. Covello. Cambridge, Mass.: Schenkman, 1980.

Robins, Philip K., and West, Richard W. *Participation in the Seattle and Denver Income Maintenance Experiments and Its Effect on Labor Supply*. Menlo Park, Calif.: SRI International, 1978.

Rossi, Peter H., and Lyall, Katherine C. *Reforming Public Welfare: A Critique of the Negative Income Tax Experiment*. New York: Russell Sage Foundations, 1976.

Schorr, Alvin L. "Against a Negative Income Tax." *Public Interest* 5 (Fall 1966):110–117.

Schuh, G. Edward. "Policy and Research Implications." In *Welfare in Rural Areas: The North Carolina–Iowa Income Maintenance Experiment*, edited by John L. Palmer and Joseph A. Pechman. Washington, D.C.: Brookings Institution, 1978.

Smith, Marvin M. "Summary of Conference Discussion." In *Welfare in Rural Areas: The North Carolina–Iowa Income Maintenance Experiment*, edited by John L. Palmer and Joseph A. Pechman. Washington, D.C.: Brookings Institution, 1978.

Spiegelman, Robert G. "Summary of the Research Findings." In *Proceedings of the 1978 Conference on the Seattle and Denver Income Maintenance Experiments*, edited by Joseph G. Bell, Patricia M. Lines, and Michael Linn. Olympia, Wash.: Department of Social and Health Services, 1979.

Steiner, Gilbert Y. *The State of Welfare.* Washington, D.C.: Brookings Institution, 1971.

———. *Welfare Options and Welfare Politics.* Washington, D.C.: Brookings Institution, 1969.

Stern, Michael. "The View from Congress." In *Proceedings of the 1978 Conference on the Seattle and Denver Income Maintenance Experiments*, edited by Joseph G. Bell, Patricia M. Lines, and Michael Linn. Olympia, Wash.: Department of Social and Health Services, 1979.

Storey, James R. "Systems Analysis and Welfare Reform: A Case Study of the Family Assistance Plan." *Policy Sciences* 4 (March 1973):1–11.

Theobald, Robert. *Free Men and Free Markets.* New York: Clarkson N. Potter, 1963.

Tobin, James. "The Case for an Income Guarantee." *Public Interest* 4 (Summer 1966):31–41.

U.S. Congress. Congressional Budget Office. *The Administration's Welfare Reform Proposal: An Analysis of the Program for Better Jobs and Income.* Washington, D.C., 1978.

U.S. Congress. House. *Administration's Welfare Reform Proposal: Hearings before the Welfare Reform Subcommittee of the Committee on Agriculture, Committee on Education and Labor, and the Committee on Ways and Means.* 95th Cong., 1st sess., September 19, 20, and 21, 1977.

U.S. Congress. House. Committee on Ways and Means. *Special HEW Report on Welfare Reform: Hearings Before the Subcommittee on Public Assistance and Unemployment Compensation.* 95th Cong., 1st sess., May 4, 1977.

U.S. Congress. House. Welfare Reform Subcommittee of the Committee on Agriculture, Committee on Education and Labor, and the Committee on Ways and Means. *Explanatory Material to Accompany H.R. 10950, the Better Jobs and Income Act.* 95th Cong., 2d sess., March 24, 1978.

U.S. Congress. Senate. Committee on Finance. *How to Think About Welfare Reform for the 1980s: Hearings Before the Subcommittee on Public Assistance.* 96th Cong., 2d sess., February 6 and 7, 1980.

U.S. Congress. Senate. Committee on Finance. *President's Statement on Principles of Welfare Reform: Hearings Before the Subcommittee on Public Assistance.* 95th Cong., 1st sess., May 5 and 12, 1977.

U.S. Congress. Senate. Committee on Finance. *Welfare Reform Proposals: Hearings Before the Subcommittee on Public Assistance.* 95th Cong., 2d sess., 1978.

U.S. Congress. Senate. Committee on Finance. *Welfare Research and Experimentation: Hearings Before the Subcommittee on Public Assistance.* 95th Cong., 2d sess., 1978.

U.S. Congress. Senate. Committee on Finance. Subcommittee on Public Assistance. *Materials Related to Welfare Research and Experimentation.* 95th Cong., 2d sess., November 1978.

U.S. Department of Health, Education, and Welfare. Office of the Assistant Secretary for Planning and Evaluation. *New Jersey Graduated Work Incentive Experiment, Summary Report.* Washington, D.C., 1973.

U.S. Department of Health, Education, and Welfare. Office of the Assistant Secretary for Planning and Evaluation. *The Rural Income Maintenance Experiment, Summary Report.* Washington, D.C., 1976.

U.S. Department of Health, Education, and Welfare. Office of the Assistant Secretary for Planning and Evaluation. *Seattle-Denver Income Maintenance Experiment: Mid-Experimental Labor Supply Results and a Generalization to the National Population.* Washington, D.C., 1978.

U.S. General Accounting Office. *Income Maintenance Experiments: Need to Summarize the Results and Communicate the Lessons Learned.* Washington, D.C., 1981.

U.S. National Research Council. *Evaluating Federal Support for Poverty Research.* Final Report. Committee on Evaluation of Poverty Research. Assembly of Behavioral and Social Sciences. Washington, D.C.: National Academy of Sciences, 1979.

Vadakin, James C. "A Critique of the Guaranteed Annual Income." *Public Interest* 11 (Spring 1968):53–66.

Watts, Harold W., and Rees, Albert. *The New Jersey Income Maintenance Experiments: Expenditures, Health, and Social Behavior and the Quality of the Evidence.* New York: Academic Press, 1977.

———. *The New Jersey Income Maintenance Experiments: Labor Supply Responses.* New York: Academic Press, 1977.

Weil, Gordon L. *the Welfare Debate of 1978.* White Plains, N.Y.: Institute for Socioeconomic Studies, 1978.

Whitman, David, and Lynn, Laurence E., Jr. *The Carter Administration and Welfare Reform, Parts A, B, C, D, & Sequel.* Cambridge, Mass.: Kennedy School of Government, Harvard University, 1979.

Williams, Walter. *Social Policy Research and Analysis: The Experience in the Federal Social Agencies.* New York: American Elsevier, 1971.

———. *The Struggle for a Negative Income Tax: A Case Study, 1965–1970.* Seattle: Institute of Governmental Research, 1972.

Index

✳

Pitt Series in Policy and Institutional Studies
Bert A. Rockman, Editor